Masters of Deception

murder and intrigue in the world of occult politics

Guy Patton

FRONTIER PUBLISHING

Masters of Deception
– murder and intrigue in the world of occult politics

© 2009 Guy Patton

Cover design: Corjan de Raaf www.rlcresearch.com
Layout: Buro kunst en drukwerk, Sylvia Carrilho

ISBN : 978-1-931882-88-0

FRONTIER PUBLISHING
P.O. Box 10681
1001 ER AMSTERDAM
Netherlands
Tel. +31-(0)20-3309151
Fax: +31-(0)20-3309150
E-mail: info@fsf.nl
www.frontierpublishing.nl

Adventures Unlimited Press
303 Main St., P.O. Box 74
Kempton, IL 60946, USA
Tel: 815-253-6390
Fax: 815-253-6300
E-mail: auphq@frontiernet.net
www.adventuresunlimitedpress.com

To Luana, Ilena and Mark

Contents

Introduction

Forty years ago, an unremarkable little book, published in France, ignited a spark that would lead eventually to a world-wide phenomenon. *L'Or de Rennes,* published in 1967 and written by Gérard de Sède revealed, for the first time, the mysterious story of a French country priest who served the parish of Rennes-le-Château. Then, documents chanced upon in the French National Library during further research introduced an enigmatic secret society, the Priory of Sion into the mystery.

De Sède's book stimulated the imagination of British author, Henry Lincoln, who produced two television documentaries (1972 and 1974) that dealt with the main themes of the enigma. Lincoln, then in collaboration with Michael Baigent and Richard Leigh, produced a third documentary (1979), followed by the best-selling *Holy Blood and the Holy Grail,* in 1982. Around twenty years later, in 2003, a novel by American Dan Brown entitled *The Da Vinci Code,* brought many of these same themes to world-wide attention. The spectacular success of *The Da Vinci Code* triggered a succession of Rennes mystery and Priory of Sion books to add to the many hundreds published since 1982.

It is my hope that this book will be viewed as not just another spin-off, but as an attempt to explain or understand several of the mysterious threads still remaining, and their wider ramifications. Four years after the publication of "Holy Blood", the authors published a sequel, *The Messianic Legacy* (1986), that sought to explore in more detail several intriguing strands of the mystery uncovered in their previous research. The result, while fascinating, left more questions than answers, inviting a third book to tie up the loose ends. Following seven years of research, I wrote *Web of Gold* (2000) to address these issues, the central theme of which was the legend of the lost treasure. Subjected to various editorial constraints, certain threads and material had to be omitted from the final draft.

Masters of Deception is the result of a re-evaluation of the main threads of the story and an attempt to unravel the web in which they have become entangled; and to view these threads against the contexts of their times. The outcome of this investigation clearly demonstrates that the initial hypothesis of *Holy Blood, Holy Grail* is untenable, as is the basic proposition of Dan Brown's novel. We will see that Gérard de Sède's story, and the subsequent Priory documents, upon which is based the hypothesis of the

Holy Blood, is not to be taken literally but rather symbolically; the interpretation of which will reveal their true motives and agenda.

Inevitably, this investigation has had to focus on the real nature, history, and motives of the Priory of Sion. This enigmatic secret society has, since 1982, attracted such extensive publicity that it has become difficult to separate fact from fiction. But perhaps even more significant, is to firmly establish any real link between the Priory and the mystery of Rennes-le-Château and its role within it. To understand the Priory, it has been necessary to delve into the twin worlds of secret societies and occult politics. The nature of a secret society makes close examination difficult, but by reading their own publications, and that of their supporters and critics, it is possible to sketch a reasonably accurate picture. In the absence of first-hand information, a best guess is used to fill in the blanks to create the whole picture. Any new information must then fit this picture, or a new scenario needs to be constructed.

The other main problem, when dealing with secret societies, is the liberal use of symbolism and symbolic language. Frequently employed by esoteric and occult writers, symbolic language is a strategy to impart knowledge or belief in a manner that can only be understood by the initiated or those on the 'same wavelength'. As a result, interpretation of such symbols may be less objective in the absence of any supporting documentation. In this respect I have tried to offer an objective, balanced, and logical interpretation.

The world of occult politics, as in the mainstream, becomes polarised into support for opposing ideologies, aims, and tactics. In examining these topics I have tried to remain impartial and no valid conclusions of my own political and religious beliefs should be drawn from this work. Descriptive words such as sinister, secretive, manipulative, and unethical, tend to carry negative connotations, but are, in fact, subjective depending on the beliefs and viewpoint of the reader. In the context of this book, such descriptions are used to reflect the contrast with the orthodox and mainstream Western political point of view.

In this age of the spirit of openness and freedom of information, political agendas, conceived and pursued in secret, elicit a response of alarm. It appears to be a fact of pragmatic political life, however, that a degree of secrecy is inevitable and even justifiable. The problem with secrecy lies in accountability, or rather the lack of it; it is naturally difficult to ensure accountability of those acting in secret. Throughout this book we will encounter many examples of individuals and groups who have pursued secret agendas with a wide range of motives. The organisational structure employed by such groups makes them vulnerable to infiltration, manipulation and subversion, whilst the general membership remains unaware. We will encounter stark examples of this, where, in some cases, the results were criminal and even fatal.

Whilst being an attempt to answer questions arising from research into the mystery of Rennes-le-Château and the Priory of Sion, this book is also a commentary on the continual evolution that has taken place in the world of occult politics. Our present era is defined by a conflict of ideologies battling for global supremacy. Besides the obvious contenders there is a third, largely unseen, power, that is playing a key role in the current struggle. This is not a clearly defined group, led by a single monarch, president, or dictator, but a network of shared ideas and visions. There are no published manifestos designed to appeal to a popular mandate; instead we find essays, correspondence and literature couched in more philosophical, metaphysical or esoteric language. In the place of public meetings, we find ideas and agendas conceived, pursued, and promoted behind closed doors in lodges or clubs composed of only initiated members. Within such organisations are members with influential positions in, or links to, the mainstream political world. It is through this interface that these occult agendas enter into and influence visible politics. This can be observed in the evolution of the European Union, the roots of which can be found in secret societies of the late 19th and early 20th centuries, and distasteful as it might appear, Nazi Germany and Vichy France.

The failure to understand and acknowledge the influence of this unseen force in domestic, European and global politics, is partially responsible for the lack of progress made in resolving current conflicts. The reluctance of mainstream politicians, and indeed historians and other academics, to take adequate account of the role of occult politics hampers the true understanding of many historical events. This topic is too easily consigned to the same fate as that of conspiracy theories. Recent revelations of CIA and British government files, due to the freedom of information act, has shown that some conspiracies, adamantly denied by the authorities for decades, did take place. No doubt, future revelations will do the same for current conspiracy theories ridiculed by the establishment. This is not to say that all such allegations are true, but that, in the world of politics, there is often more happening below the surface than above it.

I hope that the reader will be entertained, informed and stimulated by this investigation of the incestuous relationship between power and wealth and the endless drive for them. Our search will take us from the backwater of an ancient French village to the arena of global politics. We will travel through time from the Roman Empire to the present day. It is perhaps ironic that the focus of international conflict today is the very region in which our story starts two thousand years ago.

~

Chapter 1

Land of Gold

By 70 AD, the Romans were tiring of Jewish resistance in Palestine to their Imperial rule, which had come to a head in open rebellion. In retaliation, General Titus ruthlessly sacked Jerusalem, a punitive expedition that is recorded on the Arch of Titus in Rome. Sculptured panels on this Arch clearly depict the removal of the treasure[1] from the biblical Temple of Jerusalem[2], which included the Temple's Menorah (the Seven-Branched Candlestick), that great symbol of Judaism, and other treasures of similar priceless religious and real value; and their relocation in Rome. Of specific interest to those Nazis pursuing this sacred treasure nearly two thousand years later, was the fabled Ark of the Covenant, which some legends had suggested might have been included in this booty. However, other evidence shows it rather more probable that, if the Ark of the Covenant had been discovered, it may have been by the Knights Templar, the medieval order of warrior monks.

Various sources of historical record, such as the Dead Sea scrolls amongst which can be found the Copper Scroll[3], indicate the nature and general locations of this treasure in and around Jerusalem, prior to its sacking in 70 AD.

In 410, Rome was itself sacked by the Visigoths, led by Alaric the Goth. After his death, they migrated west, under the command of Ataulphus, to establish their kingdom in south-west France and northern Spain, with major centres at Toulouse, Toledo, Carcassonne and Rhedae, which many have identified with a small village called Rennes-le-Château Two hundred years later, this Visigoth kingdom was squeezed by pressure from the Franks, led by the Merovingian kings, coming from the North, and later from the Moors in the South who had crossed from North Africa through Gibraltar into Spain, in 711. Integration and intermarriage amongst aristocratic families from amongst the Visigoths and the Franks had produced Visigoth/Merovingian dynasties in the Pyrenean region. However, the rapid push north across the Pyrenees by the Moors pressured the Visigoth/Merovingian aristocracy to retreat and consolidate in their northern centres at Toulouse, Carcassonne and Rhedae. They were thus forced to transfer their vast treasure[4] from Toledo, in the face of advancing Moors, initially to Carcassonne and from there to Rhedae[5].

The Moorish advance continued to the centre of France, where it met the Frankish resistance of Charles Martel, the grandfather of Charlemagne. The Moors were pushed back into Spain where they were to remain for a further six hundred years. It is at this point that any further historical record of the treasure ceases, thus giving rise to a belief that this great treasure found its last resting place, probably divided amongst several locations, in the residual kingdom of the Visigoths. This is the region at the heart of which sits the village of Rennes-le-Château, disputedly alleged to be the site of ancient Rhedae.

The former significance and glory of Rhedae may seem unbelievable to the thousands of visitors to this pretty little hilltop village today. Its tiny church and ramshackle Château seem a far cry from the notion of a Visigothic fortress standing defiantly against the Moorish onslaught; and later as a town of wealth and culture. It is surrounded by the raw beauty of the Pyreneean foothills, and adjacent to the dramatic Corbières, delightful for their remoteness and timelessness, a dramatic setting for the one-time frontline between the Arian Visigoths, Roman Christianity and Islam. We will see, however, that whether the link with Rhedae is true or not, Rennes-le-Château has witnessed a most remarkable hisory.

A closer examination of the surrounding countryside, quite dormant today, reveals many signs of earlier activity. An area of outstanding beauty extending to some 500 square miles, it is in fact riddled with old mines, evidence of the exploitation of the vast mineral deposits in the region, including gold mines established by the Romans. The lovely little mountain-top hamlet of Auriac, barely two houses and an impressive ruined castle with magnificent views down into the valley below possessed such a gold-mine, as its name suggests. The castles surrounding these remote valleys give the positive impression that they are guarding something, and one has to wonder what. Modern roads have opened up this region, but it is still possible to see the Roman chariot ruts in the rocks of the one road that once provided the only access. Still closer examination reveals evidence of very extensive buildings and earthworks throughout the region, and particularly in the vicinity of Rennes-le-Château and its neighbour Rennes-les-Bains. It is quite clear that this area was once the focal point of substantial settlement, the purpose for which has long since gone. The ruggedness of the terrain, its relative inaccessibility, and its profusion of underground fissures, caves and mines, has added credibility to the enduring belief in these fabulous treasure deposits[6].

This period also witnessed a struggle for religious supremacy, and thus political power, between the Church of Rome, the Arian Christians (who rejected the divinity of Jesus), Islam and Judaism.

Christian Europe was divided between Roman orthodoxy and heresy, of which the most prominent was Arianism (i.e. followers of Arius, not to be confused with the racial, Aryanism). The Visigoths had converted to Arian Christianity that, by 500 AD, was dominant in Spain, Italy, Southern France, Yugoslavia – in other words the regions controlled by the Goths. Northern and Central France were occupied by the Franks who had migrated westward from the Rhine.

By the conventional expedient of assassinating rivals, Clovis established himself as sole King of the Franks, and is considered by many to be the first French (Merovingian) King. Although Clovis is known to have converted to Catholicism and to have concluded a pact of mutual support with the Roman Catholic Church, there is evidence that many of his descendants were less committed. This conveniently opened the door for the Mayors of the Palace (the medieval equivalent of present-day Prime Ministers), with the active encouragement of the Roman Catholic Church, to usurp power from the Merovingian dynasty. This suited the Roman Catholic Church's ongoing enthusiasm for the expansion and consolidation of its dominance. A result of this was the foundation of a powerful alliance between the Church of Rome and the emerging Carolingian dynasty, the greatest member of which was Charlemagne, crowned Holy Roman Emperor in 800.

Dagobert, a great-grandson of Clovis, became king of the reunified Franks in 630, and was the first of several illustrious personages to carry the name. By this time, as we have seen, a succession of court chancellors known as the Mayors of the Palace had contrived to accumulate sufficient power to challenge that of their monarchs, and had virtual control of the kingdoms of Austrasia, Neustria, and Burgundy. In 656, following the death of Sigisbert III, his five-year-old son and natural heir, Dagobert II was kidnapped by the incumbent Mayor, Grimoald, and given into the hands of Dido, Bishop of Poitiers. Baulking at murdering the young heir as he was instructed, the bishop exiled him to the monastery of Slane in Ireland, thought far enough away not to be a future threat. Meanwhile, Grimoald's own son was installed as king.

Having completed a comprehensive education and entered into the circles of Irish Celtic nobility, Dagobert married Mathilde, a Celtic princess. They moved to England, taking residence at York, where Dagobert formed a close friendship with Wilfred, the influential Bishop of York. He had played a key role at the Synod of Whitby, the dramatic confrontation between the Roman Catholic and Celtic Churches. The Celtic Church had evolved from the desert monastic tradition inspired by the teachings of the apostle Mark, and was spread north by missionaries who had travelled up the western seaboard of Europe to Ireland. Despite possibly being a more pure form of Christianity in spiritual terms, the Celtic Church was seen as an opposing force to the Roman Church and, like the Arian tradition, was branded heretical. Followers were given the choice of persecution or subjugation to the control of Rome. It was with the aim of consolidating and expanding this control that Wilfred sought to bolster the position of the rightful Christian King of the Franks.

Mathilde died giving birth to their third daughter and it is said that it was Wilfred who hurriedly arranged a second marriage for Dagobert II to a Visigoth princess, Giselle de Razès. As daughter of Bera II, the Count of Razès, and niece of Wamba, King of the Visigoths, Giselle's marriage brought together the Visigoth bloodline with that of the Merovingians. It is at this point that the history becomes vague and difficult to verify. In fact, the only information so far available comes from the secret archives of an enigmatic secret society that can be found at the heart of this tangled web of conspiracy, greed and power: the so-called Priory of Sion.

They claim that the marriage took place in the original church at Rennes-le-Château, which they identified with the fortress of Rhedae, last bastion of the Visigothic empire in France. It was from here that Dagobert, enriched and confident, was able to launch his bid to recover the throne. By 674, he had managed to become king of Austrasia, and two years later Giselle gave birth to his son and heir, Sigisbert IV. Dagobert ruled with an iron hand, dealing competently with internal squabbles amongst his rebellious nobles; even bringing Aquitaine (to the west of the Languedoc) back into his kingdom. However – and surely to the disappointment of Wilfred – Dagobert lacked obvious commitment to the Catholic Church; indeed he leant more towards the Arianism of his Visigoth in-laws.

It is accepted by historians that, in 679, Dagobert was assassinated in the forest of Stenay in the Ardennes on the order of the Mayor of the Palace,

Pepin the Fat, but with the tacit approval of the Roman Catholic Church, which felt able to support this act of political expediency in the name of suppressing heresy. The Church then endorsed the right of Pepin to assume control. According to the secret archives, Sigisbert, Dagobert's young son, was smuggled to the safety of his mother's family at Rennes-le-Château where as Sigisbert IV he eventually assumed his uncle's title, the Count of Razès[7].

The 8th century Knights' Stone[8], discovered during the restoration of the church at Rennes-le-Château in 1891, has been said to depict the young Sigisbert being carried to safety on horseback by an armed knight. The tradition further maintains that this knight, one of Sigisbert's father's trusted companions, was called Mérovée Levi[9]; his name being of Jewish origin will prove to be significant since the Merovingians themselves were considered to be of Semitic origin. Henri Buthion, former owner of the Abbé Saunière's domain, believes this sculpted stone once covered what was actually the wall tomb of Sigisbert, in the church. The chance discovery, during the excavations of a road in the village to lay a new water pipe, of other tombstones and artefacts from a Merovingian cemetery would seem to add some weight to the story.

It must be remembered that, if true, the birth of Sigisbert would be a crucial factor in establishing a dynastic alliance, through the marriage of Dagobert II, of a Merovingian monarch with the Visigoth aristocracy; as such, Sigisbert would have been held in great esteem by all his people. Had it not been for the duplicity of Pepin and the Church, he would have succeeded his father as the next Merovingian king. Coming to Rennes, he then assumed the title of the Count of Razès from his grandfather, Bera. He would also, without doubt, have been initiated into the secret of the fabulous Visigoth treasure.

But there is also an alternative tradition concerning the genealogy of Sigisbert IV. Some sources claim that he was actually the son of Bera, the Count of Razès, whose own father was the Visigoth king Wamba; Sigisbert later married Magdala, the daughter of Bridget, one of the three daughters of Dagobert II and his first wife, Mathilde. In this account, it is Magdala who was brought to the safety of Rennes-le-Château by the knight Mérovée Levis. If this version is correct, then Dagobert would have had no legitimate heir to the throne, since under Salic Law (adopted by the Merovingians) women were prevented from succeeding to the throne. Thus, while

Sigisbert IV and his descendents would still have had a right to the title of Count of Razès, they could not have laid claim to the Merovingian succession. Could it be that the creation of Sigisbert, with his Semitic genetics, and his escape story, have been manufactured in order to legitimize a future claim to the throne – and the gold?

The Merovingians continued to rule over the Frankish kingdoms in name only. The real power now resided in the hands of the descendents of Pepin the Fat, who were to form the Carolingian dynasty. Military champions of the Church of Rome, the first Carolingian was Pepin's own son, Charles Martel. Though never actually crowned king, it was the heroic Charles Martel who, as we have seen, achieved the subjugation of the Islamic Berbers (or Moors).

Meanwhile, Visigothic power became confined to the remote high valley of the Aude with its fortress capital of Rhedae. Yet while Visigothic power across the region may have waned, this concentration of activity in Rennes made something of a 'golden age' there. This is confirmed by a census report of towns of the Languedoc in the late 8th century by Bishop Theodulphe, commissioned by Charlemagne, the grandson and heir of Charles Martel, which shows Rhedae to be a city equal in importance to its neighbours, Carcassonne and Narbonne.

Charlemagne was crowned Holy Roman Emperor by Pope Leo III on Christmas Day, 800, in recognition of his extension of the influence of the Church throughout what were now Frankish domains. He granted Carcassonne to one of his commanders, in recognition of his military service, who adopted the title of Count of Carcassonne – Rhedae being one of his dependencies. A short while later, Rhedae achieved its greatest glory when elevated to the status of a royal city following the marriage of Amalric, the son of a Visigoth king, to the Frank princess, Clothilde. Rhedae was now set to enjoy a period of culture and splendour that was to last about 200 years.

Chapter 2
Conflicts of Faith and Legend

Preoccuppied with the major conflicts between Christianity and Islam, and within the Christian faith itself, it is easy to overlook the presence of possibly the oldest surviving religious sect in the region. Living largely in close-knit communities, partly for security from the ever-present fear of persecution and partly because of their strong family ties and traditions, the Jews had established several flourishing communities outside the Holy Land, of which Marseille was one of the largest. Whilst first settling some centuries before, it was in Roman times that this Jewish community most expanded its influence and wealth, primarily through trade. In the neighbouring Camargue, a marshy island at the mouth of the Rhône, a local legend arose with some variations, which claimed that, in 44 AD, Mary Magdalene, her brother Lazarus and several others, having fled to Alexandria, crossed the Mediterranean and arrived not far from the city of Marseille at the village of Ratis, now named Les Saintes Maries de la Mer. Shortly afterwards, the party split up and the Magdalene journeyed some fifty kilometres east to live out the rest of her life at the cave of St. Baume. There she evidently died in 60 AD. (This account is actually accepted by the Catholic Church which has built a mausoleum for her remains at nearby St. Maximin.)

Following the crucifixion, the followers of Jesus had been considered a political and religious threat by the elders of the Temple of Jerusalem. But since the Jewish communities throughout the Mediterranean were not under the centralised control of the Jerusalem faction, it is reasonable to believe that Mary and her close companions could have found a safe haven in the south of France. The legends surrounding the Magdalene and her arrival in France are investigated in depth by Margaret Starbird in her book, *The Woman with the Alabaster Jar*.

Mary Magdalene, the 'best loved disciple' of the Lord (possibly even his wife according to the Gnostic Gospels)[1], is believed to have been a Benjamite; Jesus was from the Benjamite's elder kinsmen the great House of Judah. Another tradition maintains that both Mary Magdalene and Jesus were of noble birth. If this is the case, her arrival in the south of France could have been even more significant for the Jewish community of the time than it was for the later Christian one.

At this point, from a synthesis of historical facts, biblical accounts and legends, an interesting scenario presents itself. On their return to Caanan after the Exodus, the land renamed Israel was divided up among its twelve tribes. It was on the border of the tribes of Judah and Benjamin that the city of Jerusalem was founded, in which Solomon was to construct his Temple. It is reported in Judges 21 that the tribe of Benjamin came into conflict with the other tribes; a great battle ensued with many casualties on both sides resulting in the defeat of Benjaminites. There was subsequently a reconcilliation but not before, according to some traditions, a large number of the Benjamin tribe had fled to seek shelter under the Phoenicians at Tyre, with whom it appears they had already made contact. Through marriage, they would have become absorbed into Phoenician society. It is of course opportune to recall that it was Hiram, King of Tyre, who sent to Solomon, the builders and materials needed for the construction of his great temple.

A great sea-faring and trading nation, the Phoenicians colonised, from 600 BC onwards, a substantial part of the Mediterranean coastline – including Marseille and Narbonne on the southern French coast and inland to Carcassonne, Toulouse and very possibly Rhedae. Some of the first Jewish communities in these cities could, therefore, have originated from Phoenician Benjaminites. Mary Magdalene could well have found there a community that welcomed her as one of their own.

A footnote to the Magdalene legend, unearthed by French researcher André Douzet, brings it even closer into the mysteries of Rennes-le-Château. One legend claims that Mary Magdalene's body was taken by a 9th century nobleman, Gérard de Roussillon, to the abbey of Vézelay – which he had founded. Gérard de Roussillon was Count of Barcelona, Narbonne and Provence, in other words Provence and Septimania, which included the region of Roussillon which extends down to the Spanish border (now known as French Catalonia). Douzet further highlights a close topological correspondence between the coastal region of Languedoc-Roussillon and the region of Les Saintes Maries de la Mer. Could she have travelled inland to Rennes-le-Château? Had Gérard discovered her body at Rennes-le-Château, and taken it to Vézelay? The true nature and history of the Magdalene is another thread, alongside that of the treasure, that has given rise to allegations of a conspiracy of silence perpetrated by the Roman Catholic Church.

With the eventual domination of the region by the inquisitorial Catholic Church, the significant role played by the Jews in the early history of France was very effectively concealed. It is often conveniently forgotten that early Christianity had grown out of Judaism; that Jesus, his family and all his disciples were Jews; and that the true mission of Jesus was probably the reformation of the Jewish religion, not the creation of a new one.

The Jewish communities flourished under the Roman administration, since the Romans were not unduly concerned about their subjects' theological beliefs, provided they paid their taxes and remained subdued. And when the Romans were displaced by the Visigoths, the effect on the Jews would have been minimal. The doctrines of Arian Christianity did not conflict with Judaism in the way that those of the Catholic Church did, so this allowed a more easy integration between the Jews and the Visigoths. There is evidence of inter-marriage between their respective aristocracies resulting in obvious Semitic names among non-Jews. For example, the name Bera occurs frequently in the extended family of Dagobert and his alleged son, Sigisbert, the Count of Razès.

Two particular facts underline the positive relationship between both the Merovingians and the Visigoths and the Jews. First, the revised Codex Euricus of 681 (based on the codified law issued by the 5th century Visigoth king, Euric), possibly the greatest legal achievement of the Visigoths in Spain, concerned itself with an examination of the existing anti-Jewish legislation and the behaviour of slaves. Jews were formerly subjected to harsh treatment by some influential sections of Visigothic society and in the second half of the 7th century were given the stark choice of conversion or enslavement. Why should the Visigoth administrators be concerned with Jewish rights sufficiently to create specific legislation? Second, both the Franks and their Merovingian rulers adhered to Salic Law as the basis of their legal framework. J J Rabinowitz, in *The Title De Migrantibus of the Lex Salica and the Jewish Herem Hayishub*, reveals that a significant section of Salic Law, Title 45 – 'De Migrantibus', is derived directly from the Talmud – that is, traditional Judaic Law. (Salic Law was derived from the legal code of the 4th century Salian Franks who had settled in the Rhine region of the Netherlands.)

Thus, the region of Septimania in the 7th, 8th and 9th centuries contained not only a very large Jewish population, but a benignly-ruled one, allowing it to exert considerable influence in society, and at the highest levels permitting integration with the Visigoth, Merovingian, or Carolingian policy. These groups can be seen to have colluded with each other to safeguard their mutual interests. For instance, following their defeat by Charles Martel, the Islamic Moors were at first driven back to seek refuge in the heavily fortified city of Narbonne – already home to a large Jewish community. Though initially content to live in mutual co-operation with the Islamic invaders, Pepin III (or Pepin the Short, the son and successor of Charles Martel) wished to drive the Islamic Moors completely out of France and to have his claim to biblical succession (the divine right to rule) endorsed by the Jews, possibly also to lay a future legitimate claim to the treasure. In return for the creation of an independent Jewish principality, he persuaded the Jews to overthrow the Islamic defenders of Narbonne. So it was, that in 768 a formal Jewish enclave was established in Septimania which owed Pepin only nominal allegiance. Professor Arthur Zuckerman examines this fascinating historical development in his book *A Jewish Princedom in Feudal France.*

Pepin also installed a King of the Jews of Septimania, whose name appears in its Frankish version as Theodoric, or Thierry, and who was acknowledged by both Pepin and the Caliph of Baghdad as 'the seed of the royal house of David', a description that had also been inexplicably applied to the Merovingian kings. From his marriage to Pepin's sister Alda, Thierry fathered a son, Guillem de Gellone.

Guillem de Gellone acquired almost legendary status in his own lifetime, inspiring a number of epic poems to be written about him in the person of Guillaume d'Orange; even appearing in Dante's *Divine Comedy* and the earlier *Willehalm* by Wolfram von Eschenbach. Guillem was one of Charlemagne's premier commanders in the continual conflict against the Moors, eventually capturing Barcelona, thus extending Frankish influence across the Pyrenees. As King of the Jews of Septimania, Guillem also held the titles of Count of Barcelona, of Toulouse, of the Auvergne and – perhaps more significantly in this quest for treasure – of the Razès, the fiefdom which surrounds Rennes-le-Château.

A highly educated man, fluent in both Arabic and Hebrew, Guillem is said to have founded, in about 792, an academy of Judaic studies at Gellone, which attracted scholars to its renowned library. On retirement from his active military career, Guillem withdrew to the confines of his academy. The partially-ruined monastery of St. Guilhem-le-Désert, the former academy, still houses a relic of the 'True Cross' given to him by Charlemagne (who in turn had been given it by the Patriarch of Jerusalem) in recognition of his military feats. Yet his adoption as a champion of Christianity in consideration of his illustrious exploits in defence of the Catholic Franks against the Islamic Moors, and his canonisation as St. Guillem, has resulted in the relegation of his Judaic origins. But this dualism has its own intriguing legacies: it is reported by V. Saxer, in *Le Culte de Marie Madeleine en Occident*, that Gellone became one of Europe's first centres for the cult of the Magdalene during its term as a Judaic academy.

The crowning of Charlemagne in 800 as Holy Roman Emperor consolidated the position of the Roman Catholic Church over a vast region that included modern France, Switzerland, the northern half of Italy, and most of Germany and Austria. But the Languedoc, with its remote mountainous regions, continued to maintain a large measure of independence: heresies fermented; individual counts wielded great power and amassed great wealth; a liberal culture flourished in which knowledge, the arts, philosophy and ethics were held in high esteem. All these attributes, of course, offered sufficient reasons for avaricious northern barons and the paranoid Catholic Church to collaborate against this enlightened oasis of Dark Ages Europe.

The successors of Charlemagne tended to be incompetent in their administrative skills; their lack of authority allowed others to make inroads into the kingdom: the Normans were able to colonise the north-western area of France now called Normandy. The Carolingians themselves finally gave way, in 987, to the Capetian dynasty; the title of Holy Roman Emperor, however, passed to the German Saxon kings, most of whom belonged to the Hohenstaufen succession. Yet the Hohenstaufens were anti-Roman Catholic. With the complicity of the Church of Rome, they were soon to be replaced by the Swiss Habsburgs, who were to remain the Holy Roman Emperors for more than 500 years. These battles for dynastic supremacy are examples of conspiracy and power agendas that have been played out in Europe until the present day.

Meanwhile, in the remote foothills of the Pyrenees, the descendants of Dagobert II continued to hold the title of Count of Razès. And, together with a few other descendants of fellow integrated Merovingian, Visigoth and Jewish families, tenaciously kept alive the memory of the fabulous treasure of the Temple of Jerusalem. One of the most prominent of these families were the Hautpouls, who in the 15th century became the Lords of Rennes and Blanchefort, and occupied the castle adjacent to the church in Rennes-le-Château. According to the researches of Lionel Fanthorpe, the Hautpoul family are descendants of the Visigoth king Atulph, an ally of Alaric the sacker of Rome. They originally settled near Mazamet, the town north of Carcassonne, where today the actual village of Hautpoul clings precariously to the wall of a gorge, in the shadow of the Montagne Noire. Atulph was known locally as the King of the Black Mountain, and a little further south is the Montagne d'Alaric.

Jean Robin's *Rennes-le-Château, La Colline Envoutée* mentions other families of possible Merovingian descent. His findings are based on an ancient document, the Charte d'Alaon, which though originating from 845, was only published in 1694. Lack of confirmation has permitted a lively debate on the authenticity of this charter, but seen together with the known antiquity of the families it mentions – the Grammonds, the Montesquiou, the Galard, the Luppe and the Comminges – Robin's conclusions would appear to be not unfounded.

Over time, historical fact and legend have certainly fused to create the powerful symbolism of an ancient bloodline, shared by the descendants of a Visigoth-Merovingian nobility, which in turn had a possible connection to the ancient biblical tribes of Benjamin and Judah. The introduction of the Magdalene into this mix adds an even more significant dimension. But fascinating as it is, the bloodline itself may be not what is most important. Surely of greater significance, politically, financially and historically is that the ancestors of these particular families of the Languedoc-Roussillon, steeped in the mysteries and traditions of the region, shared the secret of the treasure of the Temple of Jerusalem, believed to have been brought for safe-keeping to the High Valley of the Aude or the neighbouring mountains and valleys of the Corbières. We will see how the activities and agendas of an assorted range of individuals and societies, throughout the centuries, have been fashioned by a belief in these seductive legends.

Chapter 3
Legacy of the Warrior Monks

But Rennes-le-Château is not the only village in the region with an important historical past. Situated adjacent to the Roman road that extends south from Toulouse to Carcassonne and passes through the ancient market town of Limoux, is the pretty little village of Alet-les-Bains. Approached over a medieval bridge across the fast flowing River Aude, the village still contains many vestiges of its ancient past. Founded by the Romans, who named it Pagus Electensis (meaning the 'favoured' or 'chosen place'), it enjoys a naturally defensive position and hot mineral water springs, used to the present day.

Surrounded by a 12th century rampart with four fortified gateways, the village still contains many buildings of the medieval period. But it is the ruins of the great cathedral that dominates Alet. Originally an abbey, this magnificent structure was founded in 813 by Bera, Count of Razès and Barcelona, a testament to his wealth and power as lord or seigneur. Eventually (and briefly) elevated to the status of a cathedral – being the seat of a bishop – its diocese extended over a vast territory, giving its bishop great power. As with Rennes-le-Château, today's visitor will find it hard to believe that this sleepy little village was once the centre of such influence and wealth. One wonders why these apparently insignificant backwaters should have attracted such a remarkable history.

In the 12th century, the abbey claimed rights over the 'castrum de Blanca-fort'[1], a fief of Rennes-le-Château which came within the diocese of Alet. In 1119, at about the time of the foundation of the Order of the Knights Templar, Pope Calixte II personally intervened and ruled in favour of the abbey. Bernard fought this and, after 12 years of struggle, finally compelled the pope to review his decision. Of Visigoth origin, the ruins of Blanche-fort today suggest that this was not actually a castle – an allegation found in many works on this subject – but a fortified watchtower surrounded by Blanchefort lands. But most intriguing is the presence of an ancient gold-mine, worked by the Romans, that extends deep into the rocky hillside. Was it the Blanchefort tower that was so desirable or the mine underneath which could very possibly have contained part of the ancient Visigoth treasure? The 19th century local historian, Louis Fedie, claimed that the wells at the foot of the walls of Blanchefort give access to the ancient mine.

What is more, locals from the Middle Ages to today have believed that the precious metals extracted from the mine came not from a natural vein of gold but from a deposit of silver and gold secreted there by the Visigoths.

Another local story claims that Blanchefort and Rennes-le-Château are connected by an underground passageway or stream. Given the distance involved, this would seem unlikely. However, a detailed geophysics map, outlining the geological structure and mineral deposits of the region, does show a fault line in the rock strata that extends from west of the village of Granès, passing by the bottom of the west side of the Rennes-le-Château hillside before continuing to the base of Blanchefort, and finally on to the town of Arques. This is only one of a multitude of fault lines; the whole area displays such a profusion of geological activity, caused by the formation of the Pyrenean mountain range, that it would not be surprising to find many extensive subterranean galleries and cave networks. Intense geological activity also created the 1230m high Pêch de Bugarach, the most commanding peak in the whole region.

Despite a lack of contemporary documents and the inconsistency in spelling at this time, it is generally accepted that the fourth Grand Master of the Knights Templar was Bernard de Blanquefort. An alternative spelling to Blanchefort, it is possible that these Blanchefort lands in the Razès were part of the family's greater possessions, although the Blanchefort family seat was much further to the north of the Razès. The 17th century *L'Histoire Générale de Languedoc*, however, compiled by the monks at Alet, mentions the Blanquefort family too; Arnaud de Blanquefort, a valiant knight, is reported to have supported Raymond of Toulouse. It is also said that Bertrand de Blanchefort had initiated clandestine mining activities, specially importing German miners for the purpose so as to restrict communication with the locals. Indeed they were explicitly forbidden to do so, thus protecting the secret of the contents of the mine.

But there are other concrete connections between the Razès region and that Order of warrior-monks, known as the Knights Templar. Increasingly, the knights were coming to play a major political role in Western Europe – and the Languedoc in particular. Approximately 6.5km south-east of Rennes-le-Château is a rocky ridge upon which the Visigoths had once constructed fortifications and which, like those at Rennes and Blanchefort, kept guard over this isolated valley and its precious deposits. Indicated on current maps as the 'Château des Templiers', the ruins visible today are considered to be those of the Château of al-Bezun (also Albedun or Albedunum). Its lord, in the early 12th century, was Bernard Sismund d'al-Bezun. Ancient charters carrying the name show variations of Sismund – Sermon – Simon, but as an acknowledged local historian J.A. Sipra demonstrates, these are all derived from the Visigoth name Sigismund. Bernard d'al-Bezun was a member of the ancient local Aniort or Oth family (the two names often appear as interchangeable), from whom several of the noble families of the Razès were descended by blood or marriage. He changed his surname to one derived from his place of residence – now called Bézu. He was uncle to two brothers, Bonet and Pierre de Redas who were both Knights Templar, and made substantial gifts to the Templar Order, confirmed in a charter dated 22 February 1151. Donations had been made previously by other local lords, as shown in acts to this effect, kept in the abbey at Alet-les-Bains.

The village of Campagne-sur-Aude[2] still displays much evidence of its Templar past. Situated only 5km from Rennes-le-Château on the banks of the river Aude, the village has grown around a circular fort, at the centre of which is a church. Its road names today attest to its bygone role. Nearby is Esperaza, a small but lively market town whose medieval mills were granted to the Templars.

But who exactly were these medieval knights? What was the true nature of their activities? And why did they come to have such a strong connection with this isolated backwater of rural France? 700 years after the suppression of the original medieval Templars, the appeal of these almost mythical spiritual warriors is still strong. Amongst a proliferation of chivalric orders worldwide, the modern Templars are possibly the most numerous – and far exceed the number of original medieval knights. A potent mix of military virtues, such as courage, discipline, fortitude, and strength, together with the spiritual values of self-sacrifice, compassion, charity and chivalry, form a powerful archetype, which may explain something of the Order's appeal; a 'knightly' class of some description has existed in most sophisticated cultures throughout the world.

A romantic vision of the Templars appeared even in their own time through the works of writers and poets of the troubador tradition such as Wolfram von Eschenbach, who referred to them as guardians of the Holy Grail. This perception was further enhanced through the works of Sir Thomas Mallory, and later Sir Walter Scott, as well as by the integration of a Knights

Templar degree into the higher levels of Freemasonry in the 18th century. But these sources have contributed more to the Templar's legendary aspect than to historical accuracy, and without doubt, there was much more to the Knights Templar than a military force defending Christianity against Islam.

Following the political and spiritual unity that Mohammed brought to the Arab world, the new religion of Islam spread rapidly through the Middle East and North Africa, replacing the powerful Roman and Persian Empires. Palestine, and hence Jerusalem, was under the control of the Moslems by 650, and was to remain so for nearly 450 years. However, Jerusalem still operated as a fairly open city, with Jews, Moslems, and Christians free to follow their religious beliefs. With the multitude of other cults and sects also established in the Middle East, it is easy to understand how Jerusalem became a spiritual centre for many different faiths.

Of course, for the three major religions of Judaism, Christianity and Islam, Jerusalem held a special significance, the focal point of which was the great Temple, built over the rocky outcrops of Mount Sion and Mount Moriya, and dominating the centre of the city. For Jews it was the holy site of the prophet Abraham's sacrifice, and later, Solomon's Temple which housed the legendary Ark of the Covenant in its inner sanctum, the Holy of Holies; for Christians it symbolised all this and the passion, death, burial, and ascension of Jesus; for Moslems, the rock of Shetiyah on Mount Moriya was the point where Mohammed had ascended into heaven. In honour of their founder, the Moslems constructed the golden-roofed, eight-sided mosque known as the Dome of the Rock. Yet despite being a magnificent building, the Dome was seen as an affront not only to Jews but to the western Christian community and, compounded by the refusal of the Moslem Seljuks to allow Christian pilgrimages, this provided a powerful motive to launch a series of armed missions.

In 1095, at the Council of Clermont, Pope Urban II appealed for a crusade to liberate the Holy Land from the Moslems. The First Crusade was the most successful, bringing Jerusalem under Christian control. A force of knights and men-at-arms, led by some of Europe's finest nobility – and including Raymond, the powerful Count of Toulouse – entered Jerusalem in July 1099, having fought its way from Constantinople via Antioch. The leader of this victorious army, Godfroi de Bouillon, Duke of Lorraine, was elected ruler of the conquered lands but did not accept the title of King of Jerusalem; this would fall to his younger brother, Baudouin, who succeeded him the following year. This was for many highly symbolic, since it was claimed that Baudouin and Godfroi were descended from the Counts of Razès, hence from Dagobert II, and thus of the Merovingian/Visigoth/Jewish alliance. As such, they could claim a unique legitimacy to the throne of Jerusalem.

Twenty years later, it appears that three knights, Hugues de Payen, Godefroi de Saint-Omar, and André de Montbard, offered their services to the King Baudouin II, to provide security for pilgrims travelling on the roads around the Holy City. Joined shortly after by six more knights, they were offered accommodation in a section of the royal palace on the south side of the Temple site, adjacent to the Al-Aksa mosque. Calling themselves the Poor Knights of Christ[3], they appeared to do little more than carry out their stated duty of protecting pilgrims. However, some accounts have it that they were busy excavating beneath the Temple Mount, in the legendary Stables of Solomon.

However, for the first nine years, this fledgling Order consisted only of the nine knights residing in part of the ancient Temple of Solomon. This is confirmed by the Frankish historian, Guillaume de Tyre, writing in the mid-12th century. Yet the king's own historian, Fulk de Chartres, makes no mention of the knights or their mission. Does this strange omission hide a secret agenda?

Evidence of their digging under the Temple comes from a report by Lt. Charles Wilson[4] of the Royal Engineers, who in the late 1890s led an archaeological expedition to Jerusalem, in the course of which he discovered Templar artefacts at the site of the stables. Additional evidence comes from more recent Israeli investigations: a tunnel extending under the Temple Mount was identified as being of Templar construction. Because this area of Solomon's Temple is under Moslem jurisdiction, however, further excavation has been denied. It is not known whether the Templars had found something of note – treasure, documents, or other artefacts – but speculation is rife, ranging from the recovery of the Ark of the Covenant to the discovery of lost scrolls of Jesus and the early Christian Church.

The surprising scarcity of information about this early period has understandably contributed to the mystery surrounding the Templar's origins and motives. The only authenticated contemporary reference to the Templars is an account of the visit, in 1121, of Fulk V, Count of Anjou, who granted them an annuity of thirty Angevin pounds. In 1125, Hugh, Count of Champagne, the powerful overlord of Hugues de Payen, formally joined the Templars, although he had already been on crusade in 1104. This was some fourteen years before the official founding of the Templars; could Fulk have sent Hugues to Jerusalem with a specific mission? The Count of Champagne, like the Count of Toulouse, was an extremely powerful lord, with more power and influence than the King of France himself. It is possible that Hugues de Payen had been sent to Jerusalem with specific instructions to search for some ancient biblical artefact, perhaps the Ark of the Covenant.

Intriguingly, the Count of Champagne had also provided the land for the foundation of the Cistercian Abbey of Clairvaux. This was established by St. Bernard, who was the nephew of André de Montbard, one of the founding Templar Knights. Under Bernard, the Cistercian Order flourished and became a most effective international organisation, with wealth to match. It was also through St. Bernard that the nine original knights were to be transformed from a motley crew into what would become a powerful military-religious order.

Just months after the death of Baudoin I in 1126, Hugues de Payen and André de Montbard returned to Europe on what can best be described as a recruiting campaign. They were remarkably successful in not only attracting new recruits and donations of land, property and other wealth but also, and possibly more significantly, in convincing the Church to endorse their new Order. This took place in 1128 at the Council of Troyes in Champagne, only 13km from the birthplace of Hugues de Payen, under the aegis of the energetic Bernard, Abbot of Clairvaux, who also played a crucial role in drawing up the Order's 'Rule'. In 1147, Pope Eugenius granted the Templars, now called the Military Order of the Knights of the Temple of Solomon, the right to wear the now-familiar red Templar cross on their mantle. From then on, the Order went from strength to strength, establishing houses, farms and commanderies throughout Europe. Of these about one third were in the Languedoc; two of the most influential, Douzens and Mas Deu, had control over the Corbières, Razés and Rennes-le-Château – and hence by extension, any hidden treasure.

To augment their military and religious functions, the Templars developed a sophisticated administration comprising a hierarchy of posts with specific duties, both military and domestic, clerks, non-knightly workers and even translators of Arabic. These were found throughout their major centres. And by the beginning of the 13ᵗʰ century, the Templars had amassed unparalleled wealth in land, goods and precious coins, not simply through donations and revenues but from deliberate policies of financial dealing and management. This necessitated the careful keeping of records and the development of auditing skills, and with these qualifications, the Templars were soon employed on royal financial commissions and as advisers to monarchs throughout Europe. Taking advantage of these opportunities and refining their competence in financial matters, the Templars achieved a unique role as Europe's bankers.

A number of factors were encouraging the expansion of the economy throughout Europe and the East. The crusades had opened up trade routes and facilitated a massive flow of goods and raw materials from west to east and vice-versa, and it was not unusual to find political or religious adversaries who nonetheless continued to trade. The steady stream of pilgrims to the Middle East also required goods and services, and in this, shipping played a major part. The Templars maintained their own fleet and became expert in maritime trade; they were sure to establish houses in the key ports of southern Europe. Pre-eminent as merchants, shippers, and financiers, the Templars have left a lasting legacy.

The medieval world was a dangerous one. Law and order were arbitrarily applied and afforded very little protection from outlaws and bandits in open country. It would certainly have been inadvisable for anyone to travel with a quantity of money or precious goods without a small army for protection. This insecurity applied as much to ordinary pilgrims as it did to the nobility. The network of Templar fortified houses quickly undertook the function of what today would be considered a banking system. Depositing their wealth for safe-keeping at home, the traveller or pilgrim was given a letter of credit redeemable at other Templar centres, which in effect became the fore-runner of the modern cheque. It was only a matter of time before the system gained wider applications, and landowners were able to raise credit from the Templars against the security of their lands. Of course, if the owner was unable to repay the loan, this swelled the Templar coffers.

Their function as loan-agents caused some disquiet, but this didn't deter the Templars from offering such a lucrative service. Unlike the Jews, the religious beliefs of Christians and Moslems technically forbade usury – that is the loaning of money for interest. A way around this was to add a fixed commission to the initial loan – essentially interest by another name – so the more religious members of the community still found grounds for condemning this activity. Prominent Church leaders vehemently spoke out against money-lending as being as evil as avarice; Christians indulging in this practice were accused of being no better than Jews – a distorted 'righteous' anti-Semitism.

Nevertheless, the Templars remained undeterred and continued to accumulate vast wealth. It also did not deter popes and monarchs from using the Templars as their personal bankers, for collecting taxes and even raising loans. Ultimately, political expediency was to swing things against them leading to the persecution of the Order. But by then, its activities had already diversified. With the fall of the Holy Land to the Moslems in 1291, the Templars lost their original avowed raison d'être; it was time they turned their attention to a very different agenda.

Despite expanding their activities throughout Europe, the Templar's main power base was centred in the Languedoc-Roussillon and Aragon region, more or less the ancient princedom of Septimania. The Commandery of Mas Deu, on the outskirts of Perpignan, had been founded in 1132, only four years after the Order's official endorsement at the Council of Troyes. But with the original sponsors and initiators of the Order from or connected with Champagne, why would it be the Languedoc that was chosen as its principal focus for its activities? Was there something special about this region that made it particularly attractive?

A group as financially competent, and with direct experience of the ancient Temple of Jerusalem, as the Knights Templar, could hardly have been unaware of the tradition, if not the actual detail, of the presence and value of the Jewish-Visigoth treasure in the Corbières. Throughout the nearly 200 years of their existence, they were to maintain total military control over this region, exercising virtual sovereignty over its local nobility. They had received donations of a large number of lands and properties, including mills, vineyards, and farms from its lords. They were even given six châteaux by the Count of Barcelona. By the end of the 13th century, the Templars of Mas Deu were at the heart of a grand plan that aimed at nothing less than the creation of a fully independent state.

Though nominally vassals of the king of France, the counties of the Langue-doc-Roussillon and Barcelona, being far from Paris (the seat of the king), rarely fulfilled their obligations and gradually turned their allegiance to the much closer kingdom of Aragon. As the power of the Templars became formidable, the Preceptor of Mas Deu commanded much the same authority as either the king of Aragon or the sovereign Count of Roussillon. From their beginning the Spanish orientated Templars had developed as an independent power and had always exerted a strong influence over the rest of the Order. An opportunity arose to advance their ambition still further when, through a will made at Barcelona in 1162, James I of Aragon divided his kingdom. His second son was to become king of Majorca. The new kingdom of Majorca included the Roussillon and its neighbouring regions, in which could be found the great power base of the Templars[5]. They had enjoyed a close and trusted relationship with King James, so following the death of the old king at Valencia, in 1174, the Templars of Mas Deu were effectively able to establish a sovereign independent state under the titular head of the king of Majorca. Besides the Balearic Islands, this extended from Montpellier in the north to Barcelona in the south.

Rivalries within kingdoms, and between counts and cities, proved a problem for the Templars. Internal division arose as commanderies allied themselves to their local lord. This division of loyalty, combined with the wealth and power of the Templars at Mas Deu, was to prove instrumental in their downfall.

Medieval kings of all nations were habitually short of money, both from excesses of expenditure on luxury living and from continually waging war – maintaining an army was very expensive. Philippe le Bel, king of France, was no exception. He tried to enter the Templar Order, doubtless with the longer term objective of becoming Grand Master and to gain control of their military might and enormous wealth, but was denied. In other attempts to reduce his liabilities, he defaulted on loans made to him by the Lombard merchants, extracting huge taxes from them; he employed similar tactics against the Jews, even expelling them from his kingdom. As minority groups, these were fairly simple targets; the Templars would require more devious action.

In 1305, Philippe succeeded in manipulating the election of Bertrand de Goth, Archbishop of Bordeaux, to the papacy. Whether by design or by coincidence, Bertrand, who took the name Pope Clement V, was also the grand-nephew of Bertrand de Blanchefort, the Templar Grand Master, through his mother Ida de Blanchefort. He must, therefore, have suffered from a divided loyalty when he was called upon by Philippe to support him against the Templars. But he was persuaded to leave the Holy Seat in Rome to take up residency in Avignon; Philippe now had the pope fully under his control. Then, with advice from Nogaret, his able but cunning chief minister, Philippe compiled a damning list of heretical practices with which he accused the Templars.

In medieval Europe, heresy was possibly the most serious of all crimes and justified the use of extreme measures. Hence, on Friday 13 October 1307, an arrest warrant, issued by the king of France and implemented through Nogaret, ensured the immediate detention of a large number of 'Templars'. (Very few of these actually turned out to be Knights.) Pope Clement was dismayed at Philippe's actions; heresy was a religious and not a secular crime and there was no real evidence of the Templar's guilt. But politics prevailed, and within a year, Clement acquiesced. The Templar Order was officially condemned, and finally dissolved. Without delay, Philippe entered the Paris Temple, expecting to seize the Templar treasure: since the Templars had been his personal banker, he assumed they held the royal treasure along with their own. Yet with disbelief he found no trace of it – and very little in commanderies elsewhere (each commandery had its own safety deposit with some reserves of gold and silver). His principal objective was perhaps not to be found in Paris, but perhaps some 1000km south, in the remote valleys of the Corbières[6].

The fortress of Pierre d'Aniort at Albedun (Bézu), as well as the fortified tower at Blanchefort, had been destroyed in the mid-13th century. It is claimed by an avid researcher, Abbé Mazières, that the Templars from Roussillon, under the authority of Mas Deu, established a new fortified base at Bézu, within sight of the castle at Rennes. There was already a Templar fort at Campagne-sur-Aude, less than 8km away, which came under the jurisdiction of the mother house at Douzens, as well as a number of hilltop forts commanded by local lords sympathetic to the Templars, which provokes the question as to why a new base was necessary. The prevailing and enduring tradition amongst the locals was that the Templars had discovered and wanted either to exploit a hidden treasure, or to bury one of their own. Certainly, the Templars were to ensure that neither their own, nor any of the legendary treasure of the Temple of Jerusalem, would be found by anybody else, including the new King of France. Furthermore, what better place to hide the enormous Templar treasure away from the clutches of King Philippe than in the heart of the Templars' own intended kingdom?

The researches of Claire Corbu and Antoine Captier reveal a direct link between Rennes-le-Château and the Templars. A charter of the Templars of Douzens shows that a Templar family lived at Rennes even before the establishment of Alberdun (Bézu). Called Pierre de St. Jean, lord of Rhedae, he became a Templar in 1147, and progressed to Commander of Douzens and Brucafel. Ultimately, they became Preceptor and Master of Carcassonne and Rhedae, between 1167 and 1169.

An organisation as powerful as the Templars, with such an extensive network, would doubtless have had an intelligence wing. Although surprised by the speed of King Philippe's actions, it is most improbable that they would not have been aware of the factors leading to their demise, and so had prepared some contingency plans to protect their wealth. Importantly, unlike Douzens, Mas Deu was not within the realm of the king of France. It is thus quite logical that the isolated valleys of the Corbières, already believed to contain the legendary treasure of the Temple of Jerusalem, were thus also to be chosen as a secure temporary hiding place of the treasure of the Knights Templar. Following the arrest, trial, and execution of the Templar Grand Master and the hierarchy, the exact location was lost. We will see how the prize of recovering this treasure, and that of the Temple of Jerusalem, has provided a powerful motive for intrigue and conspiracy that has endured until the present day.

Chapter 4
Power, Glory, and Tragedy

The mysterious, wild and romantic Languedoc, with its curving golden coastline, vine laden plains, rugged garrigue-covered hills and secluded valleys, has also been home to riches of a quite different kind than those of ancient treasure. It has often been said that knowledge is power; power invariably leads to wealth. Certainly, wealth explains in part the quite extraordinary advance in culture found here in the Middle Ages. Following the checking of the Islamic invasion of the Iberian peninsula at the Pyrenees by Charles Martel, the Languedoc became an interface between the cultures of the Middle East and the West. In addition, Marseilles, Avignon, Narbonne, and Toulouse had been major ports since ancient times. Traffic generated by the Crusades and the resulting trade had enabled the merchants and nobles to amass fortunes to a greater extent than elsewhere in France. Together with the material trade enriching the region, a flow of knowledge and wisdom, originating from the ancient classical worlds of Greece and Rome, was allowed to flourish under the Moslems and thus came to be felt in the Languedoc.

Though the Christian Church, both Roman and Orthodox streams, had itself inherited a wealth of learning from the ancient world, it adopted a policy of strict censorship over what knowledge was fit for public consumption, fearful that such learning could constitute a challenge to its own doctrines. It further discouraged the search for scientific discovery and the development of independent thought, opting instead to 'teach' the people what it thought was necessary for them to know. The consequence was the stifling of progress in many fields, including science, medicine, and philosophy, for centuries. But the human spirit and sense of curiosity cannot be suppressed for long, and there were those who ignored, at their peril, the restrictions in the search for truth.

By contrast, the Arab world voraciously absorbed and developed the wisdom of the ancients. Within 300 years of the death of Mohammed, Islamic culture was far more advanced than that of European Christendom. Of course, the Islamic faith also had its sects and internal rivalries through which dynasties would come and go, exerting varying degrees of power and influence. One of the most successful of these was a sect called the Ismailis, who arose through a schism in 765 and coming to prominence a century later. With a strong intellectual and emotional appeal, and a respect for tradition, the Ismailis drew support from much of the Islamic world. For the intellectuals they presented a philosophical explanation of the universe, drawing on the sources of ancient and especially neo-Platonic thought. For the spiritual, they brought a warm, personal and comforting faith, with a continuous quest for the truth. Recognised as a branch of Islam today, they continue to flourish under their spiritual leader, the Aga Kahn, who claims direct descent from the Prophet.

The Ismaili cause was given an enormous boost with the emergence of the great Fatimid dynasty (named after Fatima, the daughter of Mohammed), which adopted their faith. At their peak, in the 10th century, they controlled North Africa, Sicily, the Red Sea coast of Africa, the Yemen and Hijaz in Arabia, as well as the two holy cities of Mecca and Medina. Their main base was at Cairo, Egypt. In Cairo, as in other great cities, they established the world's first universities, pre-dating Europe's own by about 200 years. However, by 1090, the Fatimid dynasty was in decline, unable to withstand the challenge posed from the more aggressive Seljuk and later Zangid Sultanate. Yet, despite political upheavals, the Islamic world continued to allow the free transmission of knowledge.

When the Crusaders of northern Europe, indoctrinated with a false vision of pagan Islamic hordes, arrived in the Holy Land on their mission of liberation, one can only imagine their utter astonishment to find such cultural sophistication. This didn't deter them from pursuing their objective with ruthless determination. But there is abundant evidence, that they did show some respect for, and even co-operated with, their pagan adversaries.

But some Europeans had already made contact with Islamic culture 300 years earlier, on the doorstep of Europe, when the Umayyad Caliphate had swept throughout the Middle East, North Africa, and the Iberian Peninsula. Within fifty years, the Umayyads were to be replaced, except in Spain, by the Abbasid dynasty, which was to found the great new city of Baghdad, which would become one of the world's most eminent centres of learning. The Umayyid prince took the title of Emir and, with his capital at Cordoba, established an independent Emirate. As elsewhere, political upheavals continued to cause disruption, but failed to hold back the flourishing Islamic culture. Irrigation enabled new crops such as cotton, rice, and oranges to be grown, as well as orchards and vineyards to be planted, on previously arid land. Spices, silks, and perfumes, all contributed to a variety and comfort of life unknown to the majority of northern Europeans.

Despite the Umayyid independence, a steady stream of scholars travelled between Baghdad and Cordoba, carrying with them scientific knowledge, literary and artistic works, and possibly most important, a sophisticated level of philosophy. Originally of Phoenician foundation, Cordoba became the capital of Islamic Spain, with a population of over a million, and the centre of learning in Europe, boasting a library of more than 400,000 books. Such was the enlightenment of its ruling body that even its Christian adversaries, engaged in a continuous crusade in the north, were treated with tolerance and respect. Cordoba, a city of illumination when Europe was emerging from the Dark Ages, attracted seekers of knowledge in their thousands – Arab, Christian and Jew alike. Schools of music, astronomy, medicine, alchemy, mathematics and many other disciplines, flourished.

Among those drawn to this beacon of light was Gerbert d'Aurillac, the future Pope Sylvester II. Some French historians have said that Gerbert, the first French pope, was the most learned man of his time to wear the papal tiara. Born near Aurillac, the capital of the Cantal region north of the Languedoc (a name which, as in other villages like Orbeilles, Auroux, Les Aurières, and Auriac, evokes the presence of gold – the word 'Or' is French for gold, derived from the Latin 'Aurum'), Gerbert was the son of a poor manager of an estate belonging to the Abbey of Saint-Géraud. As with many figures of antiquity, his life has been embellished with legend; it is not a simple task to extract the facts from the mythology.

According to French author Pierre Jarnac, Gerbert, as a young man tending to his father's flock one evening, was spotted by some monks from the nearby abbey of Saint-Géraud, staring up at the sky, counting the stars. The monks stopped to speak to him and were amazed at the apparent wisdom of his replies. With the permission of his parents, they adopted Gerbert; in the abbey he could receive a classical education worthy of his intellectual ability. He thus became a Benedictine monk, and gained a reputation as a scholar. After fifteen years, his 'free spirit' compelled him to extend his search for knowledge. In the words of Voltaire, "Science magnified his soul".

The story continues that Borel, Count of Barcelona, having returned from a pilgrimage to the tomb of Géraud in Spain, visited the Abbey of Saint-Géraud, where he made contact with Gerbert. Fired up by the enthusiastic report of Borel, Gerbert left the abbey and travelled to Cordoba to 'learn the curious arts of the Arabs who held the key to great secrets'. It is said that he was later employed by the Emperor Othon II as tutor to his son, the future Othon III, and soon enhanced his reputation as a wise teacher. A fascination with alchemy led him into the world of transmutation, the secret of manufacturing gold from base metal, in which he achieved the status of not only initiate but adept. This inevitably brought him into conflict with the hierarchy of the Roman Catholic Church, which had developed a paranoia about scientific knowledge. For its own purposes, the Church maintained a virtual monopoly over education and the dissemination of knowledge throughout Christendom, a position that gave it a power that it was determined to protect.

In the Middle Ages, alchemical and scientific knowledge were viewed with suspicion and in some cases its possessors were considered as the devil's magicians. Possibly realising where his best future lay, Gerbert managed to reconcile himself with the Church. He decided to return to Rheims, site of the baptism of Clovis, where he offered his services to Hugues Capet, claimant to the throne of France. He contrived not only to replace the Archbishop of Ravenna but, in 999, to be elected pope, taking the name Sylvester II. Gerbert's political skills and his awesome intellect kept his critics at bay and ensured his survival.

Thanks to his stay in Spain with the Jewish and Arab scholars, he is credited with introducing (or re-introducing) into the rest of Europe, the use of mercury, mechanical clocks with an escapement, the astrolabe for navigation and even distilled alcohol. Sylvester also brought back to Christendom the basis of our modern numbering system, including the zero (unknown in Roman number), and the concept of decimals. But legend also recounts a more telling incident. It is claimed that Gerbert discovered that the river flowing through Aurillac contained small particles of gold mixed in its sediment. By immersing a piece of sheepskin in the flowing waters he was able, through disturbing the sediment, to trap these small flakes in the fleece. Upon withdrawal from the water, the sheepskin glistened with gold, much to the surprise of his on-lookers. Needless to say this became further ammunition for all those accusing him of diabolical powers and, following his death in 1003, he was branded a heretic and virtually expunged from Vatican history. Such was the power and fear of knowledge.

Gerbert was only one of many who returned to northern Europe, having experienced the learning not only of the Arabs, but of Jewish scholars and even Persian philosophers. There were two well-trodden routes from Spain into France: one was the old Roman road following the coast from Narbonne down past Elne, onto Barcelona and beyond to the south of Spain; the other was the pilgrim route from Le Puy in the Massif Central to the great shrine, allegedly containing the relics of St. James, established in the 9th century in north-western Spain, at Santiago de Compostela. Both these routes passed through the Languedoc, where in the 11th to 13th centuries, during the period of the Troubadours, there was an unparalleled blossoming of literature and music at the splendid courts of the region's nobility. Using elaborate and elegant language, the Troubadours composed long romantic poems of courtly love and noble quests, recited for the pleasure of the seigneurs of the Languedoc and Provence.

Of these great literary works, *Parsifal*, by Wolfram von Eschenbach is one of the best known. It also introduces the theme of the Holy Grail, one of the most enduring archetypes of Christian mysticism. The exact nature of the Grail is still open to debate: to some it represents the blood of Christ or the chalice of the Last Supper; to others it is the quest for inner purity and the meaning of life. It could also be the secret of eternal life, the philosopher's stone, the Ark of the Covenant, or the treasure of the Temple of Jerusalem. Whatever its nature, the Grail is considered priceless, and may only be approached by those that are pure in heart.

Adopted as a Christian symbol by the Catholic Church, the Holy Grail of Wolfram's poem is given a different provenance. Despite writing for a Christian audience under the patronage of Herman von Duringen, Count of (modern) Thuringia, Wolfram did not hesitate to explain within the text, that he had learned the story from Kyot, a Provencal troubadour, who had seen the story of Parsival at Toledo, written in 'heathen' – Arabic. He later states that Kyot had himself learned the story from Flegetanis, "a Jewish scholar born of Solomon, who could read the movement of the stars". In conjunction with the rest of the Parsival story, these details of its origins are intended to show how the Grail concept transcends the divisions in the basic dogmas of Christianity, Islam, and Judaism. Wolfram also asserts his belief in a higher mission of the religious-military orders by referring to the Knights Templar as the 'Guardians of the Grail'. Without doubt the Templars were guarding something in the heart of the Corbières; could it be that the Holy Grail was actually part of the ancient treasure of the Temple? Or is the treasure the Grail itself?

Also closely connected with the Grail stories was the Cathar heresy which mushroomed throughout the region from the mid 12th century. Of uncertain origin, the Cathar teachings have much in common with those of the Bogomils of eastern Europe, based on the dualistic philosophy of the Persian Manichaeans and Zoroastrians. Despite a radically different theology in which they believed that the material world was intrinsically evil, the Cathars lived a life that was patently more Christian than the Catholics. This didn't pass unobserved by Rome. Yet although espousing an austere and spiritual existence, they were rumoured to have amassed a great treasure, and by some to have been in possession of the Holy Grail itself. Evidence certainly shows that the Cathars enjoyed the protection of local Templars, some of whom had family ties. The great lords of the Languedoc, who even if not of the faith themselves, also gave them their full support. This policy was to result in a most bloody and brutal persecution.

In July 1209, an army of nobles, knights, and men swept down from the north to besiege the town of Béziers, led by Simon de Montfort (grandfather of the famous English knight) and Arnaud-Amaury, the Abbot of Citeaux. Upon entering the town, when asked by a knight how he should recognise a heretic from a Catholic, Amaury is said to have replied, 'Kill them all, God will know his own'. This signalled the start of what was to become known as the Albigensian Crusade – named after the town of Albi, site of a particularly vicious attack.

Some forty years earlier, after Catharism had achieved a firm grip on the region, the local Catholic bishops, alarmed by the conversion of their congregations to this new faith, had alerted Rome; but it was to be many years before action would be taken. The king of France and many of his most powerful barons, pre-occupied in fighting the English who at this time held the western half of France, had little interest in an internal crusade. However, the pope offered an inducement in that all lands taken from the heretics would be forfeit to the aggressor. For over a century, the barons of the north had kept their avaricious eyes on the splendid and wealthy culture of the Languedoc, but powerful local counts, like those of Toulouse, Barcelona, Foix, and Comminges, and their vassals, had been considered unassailable. At first, the Catholic Church sent a mission to the region in an attempt to reconvert the Cathars by preaching. Despite being unsuccessful, no further action was taken until the mysterious murder of the Papal Legate, Pierre de Castelnau. Unjustly blamed on Raymond VI, Count of Toulouse, this murder provided an ideal excuse to launch a crusade.

Although Raymond was the virtual overlord of most of the Languedoc, he avoided direct confrontation with the crusading army by the somewhat cowardly strategy of taking on the Crusader's cross himself, leaving his feudal vassals to take the brunt. Of these, the young and courageous Raymond-Roger Trencavel, Viscount of Béziers, Carcassonne, Albi, and Razès, attempted to defend Béziers and Carcassonne, to no avail. The crusaders swept through this peaceful and cultured land, looting, burning, torturing and killing heretics; laying waste the castles, forts and homes of the nobility. The ruined castles still precariously perched on rocky hilltops are an enduring testament to this bloody episode. Known popularly as Cathar castles, the origins of these predate the Cathars. In some instances, they even have Visigoth foundations.

It is of particular note that seventeen of these castles form an oval ring enclosing an area of some 600km. At the centre of this is the imposing and isolated castle of Auriac. And it is within this oval of stark, silent ruins that the treasures of the Temple of Jerusalem, and possibly that of the Knights Templar, are believed to remain.

Nine years after the destruction of Albi, Simon de Montfort was killed outside Toulouse following its liberation by Raymond VI. He was succeeded by his son Amaury, who proving to be less competent, was forced to discontinue the crusade and to return home. A period of diplomatic manoeuvrings and an uneasy peace followed, the county of Toulouse was annexed to the crown of France. However, by 1240, the crusaders were back, and once again the region was subject to the ravages of fire and sword.

Twenty-five years earlier, a Spanish monk, Dominique Guzman had founded the Dominican Order of Black Friars. Charged with the mission of rooting out heresy and heretics, Dominique created the institution which would come to be known as the Holy Inquisition. Feared throughout Christendom for its extensive and ruthless use of torture, the Inquisition would become the most powerful weapon of the Roman Catholic Church.

The renewed crusade culminated in 1244 at the mountain-top fortress of Montségur ('Safe Mountain'), the siege of which was to be both tragic and mysterious, and a lasting symbol of Catharism. Following the sacking of other centres, Raymond de Pereille had allowed his castle at Montségur to become the new centre of the Cathar Church. But within a short time, the crusading army arrived at the foot of the mountain. Due to its position on the peak, an assault proved difficult, as did the cutting off of supply routes, which gave rise to ten months of siege. But the defenders finally had to negotiate a surrender with an armistice period of a fortnight. During this armistice, two heretics, Matheus and Peter Bonnet (some accounts claim two more) left the fortress by a secret and perilous route. They took with them the Cathar treasure. Speculation as to the exact nature of this has been rife ever since, but one Inquisition account mentions pecuniam infinitam, that is, a large quantity of gold and silver bullion. It is reported that there were at least two successful previous attempts to remove parts of this treasure to a place of safe-keeping.

Montségur was not the only castle to be associated with treasure; those of Puylayurens and Queribus had similar reports revealed in the Inquisition records. It is quite possible that it was passed into the hands of the Templars for safe-keeping. But it has not surfaced since in any identifiable form. Shrouded in myth and legend, the accounts that remain of both the material and spiritual treasure1 of the Cathars were even to prompt secret excavations 700 years later.

Among the crusading knights peopling this story, two in particular are significant. The first of these is the noble Guy de Levis, whose name, as we saw in chapter one, evokes Merovingian/Visigoth/Jewish connections, echoing that of Dagobert's trusted knight Mérovée Levi. The second is Simon de Montfort's lieutenant, Pierre de Voisin, who was to found a new dynasty that was to dominate the Razès.

The de Voisin family took over the mantle of Lords of Rennes-le-Château from the deposed Trencavels and were responsible for rebuilding the Visigothic castle. But why, with the pick of much more prestigious and potentially profitable lands, did they choose this isolated backwater? The only explanation is that they were aware of the precious deposits within their domain, although it is unlikely that they knew the actual details of their locations. Further east, beyond the Blanchefort tower, they constructed the magnificent donjon (keep) of the Château d'Arques[1].

Other more tangible discoveries of gold have of course been made in the area. The most bizarre must be the story, fully documented in the French national archives, of the counterfeiting of gold coins at the ruined castle of Bézu. Some twenty-five years after the suppression of the Templars in 1314, and ten years into the reign of King Philip VI of Valois, the king's treasury ministers became alarmed at the appearance of counterfeit coins in circulation. Their source was a mystery. But most surprisingly, these coins contained a higher gold content than the official currency! Extensive enquiries led them to the Languedoc and to the ancient castle at Bézu. Having withstood the ravages of the Albigensian Crusade and the Templar suppression, the fortress at Bézu had never been taken by force, but by 1340, belonged to Jacques de Voisin, the son of Pierre de Voisin, Simon de Montfort's second-in-command, who had earned a reputation in the area as a great and honest knight.

The Senechal of Paris, chief official in the royal household, sent Guillaume de Servin, his second-in-command, to investigate these activities. Arriving unexpectedly, he discovered a cave containing minting equipment and a stock of gold ready to use. Of further astonishment was that the perpetrators were not common villains but members of the local nobility: Guilhem Catalini, son-in-law of Jacques de Voisin and a nephew of the reigning Pope Benedict XII; Brunissande de Gureyo, the wife of Jacques; Pierre de Palajan, Lord of Coustaussa (a village on the hill north of Rennes-le-Château); Agnes Mayssene, de Caderone and Dame Françoise, Lady of Niort.

Surprised in their illegal deed, the counterfeiters seized Guillaume and threw him over the cliff. On noting his disappearance, the authorities went to Bézu in force, arrested the nobles and brought them to trial. They were sentenced to imprisonment and the forfeiture of their goods. Meanwhile, Jacques de Voisin, who had masterminded the operation, was away, fighting on behalf of the king, in Flanders. Hearing of the plight of his fellow conspirators, he approached the Pope and other noble families of the region for their intervention. Eventually, in 1344, the new pope, Clement VI, obtained a pardon for them from the king of France. The act of remission, in which the participants are mentioned, is held today in the French national archives.

A story almost more extraordinary than fiction, it raises a number of questions. Where had the counterfeiters' gold come from? Why would they mint coins of a greater gold content than the official currency, unless their own supply of gold was colossal, and in a form not able to be publicly revealed? Evidence perhaps of the Cathar treasure pecuniam infinitam? But this operation had also involved practically all of the nobility of the Razès, those who would have been most likely to have inherited or acquired the secrets of the treasure of the Corbières. Family connections aside, to receive a full pardon for such illegal activities was quite exceptional. Perhaps they were able to buy their freedom? All of these questions remain unresolved – but above all, the source of the gold has never been established.

There is also the most curious highlight in the history of Alet-les-Bains that occurred in the 17th century. The village, more or less in ruins following the brutal wars of religion between the Catholics and the Protestants, became a centre for activities the influence of which were to be felt throughout France. A leading light in the French Catholic Church, Nicolas Pavillon, specifically requested the position of Bishop of Alet, despite having been offered far more prestigious posts. Once established at Alet, he set about reconstructing the village and its ancient buildings. His extensive building programme included partial restoration of the great cathedral, a new bishop's palace, a school, roads, irrigation and residential properties. He also became a fervent defender of Jansenism, a formidable Christian heresy. Having a rather complex theology with undertones of Christian elitism, Jansenism generally appealed to the more intellectual, but despite both this and vehement opposition from the Jesuits, it became widespread and influential. In fact, the bishops of the neighbouring dioceses of Pamiers, Mirepoix, and Foix all became Jansenists too. But why did Pavillon choose Alet? And where did the money come from? [2]

What is more, Nicolas Pavillon, together with St. Vincent de Paul and Jean-Jacques Olier, founder of the Seminary and parish priest of St. Sulpice in Paris, became joint head of a secret society La Compagnie du Saint-Sacrement. Created in 1627, it was also known as La Cabale des Devots. Condemned for its political activities – which reached into the heart of Louis XIII's royal family – the Compagnie appeared to be trying to gain control of all the key positions of State, operating in the shadows of politics and the Catholic Church.

A very clear but extraordinary profile begins to emerge as the facts are put together. The abbey at Alet, after all, was founded by Bera, Count of Razès, descendant of the ancient Merovingian/Visigoth/Jewish family alliances we have traced. Alet now becomes the centre of a secret political society dedicated to the infiltration of the corridors of power. What is more, this is associated with the biblical Solomon, builder of the first Temple of Jerusalem. Through Olier, the secret Compagnie is also connected with the church of St. Sulpice – which will also be seen to feature in the tangled web of this saga of hidden treasure and the quest for political power.

Chapter 5

Search for Lost Gold

The association of gold with the Corbiéres, and its neighbouring area, throughout the centuries, is undeniable both in fact and in legend. This is borne out by the researches of Jean-Pierre Deloux and Jacques Brétigny[1]. In 746, the mines at Auriac were exploited jointly by the monks of the Abbey of Saint-Martin-d'Albières and the Lords of Rennes; a hundred years later they were obtained by the Archbishop of Narbonne for his diocese, and then, in 898, these rights were confirmed, but included the renewed rights of the Lords of Rennes. The mine at Blanchefort was also being worked in the Middle Ages, again under the supervision of the Lords of Rennes. But the most surprising fact is that these mines, worked from Roman and possibly Phoenician times, were considered to be exhausted of all viable sources; so what was the true source of gold 'mined' and 'minted' over the centuries?

In the mid-17th century the *Memoires de l'Histoire du Languedoc, Tome 1* by Guillaume de Catel related that German workers were imported to excavate the mines near Rennes-les-Bains. About the same time a story began circulating that concerned a shepherd called Jean (in some versions he is called Ignace Paris). Out looking for a lost lamb, Jean fell into a ditch that revealed an underground chamber in which he discovered a quantity of gold coins. Taking some coins back to his village, he was accused by some of the villagers of stealing, and stoned to death. The local lord remained strangely quiet[2]!

In 1734, Lamdignon de Basville was to write, "The Romans had mines of gold in these mountains, but as the mines were exhausted, the art of finding them was lost and the treasures are now so hidden that it is impossible to find them." But an article about Carcassonne that appeared *in Le Dictionaire Historique de Moreri 1759*, reaffirms the possibility of the continuing existence of the Visigothic treasure, including that of the Jews. Then in 1832, a keen traveller on a visit to Rennes-les-Bains, Labouisse-Rochefort, came across a local tale of the treasure of Blanchefort, valued at 19.5 million gold franks and guarded by the Devil, which he then reported in his book, *Voyage à Rennes-les-Bains*. Some years later, an archaeologist from the Aude confirmed local treasure traditions and, in 1876, a very well-respected and knowledgeable local poet and librarian, Justin Firmin from

Limoux, later to become Conservator of the local library and Secretary of the Society for Arts and Sciences of Carcassonne, carried out a detailed analysis of the known facts and popular stories concerning the treasure, and reached the same conclusion, that it must indeed exist.

Some remarkable discoveries add weight to this. In 1860, a very substantial gold ingot, made of imperfectly melted down ancient coins and weighing 50 kg, was found in a field; another 20 kg of gold was discovered on a separate occasion in a wood. Since then there have been various finds of ancient silver and gold coins, and it is alleged that some villagers at Rennes-le-Château, at the turn of the 20th century, benefited from gifts of Visigoth jewellery and other precious items, uncovered by their parish priest[3]. Understandably, the recipients of these gifts have been reluctant to discuss them, though the researcher and author Gérard de Sède4 does claim that some were shown to him. Finally, in 1928, a small partially-melted golden statue was found in the local River Blanque.

References to treasure buried in this region can also be found cryptically woven into the stories of at least two prominent French authors, Maurice Leblanc and Jules Verne. In 1905, Maurice Leblanc[5] created the character of the gentleman thief, Arsène Lupin. Leblanc's many stories of his hero's adventures contain a remarkable number of indirect references to the mysteries of Rennes-le-Château, especially that of the treasure. The extensive references demonstrate an in-depth knowledge not only of the region's mainstream history, but of the traditions, symbolism and personalities now seen to be connected with these mysteries. But even more noteworthy, these stories were written fifty years before the more recent interest in the Abbé Saunière, Rennes-le-Château and the ancient treasure. A comprehensive examination of these connections can be found in Patrick Ferté's tour de force *Arsène Lupin – Supérieur Inconnu*.

Jules Verne, a household name thanks to *Around the World in Eighty Days* and *Twenty Thousand Leagues under the Sea*, would seem to be an unlikely participant in the secret of the treasure. Born in 1828, Verne published *Journey to the Centre of the Earth* at the age of thirty-six. The novel has become a classic in the science fiction genre. But it is a far less well-known work, *Clovis Dardentor*, that links him to the mysteries of the Rennes-le-Château. An acknowledged master of puns and anagrams, he appears to have encoded messages within his stories, particularly in Clovis.

French researcher and writer Michel Lamy has extensively analysed this and other works in his book *Jules Verne, Initié et Initiateur*. It explores how Verne's membership of secret societies and association with Freemasonry probably introduced him to the mystery of the treasure. The title of Clovis Dardentor itself contains a strong clue to the hidden message of the book: 'Clovis' refers to that Merovingian king who unified the Franks and defeated the Visigoths at Vouille, pushing them back to the foothills of the Pyrenees; 'Dardentor' can be separated into *d'ardent*, the title given to the descendants of Clovis once they lost their regal power, and *or*, French for gold. Hence the title is in effect describing, 'the Visigoth gold of Clovis and his deposed descendents' – who are none other than the Counts of Razès, the Lords of Rennes, and the other ancient families of the Corbières, guardians of the secret of the treasure!

It is in the late 18th century, a decade before the French Revolution, that a very real and illustrious figure, of claimed Merovingian descent, enters the scene, whose exploits are to play a major role in the future course of events. On 8 August 1780, Luc-Siméon Auguste Dagobert, Marquis de Fontenille, Captain-Commandant of the Royal Italian contingent at Perpignan, married Mlle Jacquette-Claire Josephe, daughter of Joseph-Gaspard Pailhoux de Cascastel, Lord High Justice and a member of the Sovereign Council of Roussillon. The wedding was witnessed by Jean-Pierre Duhamel, a cousin through whom the couple had met. A man of some importance, Jean-Pierre François Duhamel was, at that time, Commissioner of Mines and Forges for King Louis XVI, and correspondent of the Academy of Sciences of Paris.

A year before the marriage, Joseph-Gaspard Pailhoux had formed an association with Duhamel and an entrepreneur, Peltier, to engage in mining activities in the region. In August 1779, they obtained permission from the Monastery of Lagrasse to reopen mines on its land, and to construct a forge and works at the Grau de Padern (the ruins of which are still visible). This permission[6] was later endorsed for a thirty-year period by the king.

As a result of his marriage, Dagobert was given a one-sixth share of the forge to which he was to add Duhamel's share having bought it. The third owner, Peltier, unable to meet other financial commitments, was obliged to sell out to Pailhoux and Duhamel. So when Dagobert finally received the gift of his father-in-law Pailhoux's holdings in 1782, he had complete control of the mines and the forges, in an area that extended from Termes in the north to Tuchan in the south and Cascastel in the east to Roco-Ne-grè, near Blanchefort, in the west. Since Dagobert was still an officer in the Royal Army, he had to appoint a manager, for whom he provided a house at Villerouge-Termenès, to oversee the mining operations. Yet it is a great surprise therefore that, despite this extensive enterprise, no record exists of any extraction of metal or other minerals!

The lands at Blanchefort, in which were found the ancient mines, belonged to the Marquis de Fleury, Lord of Rennes, who had married Gabrielle, the daughter of Marie de Negrè d'Hautpoul Blanchefort[7]. An engineer called Duboscq attempted to reopen these mines without permission; the Marquis protested, but to no avail, for Duboscq's actions were upheld by the Intendance of the Languedoc. In fact, Duboscq already held several concessions on mines in the region, granted by the king's Commissioner – who was none other than Dagobert's cousin, Jean-Pierre Duhamel. It would therefore appear that Duboscq was no more than a representative of Dagobert, who in effect had been given licence to exploit all the mines in the Corbières. Perhaps it was more than a coincidence that both Dagobert and Duboscq originated from Normandy. Evidently Dagobert had an agenda to open and search every possible mine in the region. Was he only looking for minerals or perhaps something else?

Coming from such a noble and ancient Merovingian family, it is probable that Dagobert was aware of the legend of the Merovingian, Visigothic and Temple of Jerusalem treasure, and though his marriage appears to be a love-match, it does also appear to have been remarkably fortuitous. However, to fully understand Dagobert's crucial part in future events it is necessary to dig a little deeper into his family history.

Following the usurping of the throne by the Carolingians, the Merovingian descendents of the family of Dagobert II remained in the north of France, (except for Sigisbert or Magdala, depending on which tradition one accepts, who had allegedly been taken to the Razès). Settling in what would become Normandy, this line of the family of ancient royal blood was eventually integrated by marriage into the local nobility. In the mid-16th century the Dagobert family embraced the new religion offered by Luther and Calvin, becoming Protestants; in the course of the Wars of Religion, their manorial family home near St. Lô was burned down and their archives destroyed. However, the male members of the family continued their military tradition, and many achieved notable positions in the

Royal Army. They also further consolidated their status by marrying into other noble families. To be accepted into the Royal Guard, it was necessary to establish a genealogy that confirmed noble origins; so in 1728, Robert Dagobert presented his family history to a commission. Despite the loss of their archives in the fire at St. Lô, the commission accepted that the Dagobert family were indeed of noble – and even royal – birth.

In 1685 the enlightened Edict of Nantes, which had granted restricted liberties to the Protestants, was revoked, and the Catholics embarked on a new round of persecution. Looking for support, the Dagobert family enthusiastically embraced the newly emerging groups of so-called Free-masons, which attracted free-thinking philosophers, scientists, atheists, Protestants, Jews, merchants, and bankers who were prepared to adopt the principles of Equality, Liberty, and Fraternity. Later to be assembled, in 1773, under the name Grand Orient, these early lodges were committed to the abolition of the absolute monarchy, the reduction of the power of some aristocrats, and release from the stranglehold of the Roman Catholic Church; they were later to be blamed by the monarchists for bringing about the French Revolution. Freemasonry at this time had brought together many of the great names of France who had an interest in intellectual and esoteric pursuits[8].

This was a time of phenomenal growth in the numbers of secret societies; some were direct offshoots of parent Freemasonry[9]; some of Masonic appearance but actually in opposition to regular Freemasonry; and others avowedly chivalric or of a non-Masonic basis. Generally opposed to mainstream Masonry, the chivalric orders and societies tended to support the monarchy, aristocracy and the traditional symbolism, practices and status, if not always the dogma, of the Catholic Church. It was against this background that, in 1771, the Lodge of the Reunited Friends was founded in Paris and within three years had attracted a membership of noble army officers, rich bourgois and dignitaries. One such initiate, Savalette de Lange, son of the Treasurer Royal, gave up his job as a parliamentary adviser to devote his time to his Masonic interests. This led to his appointment to Grand Secretary of the Grand Orient in 1777. Before this, however, he had persuaded his mother lodge to approve the constitution of a 'Commission of Grades and Archives', to look into the origins of Masonic rites and rituals under his presidency. This was no more than an excuse to found a new lodge, Régime des Philalethes, with the aim of acquiring as many archives from other lodges as possible in order to discover traces of lost or forgotten ancient secret knowledge! Savalette used any means necessary to accomplish his aim and carefully cultivated good relations with other Masonic and neo-Masonic groups, acquiring documents from those that had gone into dissolution.

It was in 1779 that the very experienced Freemason, the Marquis de Chefdebien, Knight of Malta, Colonel of Foot, was also initiated into the 12th and highest grade of the Régime des Philalethes – where he would have had access to their extensive plundered records. A year later, the Marquis, in collaboration with his father, founded a new rite which came to be known in Masonic history as the Loge des Philadelphes de Narbonne. Viewed by outsiders with some scepticism for its curious, apparently occult activities, the Philadelphes was in reality set up, as were the Philalethes, to poach the secrets guarded by other lodges. It was a tactic that was to prove fruitful.

In 1789, the future of France was irreversibly changed with the onset of the French Revolution and its aftermath, the Terror, which ironically in the most bloody way replaced the monarchy and aristocracy with a Republic based on the Masonic principles of Liberty, Equality, and Fraternity. It is still a matter for debate as to how much Masonic involvement lay behind the Revolution; but it is without doubt that the outcome pleased a large number of Masonic brethren, though the means may well have alarmed them. The competing Masonic and Chivalric ideologies became the core of French politics, and the most astute of politicians became increasingly adept at keeping a foot in both camps.

Within the ensuing political turmoil, the opportunity was taken by many to settle old scores and bandy about various accusations with little evidence to support them. The extremists, under Robespierre, carried out an almost indiscriminate and paranoid purge of anyone they thought may be a threat. Even the Grand Master of the Grand Orient was executed along with most of the aristocracy and the Royal Family – including the king's cousin, Philippe d'Orleans. Dagobert, accused of treason by virtue of his noble status and for suspected nostalgic sentiments for the ancien régime, was imprisoned. Awaiting the scaffold, it is said that he was saved by the intervention of his Republican Masonic brothers, who drew attention to Dagobert's popularity and competence as an army officer.

The kings of France had belonged to the Bourbon dynasty, and their cousins, who occupied the throne of Spain, decided to take advantage of the upheavals in France to launch an offensive. France desperately needed competent military officers and so Dagobert was recalled, promoted to General, and sent to join the Eastern Pyrenean Army under the command of the Marquis de Chefdebien, son of the Vicomte and Grand Master of the Philadelphes. Thus two men, ideologically divided, were brought together in an apparently common cause, the defence of France; Dagobert being a Protestant supporter of the Republic and Chefdebien being a Catholic aristocrat. This singular state of affairs was to present the Marquis de Chefdebien, who had somehow managed to escape the scaffold (probably also through his Masonic connections), with a golden opportunity to further his secret ambitions.

General Dagobert's marriage to Jacqette Pailhoux had resulted in two daughters. This lack of a male heir prompted him to leave his archives, the Arcanes des mines des Corbières, in the care of his Masonic brothers of the Grand Orient. The exact contents of these secret archives are unknown, but could they have held some knowledge relating to the legendary treasure? In the event of his untimely death – such a threat was ever present during war – they could be put to good use in support of the Masonic ideals.

Welcomed back by his troops in the Roussillon, General Dagobert had some initial success in launching his plan for the invasion of Spain; but on 18 April 1794, he died. Some eight days earlier at Montella, he had been suddenly struck by an inexplicable fever, the effect of food poisoning according to some accounts; but the mysterious circumstances have led others to believe that he was deliberately poisoned. Nobody else became similarly ill at the time, and Dagobert's cook suddenly disappeared some days before the general died.

With their family seat established at Narbonne, less than 40 km from Dagobert's home at Cascastel, and his mining operations, the Marquis de Chefdebien would have been well aware of the exploitation of the mines; it is unlikely that he would not also have known of the traditions referring to the buried treasure. The extent and secrecy of the Masonic network enabled him to gain more information about Dagobert's enterprises and eventually to acquire his archives through the Grand Orient – having possibly contrived the removal of their owner. The name of Chefdebien, and his collection of precious documents, will crop up later in this strange history, again in mysterious circumstances.

Quite coincidentally, the demise of the celebrated General Dagobert (whose tomb at Mont Louis in the eastern Pyrenees near the Spanish border is surmounted by a stone pyramid memorial, a reminder perhaps of his Masonic interests) heralded the rise of another great French officer; a general who would affect the future not only of France but most of Europe, and even further afield. Earning the nickname the 'little corporal', Napoleon Bonaparte conjurs up an image of the people's soldier, an officer who rose from the ranks and who never forgot his roots. The reality is quite different.

Napoleon was born at Ajaccio on the island of Corsica in 1769, the fourth son of Carlo Buonoparte, a lawyer, and his wife Letizia Kamolino. His father's family was of ancient Italian nobility from Tuscany who had emigrated to Corsica in the 16th century. Though truly Corsican, Napoleon was educated in France from the age of nine and continued his education in three military schools, including the military academy in Paris. He graduated in 1785 and was made a second lieutenant of artillery in the regiment of La Frère, a sort of artillery officer training school, where he continued to expand his own education in military matters. After a chequered military career tinged with political activity, he joined a Jacobin lodge whose goal of a constitutional monarchy he supported. Napoleon was finally promoted to brigadier-general following his successful recapture of Toulon from the British in December 1793.

Napoleon's military skills were then used to quell monarchist civil unrest. As a result of his success, he was given command of the army of the interior, and henceforth became acutely aware of all political developments in France. Though ostensibly loyal to the Republican Directory, he appears to have had a separate agenda, and also to have received patronage from non-Republican sources. There is no doubt that he was violently opposed to a return of the old monarchy, but he seemed equally unhappy with the system that had replaced it, the five-man executive with absolute power known as the Directory.

Successful campaigns in Europe enhanced his reputation, but his Egyptian campaign, apparently mounted to gain control of the trade route to India, proved to be a disaster. His fleet was destroyed by the British Navy whilst at anchor in Abu Qir Bay in the Nile delta. Temporarily confined in Egypt, Napoleon proceeded to utilise his innate political flair to introduce Western political organisation, administration and technical skills into the country. For over two centuries philosophers and scholars had been fascinated by this ancient and mystical land with its unique hieroglyphs, which they considered to be able to unlock lost ancient knowledge. Thus the campaign to Egypt had drawn support from many quarters, including that of some Freemasons. Napoleon was accompanied, and possibly financed, by counter-revolutionary nobility such as the Hautpouls of the Razès and the Chefdebiens – whose lodge, Les Philalethes, was dedicated to the discovery of ancient knowledge.

During his stay in Egypt, Napoleon initiated an extensive survey of ancient sites, which became the basis for much later archaeology. The most important find was a stone tablet inscribed with three parallel ancient texts that enabled the Egyptian hieroglyphs to be deciphered. According to the researches of Barbara Watterson, formerly of the Department of Egyptology at Liverpool University, the stone was found near the town of Rosetta by a soldier named Hautpoul – a name inextricably linked with Rennes-le-Château.

It has been suggested that Napoleon had a separate agenda for his Egyptian campaign other than the search for knowledge. An article that appeared in the *Gazette Nationale ou le Moniteur Universel* on 22 May 1799 reported that Bonaparte had issued a proclamation to Jews to join him in the restoration of ancient Jerusalem. From his experiences of the Revolution and the part played by the Jacobin and radical Masonic lodges, which were believed to have had Jewish financial associations, Napoleon had doubtless grown wary of such secret networks, and was determined that the new State would not remain vulnerable to further subversion. So, despite later adopting a more tolerant attitude to the Jews, it is possible that initially, Napoleon wanted to establish a Jewish State in or near Egypt to which he could exile all Jews – for their assumed support for Masonic lodges – from France. This was a strategy that may even have been acceptable to some of the more orthodox Jews, who had always dreamed of regaining a homeland.

Indeed, in 1811, James Rothschild, one of the five sons of the Jewish banking giant Meyer Amschel Rothschild, arrived in Paris to help finance the restoration of the Bourbon monarchy; an action that would have alarmed Napoleon. In general, banking and financial institutions find a monarchy more favourable for their business, since Republics or state-controlled systems of government tend to put restrictions on private enterprise.

In November 1799, Napoleon carried out a coup d'etat with the support of two of the five directors disaffected with the old administration. They set up a consulate that effectively gave Napoleon political control of France. It became clear that he did not believe in the sovereignty of the people, in the popular will, or in parliamentary debate, but instead believed that a firm and enlightened purpose, with the support of the military, could achieve anything.

Despising and fearing the masses, he imposed a military dictatorship on France with a constitution that omitted any guarantees of the rights of man or the principles of liberty, equality, and fraternity. He introduced a reform that was to be known as the Code Napoleon, that is still the basis for French civil law; but he paid most careful attention to his army who were, after all, his instrument of control. And realising the 'necessary' role of religion for the people, inspired by Voltaire, Napoleon entered into an expedient accord with the Vatican, restoring restricted rights of worship.

In time, and after surviving a British assassination plot, Napoleon came to realise that life consularship was not a secure enough endorsement. In May 1804, on the advice of Joseph Fouche, his Chief of Police, he proclaimed France an Empire, and himself its Emperor. Despite his cynicism for religion and his previous loyalty to the Republic, he wanted to be consecrated by the Pope himself, so that his coronation would be more impressive than those of the former kings of France who had never received so direct an anointing.

In 1653, the tomb of the ancient Merovingian king and father of Clovis, Childeric I, had been discovered and was found to contain arms, treasure and regalia. Amongst which were 300 miniature gold bees, a symbol sacred to the Merovingians. Surprisingly, Napoleon had these bees sewn on to his coronation robe. Equally outrageous to royalists and supporters of the Republic alike, the ceremony took place in Notre-Dame cathedral on 2 December 1804, in the presence of Pope Pius VII, who was denied the actual crowning when Napoleon seized the crown and put it on himself. Claiming legitimacy, not only from the 'grace of God', as had the Bourbon kings, but also by the will of the people, he was far more powerful than any monarch before him. His court expenditure was also to exceed that of the extravagant Louis XIV, the 'Sun King'.

Princely titles were restored for members of his family as well as an imperial nobility of hereditary counts, barons and chevaliers. Always looking to secure and consolidate his position, he surrounded the empire with a ring of vassal states ruled over by his relatives. Additionally, to gain control of the secret world of Masonic lodges who many believed to have been instrumental in the Revolution, Napoleon contrived to place his brothers as successive Grand Masters of the Grand Orient.

Possibly as a result of Napoleon's mistrust of the Masonic and neo-Masonic societies and his desire to re-invent an aristocracy, there emerged a renewed interest in Chivalric Orders. The most discernible example of this was the renaissance of the Knights Templar.

Following the dissolution of the Knights Templar in 1314, little was written about an underground survival of the Order until around 1804. But only five years after the Revolution, two doctors, one named Ledru and the other Bernard Raymond Fabré-Palaprat, claimed to have discovered documents that confirmed the Order's continuation in secret since its dissolution[10]. They alleged that the Order had re-surfaced at a convention in 1705, from which they had discovered statutes revealing the election of the Duc d'Orleans as Grand Master. Forced underground yet again due to the upheavals of the Revolution, the Order remained dormant, its archives protected by its regent, the Chevalier Radix de Chevillon. On its alleged rebirth, Fabré-Palaprat became the new Grand Master. Under Napoleon's regime, the renovated Templar Order was permitted to flourish, and succeeded in attracting some of the most prominent public figures who ensured its protection.

On 28 March 1808, Knights, resplendent in full Templar regalia, assisted at a memorial service at the church of St. Paul and St. Louis in Paris for Jacques de Molay, the last official Grand Master of the Templars, martyred in 1314. This ostentatious and lavish service, endorsed by the authorities and supposedly by Napoleon himself, was attended by an elderly and respected priest, the Abbé Pierre Romains Clouet, who was described as the 'Primate of the Order'. So the leader of the Republic and a new empire was apparently happy to accept the re-emergence of a military-religious Order that had been the sword-arm of the Catholic Church, and a relic of the medieval age of feudal kings, lords and barons. Did Napoleon believe that the Order had indeed secretly survived for the past five hundred years, and with it, the great secret of its treasures?

Napoleon's interest in the Merovingians appears to have extended beyond his coronation. According to documents deposited in the Bibliothèque Nationale in Paris, he commissioned a study of Merovingian descent from Dagobert II, who had been assassinated in 679; specifically from his alleged offspring, Sigisbert, who had settled at Rennes-le-Château. And when dissatisfied with his childless marriage to Josephine, Napoleon repudiated her in order to marry Marie-Louise, daughter of the Austrian emperor, Francis I, and of Merovingian descent. Yet Napoleon considered himself to be the heir to the empire of Charlemagne, whose dynasty had deposed the Merovingians. Was there an altogether separate explanation for his fascination with the Merovingians?

In 1810, Napoleon ordered the seizing of the Vatican archives and their removal to Paris. About 3000 boxes of material were brought back to the Arsenal Library in Paris where they were examined and catalogued by Charles Nodier and his colleagues. Nodier achieved quite a reputation in literary circles having written several books, including a multi-volume compendium of sites of antiquarian interest in France. In this he devotes a large section to the normally little-mentioned Merovingian epoch. He also wrote, anonymously, a book entitled *A History of Secret Societies in the Army under Napoleon*, in which he refers to the Philadelphes, which he states to be the 'supreme' secret society, presiding over the others. Whether this is the lodge founded by the Marquis de Chefdebien, or one of the many other Masonic groups, or even a group possibly founded by Nodier himself in 1797, is not made clear. Yet the coincidence is striking. Presumably unknown to Napoleon, he was also steeped in esoteric circles. A friend of Eliphas Levi, the renowned occultist, and mentor of Victor Hugo, Nodier eventually became an esteemed Master Mason; in 1824, he was appointed chief librarian of the Arsenal, which contained the greatest collection of medieval and occult manuscripts in France.

The common thread that appears to run through these centuries of conflict and collusion is the search for information; specifically that from the Merovingian epoch, a period of history that by the time of Napoleon was somewhat forgotten and omitted from standard historical works. Can we conclude that Napoleon, aware of the existence of the Corbières treasure, was attempting to acquire whatever information he could about it, as had many others before him? However, this aspiration was never to be realized. Napoleon's driving ambition of maintaining and expanding the empire was finally to bring about his downfall. Following defeat at the Battle of Waterloo, he was forced to abdicate in favour of his son on 22 June 1815.

Following the passing of General Dagobert and the Emperor Napoleon, the quest for the legendary treasure was of course to continue. But it is through the bizarre activities of a simple country priest some seventy years later that this hidden thread physically resurfaces. These suggest that vital documents had been carefully hidden in a secret crypt, in 1781, some eight years before the French Revolution.

Chapter 6
The Secret World of the Abbé Saunière

Abbé Bérenger Saunière arrived at his new hilltop parish above the Aude river valley, on 1 June 1885. No longer the royal fortress and vast encampment of the Visigoths, or even, in their turn, the seat of the Counts of Razès, the Hautpouls and the de Voisins, Rennes-le-Château was by then only a small and neglected village of about 300 inhabitants. From the highest point of the village, adjacent to the ancient castle of the Haupouls, Bérenger Saunière could look down on the town of Couiza, with its impressive 16th century château, ancestral home of the Ducs de Joyeuse, which during the Peninsular War with Spain, had been temporarily converted into a hospital for wounded soldiers on the orders of the late General Dagobert.

Overlooking the town, on the hillside north-east of Rennes, are perched the castle and houses of Montazels, the village in which Bérenger had been born; the eldest of the seven children of Joseph Saunière, who managed the estate of the Marquis de Cazemajou, a co-lord of Niort and cousin of the Hautpouls. In his childhood, Bérenger is said to have displayed leadership qualities and led his friends in games, of which the most popular was searching for buried treasure in the surrounding countryside.

Coming from a family of dedicated Catholics and loyal monarchists, it is not surprising that Bérenger and his younger brother Alfred decided to enter the priesthood, to the delight of their parents. Entering the Grand Seminary in 1874, Bérenger successfully completed his five years of study, and after his ordination was appointed Assistant Priest to the prestigious parish of Alet, site of the great ruined abbey, former centre of the heretical Jansenist faith and its great advocate, Bishop Nicolas Pavillon. In 1882 he was sent to the remote village of Clat, which could only be approached by a long winding track from the town of Axat, some 23km south of Couiza and Rennes. Little is known of his three year ministry in this isolated parish.

On arrival, in 1885, at the village of Rennes-le-Château, his heart must have sunk at the sight of the dilapidated state of the little church dedicated to St. Mary Magdalene. With holes in the roof, broken windows and crumbling masonry, the building had actually been condemned as unworthy of renovation and only suitable for demolition by the architect Guiraud Cals in 1883. But with a youthful confidence and determination, Saunière set about creating a 'house worthy of the Lord'. With only a modest monthly stipend of 75 Frs per month, he was obliged to borrow some money from the Commune for the essential repairs. But within months of taking up his post and commencing the most urgent repairs, he was suspended from his parish duties for making anti-Republican speeches from the pulpit and was obliged to spend nine months teaching at the Seminary in Narbonne.

Upon his return to Rennes he continued with his work even though his financial state resulted in debts with local shopkeepers. However, in 1886 he received a much welcome donation of 3000 Frs from no less a person than Maria-Thérèse, the Countess of Chambord, widow of Henri, the last Bourbon claimant to the throne of France. At first sight it appears strange to see such munificence on the part of such a distinguished person as the Habsburg Countess Marie-Thérèse towards an unknown, humble priest in a remote backwater, but it soon becomes clear that the same tentacle-like network of connections encountered elsewhere in this story can also be discerned here.

Saunière's connection to the Count of Chambord and the (monarchist) aristocracy began through his father who, working for the Marquis de Cazamejou, was a loyal servant, and as an ardent monarchist eagerly awaited the return of Henri, Duke of Bordeaux, Count of Chambord, as the legitimate claimant to the throne. The Cazemajou family had been co-lords of Niort since 1696, with their cousins, the Negrè d'Arbles. The daughter of François de Negrè d'Arbles, Marie, married François d'Hautpoul-Rennes in 1752, thus linking the Cazemajou with the Hautpoul family, Lords of Rennes and Blanchefort – those whose castle is found adjacent to the church at Rennes-le-Château. Félines d'Hautpoul had been a tutor to the young Comte de Chambord and, in 1843, the Marquis Armand d'Hautpoul had accompanied him on journeys to Germany and London where he was warmly received by Queen Victoria.

As with all other monarchists, the Count and his wife supported the Catholic Church and the renewed mission of the Sacred Heart; a Catholic institution central to the rejuvenation of the Church in France and which was seen as integral to the restoration of the monarchy. In 1870, Rohault de Fleury had initiated a scheme to erect a massive new church, dedicated to the Sacre Coeur (Sacred Heart), in order to focus attention on this growing cult. Building commenced five years later on the hill above Montmartre, in Paris. Some years before his death in 1883, the fervent Count of Chambord donated 500,000 Frs to the project, thus becoming its largest single donor.

Whether his widow, the Countess Marie-Thérèse, had heard of Saunière's endeavours through the Hautpoul connection or whether he contacted her directly is not known, but either way the donation must have seemed like manna from heaven. Saunière's own devotion to the Sacred Heart and the monarchy is in evidence throughout his former domain. It must also be recalled that Rohault de Fleury was a member of the de Fleury family that held the lands near Rennes-le-Château on which can be found the Blanchefort mines.

With fresh funds, Saunière was to continue with his refurbishment and turned his attention to the ancient altar consisting of a stone slab supported by two carved pillars (some reports claim one carved and one plain pillar), probably dating from the 9th century. According to existing receipts, he was given another small donation with which he was able to purchase a new altar; it is said that he later placed the original altar slab in a private chapel and put one of the carved pillars in a small garden in front of the church.

It was during the replacement of the altar that Saunière appears to have made his first important discovery. Actual details are sketchy and various authors give slightly varying accounts, but the consensus is that he uncovered a tomb covered by a sculpted stone, placed face down in the nave in front of the altar. In the tomb, he is said to have found some bones, some jewels, and a pot of gold coins which he told the workers present at the time were only worthless medallions.

An actual record of the restoration is not available but a rough chronology of works can be pieced together from surviving receipts. By 1891, which appears to be a critical year in the saga of Rennes-le-Château, the stained glass windows had been replaced, and the porch, with its ornate carvings and inscriptions, had been added. But it is a number of other factors that have made this year a turning point in the life of the Abbé Saunière, and that may provide valuable clues in this unfolding mystery.

In June that year, he organised a First Communion service at which some men of the village carried a statue of the Virgin Mary on their shoulders, in procession from the church and around the village, until they arrived back at the church garden. There they placed it on top of the ancient pillar.

Normally this would have been an unremarkable event, except that the pillar had been deliberately placed upside down (evident from the carving of a processional cross and an alpha and omega on its front face). On one part of the pillar Saunière had had inscribed, 'Penitence, Penitence', and in another spot, 'Mission 1891'. If the pillar is turned the right way up, then the date reads 1681 – which is also found inscribed in 'error' on the tombstone of the last Hautpoul to live in the castle. Marie de Negrè d'Ables d'Hautpoul actually died in 1781, but the inscription on her headstone reads MDCOLXXXI (1681). Given that this is factually incorrect, could there be another meaning to the inscription? The gravestone itself is not in evidence today; it is said to have been defaced by the Abbé Saunière, who wished to conceal its hidden message. Fortunately however, the original inscription had been copied by a local antiquarian and was published in the 17th edition of the bulletin of the Société des Etudes Scientifiques de l'Aude, in 1906. The illustration clearly reveals an abundance of other errors. Some so bad that, even making some allowance for the poor education of the stone mason, it is hard to believe that the person who commissioned it was content to accept it. It has therefore been suggested that the errors were deliberate, possibly part of a code. We will see that an anagram of the inscription text appears on documents, held by a secret society, published some sixty years later. Whatever the truth of the headstone inscription and its interpretation, it is obviously an important key to understanding the mystery.

Later in the year, Saunière wrote in his diary that he had, 'discovered a tomb'; not a particularly unusual event in the renovation of a church, so one must conclude that this tomb carried some special significance. Even more enigmatic is another entry in his diary, 'The year 1891, carries to the highest the fruit of that which one speaks'. Two events occurred at this time, one or both of which may help to shed some light on these entries, their possible significance undoubtedly lying at the heart of the Abbé's later activities.

In the course of replacing the pulpit, he seems to have uncovered yet another tomb, evidently of some importance, because he dismissed the workers engaged in the restoration for ten days, during which time he is said to have undertaken secret excavations in the church. Then there is the story related by his old bell-ringer, Antoine Captier (great-grandfather of Antoine Captier and his brother, Marcel, who still lives at Rennes), in which he tells how he discovered a small rolled-up parchment hidden in a glass vial that had been secreted in the top of a wooden post. This post, which originally formed part of the altar rail, had been removed and cast aside during the renovations. As a result, a small fillet of wood had become dislodged from the top of the post, revealing a cavity in which he could see the vial. Captier immediately took it to his priest, Bérenger Saunière. It is not known for certain what was written on the parchment but some believe that it contained information as to the access to the crypt, and the nature of its contents. According to some accounts, the entrance to the crypt was under the 'tomb' in the nave under the Knight's Stone. The 'tomb' had been deliberately arranged to conceal the entrance to the crypt, presumably for extra security.

These precautions are thought to have been taken by the parish priest of Rennes-le-Château, one hundred years before Saunière's arrival. In 1780, when General Dagobert married the noble Jacquette Pailhoux de Cascatel, and his father-in-law had formed the association for the re-opening of the Corbières mines, Marie de Negrè d'Ables, Dame d'Hautpoul de Blanche-fort, feeling that the end of her life was near, had summoned her parish priest, the Abbé Bigou, to her castle. Having no male heirs, she had decided to entrust the family jewels and documents of considerable importance to Abbé Bigou, requesting that these be passed in turn to someone worthy. A few years after the death of Marie, sensing the impending upheaval and danger of the Revolution, the priest placed these jewels and documents in the church crypt. This already contained the sepulchres of the Lords of Rennes and other notables. He then carefully concealed the access, leaving instructions hidden in the top of an altar-rail post. Entries in the old parish register, now on display in the museum at Rennes, confirm the existence of a 'tombeau des seigneurs' (tomb of the lords) and the approximate location of its entrance. This tomb, in which the Lords of Rennes have apparently been interred, may well be the concealed crypt[1].

From unpublished original documents, Jean-Pierre Deloux and Jacques Brétigny continue the story of Abbé Bigou and the Hautpoul secret. Fearing for his life due to his monarchist sympathies, in 1792, Bigou fled to Spain when the Revolution turned bloody, where he was to remain until his death eighteen months later. However, he had already passed on his great secret verbally to Abbé François-Pierre Cauneille, formerly priest of Rennes-les-Bains, who in turn confided it to two others. One of these, the Abbé Jean Vie, became parish priest of Rennes-les-Bains from 1840 to 1870, and the unusual inscription on his tomb in the church cemetery highlights the date 17 January, that recurrent date in the Rennes mystery. The other colleague, Abbé Émile-François Cayron, became the parish priest of St. Laurent-de-la-Cabrerisse. According to the obituary column of *La Semaine Religieuse* in 1897, Abbé Cayron had 'almost completely reconstructed his church in beautiful gothic proportions… nobody knew from where he drew the funds to finance such great repairs.' Furthermore, he also financed the education of the young Henri Boudet of Axat, who was to succeed Abbé Jean Vie as priest of Rennes-les-Bains in 1872, some thirteen years before Bérenger Saunière arrived at Rennes-le-Château.

Before continuing to investigate Saunière's unusual activities, it is instructive to look a little more closely at his elder colleague in the neighbouring parish. In 1886, after nine years of research, Abbé Boudet published at his own expense a book entitled *Le Vrai Langue Celtique et le Cromlech de Rennes-les-Bains*. It sets out to show that the true Celtic language was English, and that the key to the origin of Celtic lies in the pronunciation of words and not their spelling. Boudet was a well-respected local scholar, a member of the local Society for Scientific Study of the Aude, and so it is surprising that his book contains a number of illogicalities and wild speculations, which have led many researchers to believe that this work had a very different purpose. Evidently, he considered his book to be of some importance since he sent a copy to Queen Victoria, who replied with a note of thanks through her representative in France. A copy of the book has also been discovered in the Bodleian Library at Oxford University, accompanied by a handwritten letter from the author. Nevertheless, some researchers consider that the text of the book contains an encoded message that refers to the great secret of the Hautpouls and the treasure. Indeed, the Abbé Vannier wrote, "The Abbé Boudet is the keeper of a secret which could be the cause of major upheavals".

After his death, Boudet was buried with his brother in a family tomb at Axat, upon which is a curious headstone in the shape of a closed book bearing the weathered inscription I X I O Σ, that may possibly be the Greek word for fish (used as a symbol by early Christians). If, however, the inscription is turned upside down it becomes 3 0 I X I, which may well refer to pages 301 and 11 of his book; by a strange 'coincidence', in the original edition, page 301 is a map of the valley of Rennes-les-Bains. Signed by his brother Edmond, who is considered to have drawn it, the map contains a number of anomalies, names and features that have either been deliberately removed since, or which were purely imaginary or symbolic in the first place. Meanwhile, on page 11, there is an intriguing passage referring to 'keys' being obtained through linguistic interpretations of French, Irish, and Scottish dialects. Taken in conjunction with the place names on the map, these linguistic keys when correctly applied may reveal hidden meanings. But what is the nature of the secret Boudet held? Was this secret shared with his neighbouring priest, the young and dynamic Berenger Saunière who had embarked on an extensive and unusual renovation of his little church?

A very full and documented analysis of Saunière's building works can be found in a book by Jacques Rivière entitled *Le Fabuleux Tresor de Rennes-le-Château! – Le Secret de l'Abbe Saunière*. By the dedication service in 1897, attended by his superior, Arsène-Félix Billard, the Bishop of Carcassonne, Saunière had completed the structural renovation of the church and adjoining presbytery; reorganised the cemetery, much to the alarm of his parishioners; laid out a geometrical garden in which was placed the ancient altar pillar surmounted by the statue of the Virgin Mary; and constructed, about 15m from the Virgin's statue, a Calvary cross. Within the church, Saunière appears to have let his imagination run riot with lavish and, in some respects, bizarre decoration. Many types of symbolism can be found; some are purely Catholic, in the St. Sulpician style in vogue at the time; others are possibly Masonic, Rose-Croix, or Templar. And within this profusion of decoration, this secret message is thought to have been carefully encoded.

As in all Catholic churches, the walls are hung with the fourteen Stations of the Cross, but here they are very detailed, and run anti-clockwise around the church. They were ordered from Giscard & Son, sculptors and statue manufacturers, in Toulouse. A dedicated Freemason, Giscard's house, next door to his workshop at 27 Rue de la Colonne, is covered in Masonic symbols still clearly visible today. With this in mind, various attempts have been made to decipher the individual Stations with interesting and persuasive results, but as yet no definitive conclusions have been reached (or publicised), except perhaps for Station number one, which seems to strongly indicate the existence of the mine at Blanchefort. Saunière further commissioned from Giscard a large wall fresco, on the theme of the 'Sermon on the Mount', which occupies the top half of the west wall and appears to contain several further 'clues'. First, the hill is strewn with flowers, a hint that the location is a hill on the land of the de Fleury family; second, on the ground at the foot of the hill, there is a draw-string bag with a hole in it, through which can be seen the glint of gold; furthermore, the cross mounted on the confessional deliberately draws attention to the bag of gold. Finally, in the scenery on the left can be seen a flower commonly known as Solomon's Seal, possibly a reference to the treasure of the Temple of Solomon.

But the most unexpected feature is to be found just inside the entrance door to the church, and supports the holy water stoop: a hideous, horned, grimacing devil, in a half crouch, bearing the heavy shell-like dish. A drawing of an almost identical figure, found in a book from the library of Abbé Saunière, is labelled as being Asmodeus. In Jewish mythology Asmodeus, was king of the demons and guardian of Solomon's treasure!

Statues and other decorative features abound throughout the church, but it is St. Anthony of Padua, whose help is sought by the faithful to recover lost items, who is given a special plinth of four supporting angels; possibly a gesture of gratitude by Saunière for his important discoveries. Yet another surprise awaits the visitor to his sacristy, where part of the shelf unit on the left side opens, like a door, to reveal a small room[2]. It was said by the villagers that the Abbé Saunière would lock himself into the sacristy after he had returned, bearing a knapsack full of stones, from long walks in the surrounding hills. Why the secrecy? What was the nature of these stones? Why construct a secret room?

The strange entry in Saunière's notebook, concerning the year 1891, is accompanied by an illustration taken from the journal *La Croix*, of a baby being lifted into heaven by three angels. Below this is another illustration showing the adoration of the Three Magi with the following comment: 'Melchior; Recois, O Roi, l'or, symbole de la royauté. Gaspard; Recois la myrrhe, symbole de la sepulture. Balthasar; Recois l'encens, o toi qui es Dieu'. ('Melchior; Receive O King, the Gold, symbol of Royalty. Gaspard; Receive the myrrh, symbol of the burial place. Balthasar; Receive the incense, to you who is God'.)

Saunière's interest in this legend (the names or number of the Wise Men are not actually mentioned in the Gospels) takes on a new significance in light of the fact that three rocky outcrops, dominating the northern entrance to the valley of Rennes-les-Bains, were known in medieval times, as Melchior (Rocco Nègre), Balthazar (Roc Pointu) and Gaspar (Blanchefort); could this be yet another pointer to the ancient goldmines of Blanchefort and Rocco Nègre with their secret deposits?

The church of Rennes-le-Château appears thus to be the focus and repository of three important secrets. First, the Hautpoul archives, the contents of which may have made reference to the deposits of treasure, as well as genealogies which shed light on their family history and that of the Lords of Rennes. Second, the Hautpoul heirlooms of precious jewels, artefacts and coins, the sale of which could possibly have enabled Saunière to continue the renovation and decoration of his church, and some of which were given as gifts. Third, the unusual decoration of the church, with its cryptic references to important locations of caves and tombs, possibly relates to the sites of the legendary treasure. The keys for deciphering these clues were evidently guarded by the Abbé Boudet, and apparently revealed to Saunière in the later years of Boudet's life.

Despite the rightful scepticism surrounding Saunière's alleged discovery of ancient parchments in the crypt, much speculation has arisen as to what information they might contain. Two of the four parchments, copies of which are revealed for the first time in a book by Gérard de Sède entitled *L'Or de Rennes*, re-titled in a later edition *Le Trésor Maudit*, are Latin texts[3] from the New Testament which could well contain coded messages. De Sède writes that, being sure of this but unable to decipher them himself, Saunière went to St. Sulpice in Paris where experts in such matters could help him. The Seminary of St. Sulpice had achieved a reputation as the foremost Catholic centre for occult studies. However, there is no evidence that he did go to Paris and even the provenance of the de Sède copies is in doubt. On this basis, many have dismissed these documents as worthless fabrications. On the other hand, messages can be decoded within the passages that concur with other known evidence.

In particular, the shorter parchment has a direct reference to the thread of the Jerusalem treasure: 'A DAGOBERT II ROI ET A SION EST CE TRESOR ET IL EST LA MORT' ('To Dagobert II, King and to Sion, is this treasure, and he is there dead'). The parchment also contains the words, Redis bles, where Redis may refer to 'of Rhedae', and bles translates to corn or bread. In French slang this also means, money. Finally, its last words, solis sacerdotibus, can be translated as 'only for the priesthood'; indicating perhaps that the secret should only be passed on through priests, which has certainly been the case since Marie de Nègre d'Hautpoul de Blanchefort confided in the Abbé Bigou.

Bérenger Saunière's brother, Alfred, having become ordained as a Jesuit priest, secured a position as tutor and chaplain to the family of the Marquis de Chefdebien in Narbonne – grandson of the founder of the Masonic lodge, the Philadelphes, who had acquired General Dagobert's archives. According to Bérenger's account book, Alfred had used his aristocratic connections to obtain donations for his brother, and amongst a number of entries is one for 30,000 Frs, collected within the period 1895-1903, attributed to Alfred. There is also an anonymous entry of 20,000 Frs in the period 1895-1905, from a mysterious M. de C., generally thought to refer to the Marquis de Chefdebien. It is not impossible that Saunière was being financed to continue his excavations and researches with the intent of recovering the treasure believed to be hidden within his and neighbouring parishes. However, according to the Chefdebien family's recollections, Alfred lost his post with the Marquis after being caught rifling through private family papers – but probably not before passing on his finds to his brother! Thus, through Alfred's covert activities, Bérenger came to know the secrets held in both the Hautpoul and the Dagobert archives.

Meanwhile, having completed his work on the church property, Bérenger Saunière turned his attention to the creation of a private estate adjacent to the church. In two distinct parts, one part was comprised of a villa with ornamental garden, the other a cliff-top terrace, with the appearance and dimensions of a rampart that connected a three-storey mock gothic tower[3] and a glasshouse, all of which enclosed yet another ornamental garden. Both buildings were well appointed with the best furniture and objets d'art, and the recollection of the villagers was that he lived like a lord, frequently entertaining visitors at the villa, a claim substantiated by large bills for alcohol and other luxuries. His expenditure by this time was astonishing, and it has been estimated that a deficit of expenditure over declared income amounts to at least 250,000 Frs. The source of these funds, quite considerable for their time, has been the subject of much debate by researchers. Could it have been the discovery of a hidden cache of money, gold or precious items? Or was Bérenger being rewarded for some covert activity on behalf of rich and powerful individuals with a specific agenda?

Despite being subjected to the most intense pressure by his new bishop, Mgr Beauséjour, who replaced the amiable Mgr Billard in 1902, Saunière refused to divulge the source of his wealth. Disciplinary action was taken against him and at first he was ordered to move to the parish of Coustouge some 40 km north-east from Rennes as the crow flies, but he refused to go, having taken on a new lease of the presbytery (which was the property of the commune). He was then suspended from all priestly offices and replaced by the Abbé Marty. Saunière was so popular with the villagers that they continued to attend private services at his villa, held in the conservatory that he had arranged as a chapel. When a further attempt was made by the Diocesan authorities to confiscate his property, it was revealed that everything was in the name of his housekeeper and confidante, Marie Dénarnaud, and therefore untouchable. Saunière thus managed, at some cost to his health, to withstand the formidable and unrelenting efforts of his bishop to force him to either be moved or stripped of his wealth. Why was it so important for him to remain in Rennes-le-Château?

Throughout his ordeals, Marie Dénarnaud supported Saunière. Sixteen years his junior, she became his most trusted and loyal companion. Originally from the village of Esperaza, she had arrived at Rennes with her family in 1892, and for reasons not yet explained, the four were given lodgings by Saunière in the presbytery which he had hastened to renovate. After a while she gave up her job at the hat factory in Esperaza to attend to the priest's domestic needs. There is some evidence that her mother, Alexandrine, was unhappy with this arrangement but seems to have been powerless to stop it. Marie stayed with Saunière until his death and remained in the villa until her own demise in 1953.

As far as the villagers were concerned, they were in no doubt that their priest had stumbled across a small fortune. In fact Madame J. Vidal, a great friend of Marie (who even gave her a room in the villa on her wedding night), reported a conversation with her in which she had said, 'With what the Monsieur le Curé has left, one could feed all of Rennes for a hundred years and there would still be some left'. However, when asked why she was living such an austere life after the death of Saunière if this was so, she replied that, 'She could not touch it'. At another time she had said, 'The people who live here are walking on gold without knowing it'. In 1925 a young female teacher came to take up a post in the village school. The commune was unable to provide suitable accommodation for her, so Marie Dénarnaud agreed to let her lodge at the villa. During her four year stay, she too became very close to Marie, but found her reluctant to speak about her days with Saunière. However, her pupils were more forthcoming, and told her that their parents firmly believed that he had discovered hidden treasure. Anecdotal though this evidence is, the power of a village grapevine should not be under-estimated!

The war of attrition with Bishop Beauséjour finally took its toll on the Abbé Saunière and he died, aged 65, five days after a sudden heart attack (in some accounts a stroke) on his terrace on 17 January 1917. In the five days before his death he was treated and comforted by his close friend and physician from Rennes-les-Bains, Dr. Paul Courrent, who stayed at the villa during this time. Dr. Courrent, like the late Abbé Boudet, was a respected member of the Society for the Scientific Study of the Aude and so it is quite natural that Saunière should have bequeathed to him all the Hautpoul and Dagobert archives that he had discovered or acquired. As is customary in the Catholic Church, he was given the Last Rites in his final hours, but his old friend the Abbé Rivière, who performed this solemn duty, was said by those present at the time, to be so shocked by Saunière's last confession that from then on he became a changed man.

Secrecy had followed Saunière around like a shadow; many of his actions were clouded in mystery and innuendo with no attempt by him to dispel them. However, he was not alone. Besides the Abbé Boudet, who without doubt was a key figure in his activities, other priests appear to have shared his secrets. There is the Abbé Grassaud to whom he gave a very beautiful and expensive chalice. Grassaud was the priest of Amélie-les-Bains at the time but was later appointed priest of St-Paul-de-Fenouillet, a town southeast of Rennes, where he also attempted to renovate his church. The intriguing entry in Saunière's diary for 21 September 1891 (that pivotal year), reveals another possible collaboration. Only eight days after his discovery of an unspecified tomb, Saunière wrote in his diary,'Vu curé de Névian – Chez Gélis – Chez Carrière – Vu Cros et Secret', references to meetings with certain colleagues, at which they probably discussed his latest discovery. Nearly twenty years later, two surviving letters from these close friends refer to the fact that Saunière had access to specific money, and that, in their opinion, nobody had the right to accuse him of any wrong-doing. They also indicate that he had a duty to guard a secret which should not be revealed at that time.

It would also appear that guarding this secret was a dangerous, and in some cases fatal, affair. The aforementioned Abbé Gélis was priest of the village of Coustausa which nestles on the hillside just to the north of Rennes, dominated by its magnificent ruined castle. In 1897, the elderly Abbé Gélis, who lived on his own, was viciously attacked and killed in the kitchen of his presbytery; evidently not for theft, since nearly 800 Frs was found undisturbed in drawers. However, there was evidence that his private papers had been searched and perhaps some removed. Even stranger was that the corpse had been laid out straight, with the arms neatly folded across the chest, and a small cigarette paper, upon which was written 'Viva Angelina', was found next to the body. The priest's nephew was arrested, but eventually not charged. The incident remains unsolved.

Yet another strange death had occurred earlier in 1732, when the Abbé Bernard Monge, priest of Niort-de-Sault (not far from Le Clat, the second posting of Abbé Saunière) was found lying dead by his presbytery garden gate, having received a fatal blow to the head. The murderer was found to be François de Montroux, the appointed guardian of the young Marie de Nègre d'Arbles, who was later to marry François d'Hautpoul, the Lord of Rennes and Blanchefort. Montroux was banished for his crime, but was found to have lent money to François d'Hautpoul in order to purchase the presbytery.

Three generations later, when the author and researcher Gérard de Sède interviewed the erudite local historian and former lawyer Abbé Mazières, he was warned that, "This Rennes affair is very gripping, but I must warn you it is also dangerous…." The question is why?

Chapter 7

Hidden Agendas, Occult Dreams

The secrecy in which Saunière surrounded himself and his activities is indicative of his involvement in a world in which powerful unseen forces played out their hidden agendas. We know he held a vision of France that was diametrically opposed to the liberal democratic Republic in which he lived. This vision was of a society with echoes of feudalism in which a partnership between the Catholic Church, the aristocracy, and the monarchy would provide a paternalistic government for its people. It looked back to a fusion of the pre-Revolutionary state of the Bourbon monarchs, the Holy Roman Empire of Charlemagne, and even the age of the unification of the early Franks by the Merovingian king, Clovis I.

Living under a Republican administration openly antagonistic to monarchical aspirations, it was inevitable that the existing network of lodges or secret societies would prove irresistible for infiltration by those dedicated to realising this vision. Even previously non-political but influential networks could be subtly infiltrated at an administrative level and exploited either for their contacts or to provide a cover for another agenda.

The dissent harboured in, and indeed nurtured by, the times in which Saunière lived was one that had been brewing for centuries. Following the Reformation in the 16th century, the Catholic Church had found itself an adversary in Protestantism. This could not be suppressed by the traditional means it applied to heresy, vigorously wielded by the Inquisition. Even the founding of the austere Society of Jesus by Ignatius Loyola in 1534, commonly known as the Jesuits, dedicated to the defence of Catholicism, could not stem the flow of conversions to Protestantism. Modelled on the old Order of Knights Templar, the Jesuits were the sword of the Church, except that skill at arms was replaced by intellectual study and debate. In time they were to become a major influence within the Vatican, involving themselves in diverse strategies for undermining and destroying enemies both within and outside the Church. After a succession of religious wars and persecutions, both Catholics and Protestants remained firmly entrenched in European society and politics. In France, the Church of Rome remained in overall control until the Revolution, which dispossessed it of its extensive property and many of its wealthy aristocratic supporters by means of the guillotine during the terror. Even after Napoleon's accord with the

Vatican, the Catholic Church never recovered its former power.

In Great Britain, the religious battle for the monarchy had been won by the Protestant Hanovarians following the final collapse of the Stuart cause. Nominally Catholic and with a history of dynastic marriages (Mary, Queen of Scots, daughter of James V and Mary of Lorraine, had married the Dauphin, afterwards Francis II of France), the Stuarts, with Scottish roots, looked to their French cousins for support. Following the execution of Charles I, his family sought protection in France and were granted a safe haven at the palace of St. Germain-en-Laye, outside Paris. It was not long before the royal guests were joined by members of the Scottish no-bility and Jacobite supporters who, determined to restore their monarch and power in Britain, organised a network of Masonic lodges[1] through which they could communicate and conspire. Becoming generally known as Scottish Rite Freemasonry, independent lodges proliferated throughout France. Among these by 1730, there were some that had no direct link to the Stuart cause, their members being attracted by the rites, rituals and social benefits. And being mainly Catholic and aristocratic, these lodges attracted the flower of French nobility. It was inevitable that a rival sys-tem would be established, and one soon grew, affiliated to the Hanoverian Grand Lodge in London (formed in 1717). This drew its members from Protestants, Jews, minor aristocrats and the bourgeoisie. Soon, this French wing, displaying typical Gallic independence, decided to break with the English administration and formed the Grand Lodge of France.

The majority of lodges and their members were not in fact politically ac-tive; by and large their motives were social, an extension of the gentle-man's club. However, part of the attraction was in the sense of mystery, maintained by an element of secrecy and a strict hierarchical structure; the concept of initiations and degrees of office engendered a powerful feeling of exclusivity and elitism. In itself, this could be considered harmless, but it was these aspects, coupled with the widespread network of lodges, that made Freemasonry and other similar secret societies so attractive and vul-nerable to exploitation by subversive agents. This potential has certainly been exploited over the past 250 years, and it still gives outsiders cause for suspicion and alarm.

In effect, the French Revolution, though essentially atheistic, could be seen as a victory for the Masons of the Grand Lodge of France. These had a clos-er affinity with the aims of the Revolutionaries than those in the Scottish

Rite and the other neo-chivalric Orders. In fact, the convergence of their aims led to accusations that the French Revolution was inspired, if not led, by Masonic politics. There was indeed a network of left-wing 'Jacobin' political clubs, named after the Jacobin convents in which they held their first meetings, who actively campaigned for popular support; their agitation led to the escalation of internal conflict and ultimately, full revolution. But these clubs have never been shown to be Masonic in nature, although it is possible that some of their members were also Masons.

By the time of the Abbé Saunière, French politics were polarised between Republican and Monarchist camps, each with its own supporting network of Masonic and para-Masonic lodges; but despite having temporarily lost power, the Monarchists were hopeful of an early restoration. An investigation of many prominent supporters of both sides reveals no clear distinction between aristocrats and commoners and their relative affiliations; Napoleon's new aristocracy, created mainly from the military and the bourgeois, did not necessarily support a monarchy.

But the choice between king or president was not solely a political decision, for the monarch was considered by many Catholics (and of course the Church itself) to rule by divine right. This implied that a monarch could enlist the spiritual help of heaven. To monarchists, theirs was the only possible option if France was to be protected from her enemies. By implication, French politics were once again experiencing the manipulation of the unseen hand of the Church of Rome.

The researches of French writer André Douzet have revealed that the Abbé Saunière had spent some time in the city of Lyon, known as the occult capital of France. In this context 'occult' refers to an interest in the supernatural, magical and mystical aspects of life; not to be confused with black magic or Satanism, though the boundaries of each sometimes become blurred. Correspondence addressed to Saunière shows that he was in contact with a secret society in Lyon, called the Martinists, and that he often stayed at a house two doors away from that of Joanny Bricaud, a prominent Martinist. As is typical in Lyon, their houses were even connected by an underground passage allowing unseen movement between houses.

Employing a strange blend of esoteric magic, initiatory rites and Catholic symbolism, the Martinists attempted to connect with the invisible, that is, the spiritual world. We will look in detail at Martinists beliefs and the role that Martinism played in the politics of Saunière's world, in the following chapter.

Martinism had started in the mid 18th century with Martines de Pasqually, of Portugese-Jewish ancestry, whose family had converted to Catholicism, and who claimed to have obtained secret knowledge from an old Dominican family. The Dominicans were responsible for operating the Inquisition, in the course of which they had amassed a huge quantity of so-called heretical documents, from which they were able to build up a corpus of secret and unpublished knowledge. This knowledge could well have included some details of the treasure, from information obtained during the Cathar inquisition. From his interest in mystical Christianity, Pasqually had also developed a cosmogony built around the figure of Christ, but which also introduced elements of esotericism and the Jewish cabala, resulting in his founding of the neo-Masonic Elus Cohen ('Elected Priest', where Cohen is the Hebrew word meaning priest). It is interesting to note the choice of Jewish symbolism in this otherwise mystical-Christian society, and the elite status of his initiates.

He was succeeded by his former secretary, Louis Claude de Saint-Martin, who had been initiated into the Elus Cohen in 1765. On an outwardly spiritual level, the original Martinism offered a system by which 'man' could reconnect with his divine self, and so attracted those seeking such a spiritual goal. Saint-Martin maintained the focus on Christ but added elements of magic and initiation – which brought Martinism closer to the world of Freemasonry. However, despite its avowedly spiritual role, Martinism was soon to play a political role of some importance.

By the time of Saunière's involvement, Martinism had come under the control of Papus, the pseudonym of Dr. Gérard Encausse, a healer and occultist who had organised a Martinist lodge system of which the majority of members were priests interested in mystical Catholicism. But, as with many secret societies, break-off groups founded their own sects. Even the Philadelphes, founded by the Marquis de Chefdebien a century earlier, and dedicated to the acquisition of Masonic secrets and archives, are shown to have displayed Martinist influences. But interestingly, the Martinist symbol of two interlocked triangles like a Star of David, but with one white and one black triangle is also to be found in the region of Rennes-le-Château. For instance, on the bedhead of the deathbed of Marie de Nègre Dame d'Hautpoul de Blanchefort, in the Hautpoul castle, is engraved the

Hautpoul coat of arms, alongside a six pointed star. The Martinist symbol, displayed at all lodge meetings, is also composed of black and white interlaced triangles, forming a hexagonal star. And in the Dossiers Secrets, a collection of documents purporting to reveal the true history of Rennes-le-Château, an illustration shows the plain blue badge of the village but with a Martinist star imposed at its centre.

What is the significance of this ancient symbol in the context of the Hautpoul family and the village of Rennes-le-Château? The interlocking triangles form not only the Martinist symbol, and the Star of David, otherwise known as the Seal of Solomon, but also the symbol of hermeticism representing the philosophy of 'as above, so below', meaning that the state of the Heavens is reflected on the Earth. This philosophy is considered to have been passed down from ancient civilisations that are thought to have had a greater knowledge of man and his place in the cosmos; and to have had access to sacred techniques such as astrological divination, alchemical transformations and the ability to transcend the physical world. Christians believed that this ancient knowledge or 'gnosis' is contained in the teachings of St. John the Divine, especially in his Revelations. This is the basis of esoteric Christianity that appealed to the more intellectual, endorsing their belief that the Catholic Church was a repository for such lost knowledge.

It was generally believed in the occult world that the Martinists possessed arcane secrets and that they followed a hidden agenda. Despite the profusion of Masonic and secret societies, the Martinists attained a pre-eminent status attracting and influencing some of the greatest names in occult circles as well as a large number of Catholic priests. The involvement of priests was not frowned upon, for Martinism was not a Masonic organisation and didn't suffer the same condemnation from the Catholic Church. In fact, in view of its predominant Catholic and monarchist affiliates it may even have been encouraged by the Church. Nevertheless, after the time of Saunière's involvement, Martinism appears to have become increasingly more political than spiritual, participating in the veiled world of occult politics.

Yet another prominent devotee of esoteric Christianity, Josephin Péladan, had also been initiated into Martinism. Shortly afterwards, he founded the Order of the Rose-Cross and the Temple and the Grail with the support of Papus, head of the Martinists, and an imaginative occult poet, the Marquis Stanislas de Guita. This was an attempt to revive the ancient and mythological Rosicrucian brotherhood[1] of the early 17ᵗʰ century; a mysterious and unidentified body that as well as promoting a subversive philosophy had also been credited with the possession of ancient secrets. Rosicrucian symbols are to be found in profusion in the church at Rennes-le-Château; an indication that Saunière – or his mentor – was actively involved with this neo-Rosicrucian revival.

Taking the pseudonym Sar Merodack (of Assyrian origin; Sar meaning king, and Merodack, an Assyrian god), Péladan established the Salons de la Rose-Croix in Paris, in which he mounted exhibitions with the aim of restoring what he considered to be 'Ideal Art' based on traditional and Catholic influences. Very successful for five years, the Salons attracted many accomplished and distinguished exhibitors; it is even reported that Debussy would arrive almost every day to play the piano. The connection with Debussy is significant since he is cited as a Grand Master, like the famous alchemist, Nicolas Flamel, and Charles Nodier before, of the secret society that claims to have acted as guardian of Rennes-le-Château and its great secret: the Priory of Sion.

Péladan himself left a considerable body of literary work dedicated to Catholic occultism, mysticism and magic. In 1889 he had made a visit to Jerusalem and on his return claimed, without any supporting evidence, to have discovered the true site of the Tomb of Jesus; not in the Holy Sepulchre as generally believed but under the Mosque of Omar. That site, one may recall, formed part of the dwelling occupied by the Knights Templar on their arrival in the Holy City. No further explanations were ever given publicly, but despite his devotion to the Catholic faith, he firmly believed in the mortality of Jesus. As well as his Martinist and Rose-Croix affiliations, Péladan had connections with the Order of Knights Templar since he had been invested into the reconstituted Sovereign and Military Order of the Temple of Jerusalem, and according to the Order's history, became Regent for two years (in place of a Grand Master) in 1892.

By the late 19ᵗʰ century the French occult world was a close knit group of often competing lodges, sects and individuals, with alliances being continuously formed and broken. Out of this mêlée of esoteric mysticism, Templarism and Masonry, a new network of secrecy and influence arose that was to become highly significant in later French and European politics. This very same network is found inextricably linked with the search, acquisition, and transmission of archives relating to the hidden gold. But an equally effective phenomenon, directly connected with the Catholic Church, also manifested itself and came to play a major role in the politics of the time: that of miraculous apparitions.

The Catholic-backed monarchist cause came to a head in 1876 with the French National pilgrimage to Lourdes by monarchist supporters to crown the Virgin Mary as Queen of Heaven, thereby enlisting her spiritual aid in their cause. Lourdes, located in the foothills of the French western Pyrenees, had been, in 1858, the site of the famous visions of a young shepherdess named Bernadette Soubirous. She claimed to have seen the Virgin Mary no less than eighteen times in a grotto above the Gave de Pau river; and miraculously, a spring of fresh water began to flow that has apparently healed the afflictions of the faithful that have visited the site ever since. Whatever the truth behind the events of 1858, Lourdes has become a powerful symbol of the true faith, and one of the leading tourist sites of the world, attracting in excess of 4 million pilgrims annually (supposedly more than visit Rome or Mecca).

The Catholic monarchist movement had already moved into higher gear, as previously mentioned, through the cult of the Sacred Heart.[2] Resurrected by Rohault de Fleury (whose family were intimately linked with Rennes-le-Château and Blanchefort), the cult of the Sacred Heart drew its original inspiration from the prophetic visions of a nun, Sister Alocoque, who in 1671 claimed to have seen Jesus with his heart exposed and bleeding. He told her that France would only be protected from her enemies if the nation fully embraced the worship of the Sacred Heart.

In 1873, a former nun, Constance Estelle Faguette, also had a vision of the Virgin Mary. Born in 1843 near Châlons-sur-Marne, at the age of eighteen she became a novitiate with Augustine nuns, but was forced to leave after two years having suffered a knee injury. She obtained a position as a servant in the household of the Countess of Rochefoucauld at the château at Pellevoisin. For ten years she travelled between Paris and Pellevoisin until she became ill with a lung disease. She wrote a letter to the Virgin Mary asking for succour, which was placed at the foot of her statue. During her illness, the Rochefoucaulds paid for her comfort and, not expecting her to live, they also made burial provisions. But, as though on cue, the first of her fifteen visions of the Virgin Mary occurred, which often showed the Devil being overcome by the Virgin, and the request that she erect a marble tablet at Pellevoisin, if she was cured. In the vision the marble tablet appeared with a golden rose in each corner and, at the centre, a heart with flames emanating from the top. Needless to say, Estelle was healed, continued her working life in the service of the Rochefoucaulds, and lived until the age of eighty-three. She had two further visions in later life, one of which endorsed yet another message, one that had been received in 1846 in a vision at La Salette. Pellevoisin never achieved the status of the other pilgrimage sites and remained a rural backwater; the visions were never adequately investigated, and, indeed, the whole episode is highly suspect. Is it just a coincidence that Count Antoine de la Rochefoucauld was a founder member with Péladan of the Order of the Rose-Croix Catholique, and initially financed the Salons de la Rose-Croix?

Amongst its profusion of curiosities, the domain of the Abbé Saunière contains a number of clear indications of his devotion to the monarchy and the Sacred Heart. But one of the most enigmatic of his religious features is that ensemble of the statue of the crowned Virgin Mary placed on the upside-down ancient pillar, on which he had engraved the words, 'Penitence, Penitence' and 'Mission 1891'. Whereas the crowned Virgin relates to the visions of Lourdes, the Penitence, Penitence exhortation refers more appropriately to the vision witnessed some twelve years before those of Bernadette Soubirous in September 1846 at La Salette, near Grenoble in the French Alps. There the Blessed Virgin appeared to a poor, innocent, fourteen-year-old shepherdess, Melanie Calvet, and her young companion, Maximin Giraud. The message revealed to these two naïve children, as interpreted by their confessor Jean-Marie Vianney, the Curé d'Ars, was a warning that if the French people did not reform their ways and return to the teachings of the Church then they would be abandoned by Jesus Christ. A final part of the message, known popularly as the Secret of La Salette, is said to have been passed only from pope to pope and never revealed; it is alleged to be a political criticism of the Church and the papacy. As with the vision at Lourdes, the story has a monarchist undertone. One Charles Naundorff protested that he was the natural son, previously assumed dead, of Louis XVI and backed by a sect of Catholic Church reformers, the 'vision' of La Salette appears to have been stage-managed to promote his cause.

The nine-year-old shepherd boy, Maximin, later confessed to Jean-Marie Vianney, the Curé d'Ars, that he did not actually see anything and had to some extent been led along by Melanie. The Curé, upset by this, complained to his superior, Philibert Brouillard, the Bishop of Grenoble, who advised him to return home and say nothing. It later transpired that the 'vision of the beautiful lady' was really Constance de la Merlière, a local eccentric who enjoyed dressing up, and who after the 'apparition', was spotted in several places wearing the same dress as described by Melanie. Accused by two priests of deception, she brought about a defamation case which she subsequently lost despite the efforts of her lawyer.

The case highlights a strange collaboration. Constance de la Merlière was a fanatical monarchist, but her lawyer was Jules Favre, an ardent Republican and member of the Les Coeurs Reunis lodge of the Grand Orient at Toulouse. Reconciling this courtroom collaboration is somewhat of a puzzle, except that the outcome of the trial appeared to discredit both the Church and the restoration movement, to the obvious satisfaction of Jules Favre, who probably suspected this result from the outset. Despite this revelation of trickery, La Salette continues to be a pilgrimage site drawing thousands of pilgrims each year; a practice that has never been discouraged by the Catholic Church.

Still more coincidences arise from the La Salette incident; a rare statue of Jean-Marie Vianney, the Curé d'Ars, can be found in the little church of Bézu, a village only 6.5km from Rennes-le-Château. Melanie Calvet, the young shepherdess, turned out to have a famous relative, the opera singer Emma Calvé (originally Calvet but changed for professional purposes), who was closely associated with the Paris occult circles with whom the Abbé Saunière is believed to have made contact.

A certain mystery surrounds Emma Calvé. Born in 1858 at Decazeville, she spent much of her adolescence in the mountain village of Bastide-Pradines, which is close to the preserved Templar commanderies of St Eulalie-de-Cernon, La Cavalerie and La Couvertoirade. After her initial success in the Opera, she donated money to finance a sanatorium at Cabrières, north of Millau, but by the end of 1893, her diary shows that she was 100,000 Frs in debt. However, a year later she had paid this off and had begun the purchase of the delapidated château at Cabrières.

Though at one time the lover of the renowned Paris occultist, Jules Bois, her rapid change in fortune has been attributed to financial help from the Abbé Saunière, with whom she was alleged to have had a close relationship. They are said to have met during his visit to Paris[3]. Whilst researching the history of her ancient home, she also discovered that the old family of Cabrières had possessed a copy of the ancient alchemical and cabalistic work of Abraham the Jew, the text studied by the celebrated alchemist Nicolas Flamel. Confirmation of this can be found in a book, *Trésor des Recherches et Antiquites Gauloises et Françaises* by Pierre Borel, published in Paris, 1655. During a visit to M. de Cabrières' château, Borel claims to have seen the original book used by Flamel.

Towards the end of her life, Calvé experienced further money problems and sold the château to Madame Aubin, a former tutor to the Habsburgs. She died after an illness in 1942, in an apartment in Millau. Although it has not been possible to verify her alleged relationship with Saunière, there is no doubt that they frequented the same occult circles[4].

Other members of these circles appear to have had a direct influence on Saunière; such as the eccentric Eugène Vintras and his devotee the Abbé Boullan, who had a strange relationship with the nun Adèle Chevalier, a friend of Melanie Calvet whom she had met at La Salette. For their rites and rituals they adopted the symbol of the upside-down cross, which represented not only the martyrdom of St. Peter but also the secret inner teachings and traditions of the Catholic Church. This could explain Saunière's action in placing a crowned Virgin Mary over an upside-down cross.

Although the events at Rennes-le-Château took place only a hundred years ago, and some sons and daughters of Saunière's parishioners are still alive, teasing out fact from fiction has proven remarkably difficult. One analyses the available evidence together with suggestive but unproven allegations in an attempt to discern the truth, but the secrecy surrounding many of Saunière's activities inevitably compounds the problem. Gérard de Sède in his book, *L'Or de Rennes*, provides an account which helps to provide a much disputed but a surprisingly coherent overall picture[5].

De Sède writes that having discovered the parchments in the crypt and realising that they had a potential value, Saunière made accurate copies and attempted to decipher them. After a couple of years of studying them without success, despite the assistance of his erudite colleague Abbé Boudet, he sought the advice of his co-operative bishop, Mgr Billard. It was Billard who suggested that Saunière take the parchments to the Seminary of St. Sulpice in Paris, where he would find experts in ancient and esoteric documents. He gave him a letter of introduction to the Director of the Seminary of St. Sulpice, the Abbé Bieil, and advanced him his travelling expenses. During his stay in Paris, whilst the parchments were being studied by specialists, Saunière is believed to have stayed with the nephew of Abbé Bieil, one Monsieur Ane, a creator of religious imagery. It is here that he is said to have met another nephew of the Abbé, the young novice priest, Emile Hoffet, who later became an expert on occult matters and Freemasonry, amassing a prodigious library of esoteric works[6].

But just as the accuracy of the story of the trip to Paris is questionable, so the saga of the parchments themselves is mysterious. Those documents supposedly taken by Saunière to St. Sulpice were evidently confided to Émile Hoffet for further study probably after the death of his uncle and remained secreted in Hoffet's library until his death in 1946. The parchments were then acquired – whether bought or stolen is not clear – by a group claiming to be representatives of the London-based League of Antiquarian Booksellers, who applied, and apparently received permission, to export three of the documents to England where they were deposited in a strongbox at Lloyds Bank International. Other accounts add that these three documents were at first inherited by Saunière's niece, Madame James, who then sold them, not appreciating their value, to the League of Antiquarian Booksellers. Certainly, after the death of the Abbé Hoffet, Marius Fatin, archaeologist and owner of the castle at Rennes, received a letter from this enigmatic League stating that his castle was a site of great historic importance, having been the home of Sigisbert IV. The letter also refers to the purchase of the parchments from the library of Émile Hoffet by the League, and even their initial discovery by Saunière.

But who are this mysterious League of Antiquarian Booksellers[7]? And why would a British antiquarian book society be so interested in parchments relating to a somewhat obscure (especially for the British) Merovingian line? What was their interest in the fate of their descendants and the castle at Rennes? Meanwhile, events show that Saunière's own copies, and the documents stolen by his brother from the Marquis de Chefdebien, were confided to his friend and physician, Dr. Courrent, just before the priest's death.

The trail of the parchments, the conspiracies to acquire them, and the extraordinary figures behind the League of Antiquarian Booksellers, are fascinating in themselves. But this is more than an adventure story: its twists and turns have far-reaching, and increasingly sinister, implications.

The Abbé Saunière's initiation into the Martinist Order brought him into the midst of a shadowy world of secret societies, whose devotees' activities can be detected throughout Europe. At first sight these mystical preoccupations appear no more than harmless and even laudable (or laughable!) attempts to acquire spiritual knowledge and development through secret teachings, rites and rituals. However, a closer look soon reveals that the hard edge of politics is never far away.

In the tangle of 19th century occult societies some individuals stand out from the rest. One of these was Alphonse Louis Constant (later adopting the name Eliphas Levi). Born in Paris in 1810, he entered the higher seminary of St. Sulpice at Issy to complete his training for the priesthood. It was here that he found an interest in magic. However, having fallen in love with a young woman, he was obliged to resign from the ministry. He then met Flora Tristan, a leading light in working class and feminist movements, through whom he was introduced to the great novelist, Honoré de Balzac, a Catholic occultist much influenced by Martinism. Influenced by these and other philosophies Levi, dedicating himself to a transformation of society and the abolition of social inequality, wrote a number of books which at times brought him into conflict with the Catholic Church. He was much admired for his openness and belief in occult sciences by progressive artists (and later by the Surrealists), who coincidentally also admired the alchemist Nicolas Flamel. Levi firmly believed that through the practice of magical rites he could enlist the help of 'higher powers' to bring about desired personal and social changes and even miracles to rival those of the authorised religion.

One vision of social change was called Synarchy[8] or joint sovereignty; a tripartite government comprising three essential functions based on education, justice and economy. Synarchy was the idealistic brainchild of Saint Yves d'Alveidre, who had married Balzac's second wife, through whom he acquired considerable wealth as well as the title, Marquis d'Alveidre. He also believed in the tradition of Agartha, the existence of an underground city in the centre of Asia, the home to great masters of science and wisdom, from where would come the enlightened King of the World. He also wrote a number of books, including *Les Missions des Juifs* (The Mission of the Jews), and *La France Vrai* (The True France), in which he develops his synarchist ideas. The concept of Synarchy would later be adopted into strands of para-Masonic politics, and when integrated with Martinism produced the esoteric and politically active Ordre de Martiniste-Synarchique.

But of all the extraordinary personalities involved with these esoteric societies, one of the most remarkable and influential was Papus. Born in Spain as Gérard Encausse, but brought up in Paris, he began his career studying medicine but abandoned this to study occultism. He was initiated into Martinism, which he then started to reorganise, setting up a network of lodges, the first of which was in Lyon; and which would have existed at the time of Saunière's participation. He assisted Péladan, the fanatical Catholic monarchist, to found the Cabalistic Rosicrucian order, and became a central figure in the distribution of occult ideas, writing no less than 260 works. Returning ultimately to his medical interests, he developed and published a philosophy of anatomy and, in 1897, opened a school of hermetic sciences. Acquiring a reputation for alternative healing and medicine derived from the occult, he was summoned to the court of the Russian Czar Nicholas II where esotericism and spiritualism had become as popular as they had in the salons of other branches of European high society. From the early 1800s, secret societies, including Martinism, had enjoyed changing fortunes at the Russian court and even during most influential periods was mistrusted by those fearful of subversive or revolutionary politics. At a magical séance held by Papus, he supposedly invoked the spirit of the Czar's late father Alexander III, from whom he interpreted advice on how to deal with the growing social unrest in Russia. This episode clearly demonstrates the political influence some secret societies can exert even on an administration as powerful as the Russian court.

But this was not the court's only source of advice and influence: the Czar and Czarina had fallen under the spell of the 'mad monk' Rasputin, following his alleged cure of their son from haemophilia. Many were alarmed at the enchantment of the Russian royal family and court by this dirty, unkempt and apparently amoral sham holy man; some believed that he was the representative of secret Masonic societies plotting to bring about the downfall of the ruling Romanovs. Papus himself warned against the power of Rasputin and the danger of listening to his advice.

It is at this time that the highly anti-Semitic Protocols of the Elders of Sion also appeared at the Russian court. This document was purported to be the minutes of a World Jewish Congress that had taken place at Basle, Switzerland, in 1897, at which a plan had been agreed by Jews and Freemasons to achieve financial, and hence political, world domination.

Generally regarded as a fake, the origin of the Protocols remains unknown.

It is possible that they were composed and published by the Martinists to discredit the growing Jewish and Masonic influences bearing on the court. As in the case of Rasputin, these influences were also considered by the Martinists to be aimed at weakening the power of the Czar and to bringing down the Romanov dynasty. Whatever the reality of their origin, the Protocols have been used as justification for continued anti-Semitism by many right wing nationalist organisations ever since.

Geographically, St. Petersburg is a great distance from Rennes-le-Château. But the network of lodges and secret societies brings them much closer together than the map belies. Saunière's Europe at the turn of the 20th century was one of competing inter-related dynasties; the Habsburgs ruling an Austro-Hungarian Empire, Germany united with Prussia under Bismark, the Romanovs reigning over Russia, Great Britain and her Empire ruled by cousins of the Russian Czars and German Kaisers, the Bourbon kings still on the throne of Spain, even if displaced from France by the Revolution. However, the sands of time were running out for many of the 'old order'; rumblings of discontent from the people about the way they were ruled, the fragile alliances between these competing dynasties, were to sound the death knell for some, and major upheavals for others. Against this background it is easy to understand why secret societies proliferated and in many instances became drawn into the political arena, taking up positions supporting conflicting factions with separate agendas. Without doubt, the role of secret and occult societies was far more significant in this conflict than conventional history relates. We will discover traces of underground intrigue and conspiracy underlying the evolving politics of Europe from this time until the present day.

In 1889, yet another curious and unexplained episode enters the mysterious history of Rennes-le-Château. It concerns the visits to Abbé Saunière of an individual who called himself Jean Orth, but who was in reality the Archduke Johan Salvator von Habsburg. A nephew of the Emperor Franz Joseph, Johan was also cousin to Crown Prince Rudolph, whose death in 1889 at a hunting lodge at Mayerling was believed to have been a suicide pact with his mistress Mary Vetsera. The suspicious circumstances have prompted several alternatives. Shortly after this tragedy Johan renounced his inheritance and titles, incurring the wrath of his uncle, the emperor, and exiled himself from the Empire. He took the surname Orth from the name of his family castle. His arrival in Rennes was recorded by the local police at Couiza, who were informed by Doctor Espezel from the neighbouring village of Esperaza. Concerned by some aspects of Saunière's public life, Doctor Espezel was suspicious of any strangers who visited the priest. It is said that Jean Orth and Saunière opened accounts in the same bank with consecutive account numbers, and that a large sum of money was transferred into Saunière's account. Then in 1890, having acquired a master's certificate in the merchant navy, Johan set sail for South America on the Saint Margaret; there is no reliable evidence to indicate that he was ever seen again.

Two further facts, though in themselves obscure, link the mystery of Rennes with the Habsburgs. First, the Count of Chambord (whose widow had donated 3000 Frs to Saunière) and the Archduke Johan Salvator were cousins by virtue of sharing their maternal grandfather, Francis I, king of the Two Sicilies. Second, after his unfortunate death, Rudolph had left behind a locked strongbox, said to have contained coded documents and other items of great importance to the Habsburg Empire. This was later passed to Johan, who gave it to his faithful mistress, Milli Stubel, for safe-keeping. Mystery still surrounds the fate and contents of the box, though Otto von Habsburg, his oldest surviving descendant, claims to possess it. The Habsburgs had already acquired the legendary 'Spear of Destiny'[9], believed to have been used by the centurion Longinus to pierce the side of the crucified Jesus, so it is quite conceivable that, being aware of the great biblical and symbolic treasure hidden near Rennes-le-Château, Johan, perhaps on behalf of others, wished to support Saunière in his researches.

By way of a footnote, 1975 saw a visit to Rennes-le-Château by Mgr. Archduke Rudolphe of Habsburg, the sixth child of the Austro-Hungarian Emperor Charles IV and Empress Zita. According the authors Gérard de Sède and Jean Robin, and confirmed by the researcher Pierre Jarnac, Rudolphe interviewed well-informed locals concerning the Saunière affair about which he already appeared to have extensive knowledge. He then interviewed two Rennes experts at Carcassonne, Mgr Boyer, the Vicar General, and the Abbe Mazières; Rudolphe paid particular attention to the story of his ancestor's vist to Saunière. Jarnac's researches further reveal that a police file still exists containing some details of a judicial enquiry, following Saunière's death in 1917, into the source of his revenue. Although the nature of the evidence is now unknown, the enquiry did conclude that he had been 'trafficking in gold with Spain'. So did Saunière indeed find some part of the ancient treasure? Or was he just an intermediary for more powerful forces?

Chapter 8
Spiritual Quests, Political Visions

So, by the dawn of the 20th century, the little mountain village of Rennes-le-Château had recovered a little of its past glory. An extract from a report of a visit in 1905 by the Society for Scientific Study of the Aude states: "suddenly, we discovered a beautiful crenellated wall, a beautiful villa, a recently constructed tower... a beautiful pleasure garden sheltered by a beautiful terrace from which one may enjoy a beautiful panorama; without contradiction, an oasis lost in the middle of a desert. [...] All this is the beautiful domain of the Abbe Saunière." Furthermore, the villagers spoke of important strangers to the village who were royally entertained by their priest at his new villa, evidence supported by invoices that reveal the purchase of copious amounts of food, wines, and spirits.

There are also several extant letters from priests thanking Saunière for his excellent and generous hospitality during their stay. But what was it that drew such important people to this backwater parish? How could his fellow country priests have accepted such a strange and lavish lifestyle from one of their own? The answer may well lie in Saunière's involvement with Martinism[1].

A central belief of Martinism is that man can re-discover his spiritual or divine self, the state in which he was before the biblical 'Fall'. Very closely related to this is a second belief that, with training and enlightenment, one can contact the 'unknown', that is, the spirit world. Initiates were instructed that these were their goals, and both could be achieved through magic rites and rituals, focused on the figure of Christ. Adherents from the priesthood itself would have considered themselves to be on a spiritual quest for an even higher purpose than that which they provided for their own congregations.

The belief in and objective of contacting one's higher nature is common to many occult organisations and philosophies. Coming from America in the late 19th century, Spiritualism had quickly taken hold in Europe and soon gained notable adherents, such as the writers Victor Hugo and Sir Arthur Conan Doyle. Even Queen Victoria was said to have received messages from her beloved Prince Albert through the mediumship of John Brown, a worker on her Balmoral estate. There is no doubt that she developed a very close relationship with John Brown, but always remained devoted to her late husband. Papus, that great organiser of Martinist lodges in France, achieved great influence through holding séances and invoking spirits. It is quite conceivable that, having become immersed in Martinist activity at Lyon, Saunière himself had founded what was essentially a lodge at Rennes-le-Château where personal spiritual development and séances could take place. However, being aware of the remarkable history of the region, is it not also possible that Saunière and his compatriots believed that through contacting the spirits of the ancient lords of Rhedae, or perhaps the Knights Templar, they could discover the exact locations of all the legendary treasure – or even wilder, perhaps political, ambitions?

For Saunière this would not have been for mere personal gain. It would have enabled him and his associates to realise their passionate objectives: the restoration of both the power of the Catholic Church and their lost monarchy. Ownership of the treasure would have both funded their cause and given it sanction, considering its symbolism. Belief in the ability to contact the 'world of spirit' through the active involvement of Saunière, may well also explain the actions of his confidante, Marie Dénarnaud, after his death. After all, in *L'héritage de l'Abbé Saunière*, Antoine Captier and Claire Corbu recount that Marie would go to the cemetery and the grave of her priest every night, as if she had a pre-arranged meeting with him. They also note that immediately after the death of Saunière on 22 January 1917, she went around the village, in obvious distress, shouting, 'Mon dieu ! Mon dieu ! Monsieur le curé est mort… Maintenant tout est fini…' ('My god! My god! The curé is dead … Now everything is finished'). Did Saunière have psychic abilities? Had he himself acted as a medium for his initiates? According to the accounts of his parishioners, their priest certainly had great charisma – a quality often found in psychics. He was also adamant about remaining at Rennes-le-Château, despite the enormous pressure exerted on him, by his later bishop, Mgr. Beauséjour, to account for his wealth and lifestyle[2]. Surely something of great magnitude was keeping him there.

A close examination of the ground plan of the domain, painstakingly surveyed by Alain Féral, artist, researcher and long-time resident of the village, reveals a remarkable and complex underlying geometry. Buildings and features of the estate have been very deliberately laid out to create regular pentagons in the church garden and the villa garden respectively, and an irregular but cyclic pentagon in the Tour Magdala garden. All three are perfectly integrated with a giant regular pentagon which dominates the complete site. Such a rigid geometrical construction cannot possibly have been accidental. Is this precise plan confirmation of Saunière's intention to establish and occult or spiritualist centre at Rennes-le-Château?

The pentagon is arguably one of the oldest and most universal of symbols. Pentagonal geometry contains the 'golden section', a constant ratio (like that of pi) often found in nature, which was revered by architects and philosophers of the ancient world as a manifestation of the divine. It is also the symbol for man within the universe, as illustrated in the famous drawings of Albrecht Dürer and Leonardo da Vinci. But the pentagon, and its derivation the pentagram (a five-pointed star), are most popularly known from their use in magical rites, and are exemplified by the hermetic drawing of Eliphas Levi. This prominent occultist and magician of the mid-19th century believed that 'the original alliance of Christianity and the science of the Magi are essential'. In other words, the path to spiritual truth is found in a fusion of Christian teachings with knowledge and wisdom from the classical world – a belief parallel to that of the Martinists.

By comparison with another site, this pentagonal geometry takes on a further significance. Paray-le-Monial, a town in the north of the Massif Central and site of the Sacred Heart visions of Sister Alacoque, became a major pilgrimage site from the late 17th century, attracting many thousands of the faithful. The town is dominated by the 11th century basilica, with the Chapel of the Visitation, site of the famous apparitions, only a short distance away. But of greater significance to our story is the Museé Hiéron. Outwardly a museum displaying art and artefacts connected to the Eucharist, it was also home to an enigmatic and secretive institution, the Hiéron du Val d'Or[3]. Esoteric in nature, it had an ambiguous relationship with its devotion to the Sacred Heart, but laid great emphasis on adopting ancient Celtic sites and the use of sacred geometry; it even occupied a building arranged in the shape of a pentagon.

Amongst those connected with the Sacred Heart centre was the writer, artist and archaeologist, Louis Charbonneau-Lassay. Attracted by the world of Christian symbolism, heraldic signs and sacred geometry, Charbonneau was particularly interested in the Knights Templar and the possibility that they had discovered some ancient knowledge. Over the years he had accumulated a priceless collection of weapons, jewels and coins, from the Gallo-Roman and medieval periods. The exact source of these finds is unknown, but since Saunière and Lassay were both devotees of the cult of the Sacred

Heart and probably both members of the Hiéron du Val d'Or, it would not be surprising if he had discovered some in the region of the Corbières.

Jean-Luc Chaumeil claims that one hidden agenda of the Hiéron was the creation of a new Habsburg and Vatican-dominated Holy Roman Empire, based much on the same model of a hierarchical, paternalistic elite favoured by many monarchists and aristocrats at the time, yet in direct opposition to the liberal democracy of the Republic of France, which they identified with evil. From his pulpit in October 1885, during local elections in the Aude, the Abbé Saunière fulminated against the Republic, encouraging his parishioners to vote against it saying, 'Les Republicains, voilà le Diable a vaincre et qui doit plier le genou sous les poids de la Religion et des baptises. Le signe de la croix est victorieux et avec nous…' ('The Republicans, there is the Devil to conquer and who must bend under the weight of the Religion and the baptised. The sign of the cross is victorious and with us…'). This leaves little doubt of his opinion of the Republic and its non-Catholic supporters.

The superiors of the Sacred Heart cult at Paray-le-Monial produced a magazine called *Regnabit* (He Will Reign), with articles submitted by Charbonneau-Lassey and such famous Christian-esotericists as René Guenon, a great adherent of spiritualism and, initially, Freemasonry. Guenon got to know Papus and other esotericists but also found himself drawn to Hinduism, Sufism and Islamic esotericism; eventually, after the death of his first wife, he converted to the Sufic branch of Islam. He also considered all branches of esotericism to have the same roots. However, as a traditionalist, he was involved in extreme right-wing activities and wrote, 'History clearly shows that the failure to recognise a hierarchical order (based on the supremacy of the spiritual over the temporal) has the same consequences in all places at all times; social instability; confusion of duties; domination by the lower orders; and intellectual degradation.' Guenon was also a disciple of Saint-Yves d'Alveidre whose synarchic concept of government was adopted into Masonic politics. Later, synarchy became allied with Martinism, and is now the esoteric agenda of anarchists. Guenon also adopted Saint-Yves' belief in the Central Asian-centred underground kingdom of Agartha, which he believed could be either actual or symbolic. Further, these metaphysical obsessions led him to an association with another strange occult group called the Polaires, whose origins – actual and legendary – are as obscure as its beliefs.

The Polaires[4] and their relationship with other occult societies and individuals are reviewed in detail by Joscleyn Godwin in *Arktos : The Polar Myth*, which reveals some interesting coincidences. The sign of the Polaires is quoted as the sign of two interlaced triangles, the same symbol as that of the Martinists and of course of Judaism. But more significant is that during 1929 and 1930, this group is alleged to have undertaken excavations and research for historical documents in the ancient Cathar region south of Carcassonne around the valleys of the rivers Aude and Ariège.

Also at this time, an awareness of the significance of the Cathars had slowly developed in England, within the esoteric society the White Eagle Lodge. At séances held in the lodge, the spirit of Conan Doyle was believed to have communicated, through the medium Grace Cooke, that he was working on the astral plane with a Rosicrucian initiate supporting the work of the Polaires. Later messages, received in 1937, revealed that something of great importance, but not actually defined, was hidden in the Cathar region, and that members of the Polaires should mount another expedition to the area. There they would make contact with someone called Walter.

This person can be identified as Walter Birks who, having studied history at Oxford University, taught in England and France, until his unexplained decision in 1937 to go to the Pyrenees to recover the lost traces of a 'Brotherhood'. His stay in the Ariège and the people he met are recounted in his book *Treasure of Montségur*, written with the collaboration of R.A. Gilbert[5], today a high-ranking Freemason and occultist. Much space is devoted to examining the nature of a 'spiritual' treasure, but confirmation is also given of a huge material treasure possessed by the Cathars. Walter Birks, later to be an army major and recipient of an MBE, claimed also to have worked for British Intelligence and it seems hardly credible that such a man should undertake this sort of venture in so remote a region of France without a very substantial reason.

But seven years before the arrival of Walter Birks, another grail devotee had made his mark. Hard on the heels of that first group of Polaires in Cathar country, was a young German named Otto Rahn who in his search for the Holy Grail was to find himself involved in a sinister and ultimately fatal agenda. Evidently blinded by idealism, Rahn initially supported a regime dedicated to German national regeneration. The pursuit of this aim was to dramatically affect world history through the horrors of World War II, but its roots can actually be found in European events some sixty years before.

After all, whilst young Bérenger Saunière was growing up in the little tranquil village of Montazels, perched on a sunny hillside overlooking the sparkling river Aude, the great dynasties of Europe were already edging towards disaster. France had of course already experienced a bloody revolution, and had replaced an absolute monarchy with the relatively democratic Republic. However, in most of the rest of Europe, the power still resided in hereditary dynasties. The Romanovs remained in Russia, the Habsburgs in Austria and Hungary, the Ottoman Empire of the Turks persisted, and Kaisers still ruled Germany. But the Crimean War of 1851 saw the beginning of the disintegration of these empires, completed after the Great War, sixty-six years later. Even so, the effect of Napoleon's conquests, both those successful and those attempted, resulted in a sense of insecurity that stimulated a fierce sense of nationalism that would dictate the foreign policies of most European countries. Pre-occupation with expansion of territory or the protection of existing borders took priority over domestic policy; increasing symptoms of social unrest went unheeded.

This was also a situation easily exploited by the secret societies now gaining political influence. Conventional historians tend to overlook the role of secret societies in these turbulent events, not believing that they have any real effect or significance in politics. On the contrary it can be well argued that the majority of political activity in any era is motivated by hidden agendas conceived in secret.

Operating from the shadows, and sometimes carefully concealed within outwardly harmless esoteric or chivalric organisations, the agenda of these groups has included objectives ranging from the recovery of ancient treasure in the Corbières to political control within other regions of Europe. Driven by greed, ideology, religious zeal or political ambition, these unseen forces can exert powerful but barely traceable influences. Detection of such forces at work is hardly new. The 18th century British statesman and Prime Minister, Benjamin Disraeli, had an interest in secret societies and the occult, and spoke out about the threat that they posed in Europe. In his novel *Coningsby*, he stated that 'the world is governed by very different personages to what is imagined by those who are not behind the scenes' – a statement that shows either great perception or inside knowledge. One of Disraeli's closest friends was Edward Bulwer-Lytton, 1st Lord Lytton of Knebworth. His interest in the occult stemmed from his days at Cambridge. Despite becoming a very active Member of Parliament he maintained an interest in the theatre, literature and esoteric pursuits. He enjoyed high status in occult circles and he was visited in 1854 by that famous Paris occultist and magician, Eliphas Levi, who considered Lytton to be one of the principal exponents of occultism in Britain. Unconfirmed family sources claim that Lytton was even a Rosicrucian[6] initiate, and without doubt his esoteric book *Zanoni*, is in large measure a reflection of Rosicrucian philosophy. It further enhanced his reputation in occult circles, and had an impact on the anti-Christian esotericism of Madame Helena Blavatsky, the Russian medium who was to found the Theosophical Society. Attracting members from other esoteric societies, the Theosophical Society was also to take a more political stance under the later leadership of Annie Besant, who campaigned on a number of social issues, and it became affiliated with the Masonic Grand Orient Lodge of France.

Bulwer-Lytton's *The Coming Race* had not only even greater impact on the Theosophists but also influenced the mystical elements of German nationalism. From this arose the Vril Society, a German mystico-political group that adopted the swastika as its emblem. This society, and others, associated the writings of Bulwer-Lytton and the occult philosophies of the theosophists with a dangerous mix of anti-Semitism, extreme nationalism and a belief in root races or racial supremacy. This was also adopted by extreme right-wing groups, of which a prime example was the Ordo Novi Templi (The Order of the New Templars), founded by Lanz von Liebenfels in 1907. This promulgated a right-wing, racist, anti-Semitic agenda, using an erroneous interpretation of the medieval Templars' mission as justification. Through a network of similar groups and by supporting pro-Serbian nationalism, the ONT was even able to play a major part in bringing about the assassination that sparked the tragedy of 1914.

During the 1920s, whilst the seeds were being sown for Adolf Hitler to take power in Germany, the ONT acted as co-ordinators for right-wing groups in Europe. And, although prohibited in 1941 by the Nazis, who had a paranoid fear of secret societies, the philosophies of the ONT, and the later German Order and Thule Society, were readily adopted by Hitler and his inner cabal, forming the basis for the political creed of the National Socialist Party.

The extreme right-wing politics of the Nazi party were in direct contrast to the Polaires and their quest for the spiritual – and admittedly material – treasure of the Corbières. Yet unwittingly, Otto Rahn, driven by a passionate desire to discover this Holy Grail, was to become fatally entangled with the ruthless politics of the Nazi high command.

Chapter 9

Seeking the Grail

Convinced he had cracked a code in the pages of Wolfram von Eschenbach's classic novel *Parsifal* that identified the hiding place of the Treasures of the Temple of Solomon, Otto Rahn travelled to the South of France to find these legendary Grail treasures. Rahn was possibly ordered to the Languedoc by Hitler and his inner circle to find these ancient talismans of power. Whatever the reality, the enigmatic character of Otto Rahn, his own quest for the secret of the Cathars, and the nature of his pre-war activities, reveal a lesser known agenda of the Nazi party. The scarcity and dubious reliability of biographical sources relating to Rahn, and his eventual membership of the SS, has always made an objective assessment of him difficult. However, his idealistic obsession with the Grail quest was to conflict with his role of a soldier and the sinister aims of the Nazi principals with disastrous consequences.

According to his SS file, he was born on the 18 February 1904, at Michelstadt, to Karl Rahn and Clara (née Hamburger); Otto was Jewish on his mother's side – a fact that may help to explain the mystery surrounding his later SS career and untimely death. In his second book, *Lucifer's Court*, he recalls that, at an early age, he was introduced to the Grail romances by his mother; but his adult passion for Wagner, who had immortalised the story of Parsival[1], led him to study this epic work of Wolfram von Eschenbach. After an extensive academic education, this fascination led him, in 1931, towards the Pyrenees and the Languedoc, where he embarked on research of the Cathars, Templars, troubadours and Visigoths. He sought in particular the secret of the Grail that he thought had been known by the Cathars and Wolfram von Eschenbach. He believed, somewhat idealistically, that the power of the Grail could unify Europe.

Staying at a guest house in Ussat-les-Bains in the Ariège valley, Rahn's thorough investigation of the ancient Cathar sites, including the ruined fortress of Montségur, soon brought him into contact with Antonin Gadal, the acknowledged local champion of Cathar legends. Delighted to have found a fellow enthusiast, Gadal gave Rahn great support in his researches and later the two were to maintain a long-term correspondence.

It was from Antonin Gadal, known locally as the 'Cathar Pope' (Rahn also referred to him as his Trevrizent, Parsival's uncle), that he got many of his Grail theories. However, Déodat Roché, a noted academic authority on the Cathars, was less impressed by Gadal, and became somewhat suspicious of Rahn's motives. Indeed, one incident is reported, to the effect that Rahn was discovered faking Cathar engravings. In any case, Rahn's stay in the region came to an abrupt end in September 1932, as a result of embarrassing financial circumstances following the non-payment of debts, partly arising from a lease that he had taken out on the Hôtel Marroniers. After a brief stay in Paris he was forced to return to Germany, where in 1933, he published *The Crusade Against The Grail*. Whilst not well received as an academic treatise, the book immediately found great favour with the Nazi Party. Himmler is reported to have expressed great enthusiasm for it, and even to have given a specially bound copy of it to Hitler as a birthday present.

Despite their lack of academic merit, Rahn's researches and publications must have created a significant impression. On the 29 February 1936, an SS Divisional General, Karl Wolff, wrote to the SS recruitment office to convey Himmler's personal wish that Rahn be admitted. Evidently his Jewish parentage had not been discovered and he was formally accepted into the SS on the 12 March 1936. The following May, he joined the personal staff of Reichsfuhrer of the SS, Heinrich Himmler. The depth of Rahn's commitment to the Nazi cause is unknowable, but it is generally accepted that, while he supported its ideology and mythology, he was very much less enthusiastic towards its military aspects and the practical application of Nazi philosophy.

Two years later, in 1938, Walter Birks, who, as we have seen, had been drawn to the region the year before by his contact with the White Eagle Lodge, visited the Languedoc and was introduced to a character of very different nature. Calling himself Natt Wolff, he presented himself as an American, though the locals were convinced from his accent that he was German and possibly a spy. It soon became apparent to both Birks and the local residents that Wolff was obsessed with the Cathar treasure. They concluded that his sole motive was to profit financially from the Cathars; either by finding their treasure or by exploiting the mini-tourist industry that had developed in the region. Wolff, usually surrounded by 'suspicious-looking German and Spanish refugees', further upset the locals with his general deportment and behaviour, drinking heavily, and womanising. Given this, one wonders how serious his intent in the region was; he also manifestly lacked any entrepreneurial dedication.

There is a suspicion that Natt Wolff was in reality Karl Wolff (later to become an SS general), and that he was indeed a German spy. His purpose being to further investigate the claims made by Otto Rahn, his unpleasant persona could have been adopted as a deliberate cover to conceal his true identity. Possible confirmation comes from assertions in a book by the grandson of Paul Bernadac who owned the guest-house at Ussat-les-Bains where Rahn stayed in 1932. Being an enthusiastic potholer with an interest in the local history, Paul had accompanied Rahn on several occasions; details of which he had apparently passed on to his grandson, Christian.

In Christian Bernadac's *Le Mystère Otto Rahn : Du Catharisme au Nazisme*, it is reported that during his visit in 1932, Rahn was accompanied by Natt Wolff. Travelling on an American passport, he claimed to be on a US government photographic project. According to police files, Wolff used two passports with different details, giving rise even then to the suspicion that he was a German spy; he was eventually expelled on the orders of the Minister of the Interior.

Walter Birks, however, was less convinced that the presence of Rahn and Wolff could have been in any way connected with Nazi ambitions. His distaste for Wolff might be a clue to this, in that his own sense of cultural refinement and academic taste probably precluded a character such as Wolff from being anyone of consequence. As he himself put it, 'The man was a chump who thinks he can get rich quickly, but in fact thinks of nothing but his aperitif and his dogs'.

It is not really surprising that following the publication of his books, Rahn should have been invited to join the SS. His quest for the Grail, his interest in romantic and chivalric heroes, his attraction to Celtic/Nordic philosophies, and his commitment to National Socialism would all have endeared him to the Nazi propaganda machine. But even more, he was thought to have uncovered the legend of the lost treasure of the Cathars, the Holy Grail itself.

Membership of the SS would necessarily have exposed Rahn to the harsh realities of the Nazi regime. His own scholarly and ideological interests would soon have been at odds with the more militaristic preoccupations of Nazi officialdom. The four-month tour of duty with the Oberbayern, at a training camp in Dachau where guard duty at the concentration camp was regularly assigned, could well have stretched his Nazi sympathies too far. Perhaps even to the point where, despite his previous usefulness to the party, he had now become a liability.

In March 1939, Otto Rahn was reported killed in an Alpine skiing accident. However, that is itself shrouded in mystery; not least because no body was ever found. Further, an obituary notice in *Berliner Ausgabe*, announcing that Rahn had died in a snowstorm in March, did not appear until 18 May, and a week later on 25 May another obituary appeared in the SS newspaper *Das Schwarze Korps*. Interestingly, both obituaries were signed by an SS officer named Karl Wolff; and it further appears that Rahn had resigned his commission in a letter to Karl Wolff dated 28 February 1939. The day after, Wolff wrote a letter to the SS office of Racial Questions, informing them that Otto Rahn had been unable to produce the required certificate of racial origin. He was officially dismissed on 17 March 1939. But on the 17 July, Rahn's father wrote to a German writers' association, informing them that his son had died in a snowstorm at Ruffheim, on 13 March 1939 – four days before his dismissal.

There was also talk shortly before Rahn's death of an enquiry into the nature and outcome of his unsupervised activities in the Corbières. According to Hans Jurgen-Lange in his book *Otto Rahn: Leben & Werk*, Rahn had been visited at the Hôtel Marroniers by the German singer and actress Marlene Dietrich and her friend Josephine Baker, the black jazz singer; both of whom, disenchanted by the society being cultivated by the Nazi party, spent much time in Paris frequenting the occult circles. These were the very same circles which attracted the romanticists, surrealists, esotericists, and free-thinkers of the time; and those that have formed the backbone for the transmission of occult traditions from the 18th century to the present day. These same elite intellectual circles had attracted Debussy and Victor Hugo (both supposedly Grand Masters of the Priory of Sion); and they fashioned the world in which the Abbé Saunière and the opera singer Emma Calvé had found themselves some fifty years before.

A passionate Francophile, Dietrich was a close friend of the great French artist, poet and film-maker Jean Cocteau, also said to have been a Grand Master of the Priory of Sion. By his early twenties, Cocteau had established himself in bohemian occult circles with occasional forays into spiritualism. His World War II activities are unclear, but he denounced the Vichy government and may have worked secretly with the Resistance. It is also said that Dietrich had been a close friend of André Malraux, yet another high-ranking member of the Priory, a Resistance hero and member of De Gaulle's post-war government. Both Dietrich and Baker received the Légion d'Honneur, Croix de Guerre, and the Resistance Medal in recognition of their ardent anti-Nazi commitment. But what were they doing down in this remote region of France in 1932? Are these associations merely another strange coincidence in this mysterious web centred on this remote region in the south west of France?

Perhaps inevitably, there have been more recent historians who have ventured that Rahn did not die in 1939[2]. It has even been suggested that Otto Rahn transformed into Rudolf Rahn, the German Ambassador appointed to Italy in 1943; and it was SS General Karl Wolff who agreed the German surrender with the Allies in Italy in 1945. If he was indeed spirited away it does suggest that he was up to something, and it is not unreasonable to accept that Karl Wolff, using the pseudonym Natt, was involved with Rahn, and with others in 1938, in the search for the Grail treasure. It is unlikely now that the truth will ever be known for certain.

It is similarly unlikely that Walter Birks' dogmatic dismissal of any strange activities should be accepted without question. He had first-hand experience of Wolff, and this may have clouded his judgement, both of the man and his purpose. He may also have had his own agenda. In the bizarre history that has coloured the parallel valleys of the Aude and the Ariège, little appears to be what it seems.

Before moving onto the war years, it is important for this story to grasp why this region, its promise, and these activities would have had significance to the Nazis; and how that significance evolved during their twelve years ruling Germany. During the early years of Nazi rule, the Party was clearly in the ascendant. Everything was apparently going as planned: the currency had stabilised, affluence was apparent everywhere, autobahns (as part of a work creation scheme) were mushrooming throughout Germany, and there was a sense of purpose and vigour. Morale was at its highest level for a quarter of a century. It can be no surprise that Hitler was held in such high esteem by what seemed like the whole of Germany, and that the Nazi Party in consequence enjoyed almost universal support.

The tone of Hitler's speeches makes it very clear that Nazism sought to justify itself by resorting to the esoteric. The 'divine inspiration' for his philosophy included high-blown notions of reincarnated Teutonic Knights (of which Hitler saw himself as one), present day realisation of Nordic folklore, and the perceived supremacy of the Aryan Race. It all struck the right chord with the once proud German nation. Success was once again breeding success, and generating yet further success. The return to invincibility, in the face of the current evidence, was impossible to doubt.

Many scholars acknowledge that Nazism became a substitute religion. Its mass rallies were very carefully organised to provide the participants with a mystical experience, similar to that found by many devotees at a Catholic High Mass; a great deal of sophistication went into establishing rites and rituals to complete this psychological manipulation. The Nazi salute, the swastika (ancient symbol of the sun), the red Nazi flag (symbolic of the blood of its early martyrs), and the magnificent uniforms and decorations worn by Nazi officers, are but a few manifestations of this.

In preserving this euphoric momentum, it is easy to comprehend the pride with which Hitler presented to his nation the so-called Spear of Destiny, said to be the spear which pierced Christ's side on the Cross. Hitler had acquired this from the Hofburg Palace in Vienna, when Austria became part of Germany by virtue of the Anschluss agreement in March 1938. It was brought back to Germany and housed in the magnificent German National Museum at Nuremberg that was, and still is, the great centre of Germanism, a centre devoted to a pride in Germany and its characteristic traditions. The Spear of Destiny and the royal emblems of the Holy Roman Emperors had been previously kept at Nuremberg from 1424 to 1796; Nuremberg was chosen to host the greatest of Nazi rallies. That it was selected as the site for the Allies' war crimes' trials, cannot have been lost on either the victors or the vanquished. Whether the Spear was authentically that used to pierce Christ's side was irrelevant; the national mood of the time was totally receptive to accepting anything that glorified the Reich and its Fuhrer.

The legends and mysteries surrounding the nature and history of such treasure, but most particularly acquiring further such artefacts, must have been music to the ears of the Nazi leadership. Imagine the tempting possibilities of acquiring the Grail cup, supposed to have caught Christ's blood from the Cross, or even the Ark of the Covenant. The sheer symbolic value of such treasures falling into Nazi hands after 1500 years, would have been incalculable.

It is well documented that both Hitler and Himmler had a profound interest in esoteric issues, and the SS was indeed modelled on those ancient warrior-monks, the Teutonic and Templar Knights. Himmler was contemplating a resurrection of a 'Round Table of Knights', which was to have had its headquarters at the small town of Wewelsburg in Westphalia. Throughout the War he continued the restoration of the ancient castle at the centre of the town. The crypt of the north tower of the castle was to contain the sacred flame, representing the centre of the world of the Third Reich, around which his knights would meet for highly symbolic rituals. Much to Himmler's chagrin, he had failed to gain personal possession of the Spear of Destiny, which he had hoped to keep at Wewelsburg. However, Hitler did allow him to make a copy, which was displayed in a place of honour in the castle.

Nazi activity continued in the remote region of the Corbières throughout the war, even though far removed from the front lines of conflict. In 1943 a group of German scientists, including geologists, historians and archaeologists, camped out below Montségur, under the protection of the local French Milice[3]. It is said that they carried out excavations throughout the surrounding area; the very area researched by Otto Rahn. At much the same time, eye-witnesses recall a Nazi division of engineers involved in clandestine activities at various locations throughout the Corbières, in the region of Rennes-le-Château. Specifically mentioned by local residents to the avid researcher Roger-René Dagobert, were the areas of Auriac, St. Paul-de-Fenouillet, Embres-et-Castelmaure, Durban-Corbières and several others – the exact region surrounded by the ring of ancient Cathar castles that encloses the supposed sites of the Visigoth treasure.

This continued activity in the Corbières was evidently a last ditch attempt by a small cabal of Nazi superiors, that included Heinrich Himmler, Alfred Rosenberg and Martin Bormann, to acquire for themselves this legendary treasure before it was too late. Indeed, Bormann entrusted this delicate mission to a man already charged with acquiring wealth for the 'Brotherhood'. Known somewhat affectionately as Scar, as a result of a facial injury, Otto Skorzeny was the most gifted commando to appear on the stage of World War II.

Skorzeny was a flamboyant officer of great courage, panache and initiative; his individualism made him ideally suited to the role of adventuring troubleshooting go-getter into which Hitler cast him. He is best remembered today as the officer sent by Hitler to rescue Mussolini when the Italians, disillusioned with their dictator after a series of defeats, had ousted him and imprisoned him in a hotel atop the Gran Sasso Mountain. Skorzeny was later credited as being the man who set up and ran ODESSA, the world-wide organisation that successfully helped former SS officers escape from Europe.

Early in 1940, having been seconded to the 1st SS Division (Heavy Artillery), Skorzeny was sent to France. Following the French Armistice, he was granted leave for a 'short and pleasant' interval in the south of France after which he was sent to Holland. In December of that year, as an engineer officer, he accompanied the 2nd SS Panzer Division Das Reich to France, which was then to be followed by three months of inactivity. Skorzeny's autobiography, *Skorzeny's Special Mission*, is pointedly vague about the purpose of this assignment. However, at a time when the Eastern Front was opening up with initial excitement and success, Skorzeny's own description of his time in the south-west of France as being a period of rest and inactivity stretches the imagination. Furthermore, by his own account, his visit was followed by several further visits. For a man with such a high-flying career, it is unlikely that there would not be a more major significance behind these visits, attractive and agreeable though that part of France undoubtedly is.

Hitler sent for Skorzeny in June 1941, and he was dispatched to Poland to fight the Russians. The turning point in Nazi fortunes had been reached: after an eight-year period of almost incredible achievement, began a four years period of Gotterdamerung, which was to destroy Germany, leave it humiliatingly divided, and occupied by foreign powers for the next half century. However, Skorzeny, a born survivor, was to carve out a place in Nazi military legend for himself. By 1943, having successfully carried out the rescue of Mussolini, Skorzeny was as close as a Major could be to the centre of power. Congratulated by Hitler and Himmler, and awarded the Knights Cross of the Iron Cross, the contacts and connections which he had earned and cultivated, made it quite certain that he had a better idea than most of the realities of the then current situation. Interestingly, Skorzeny was even to marry the daughter of Hjalmar Schacht, Hitler's financial genius. He had been accepted into the heady world of the Nazi elite.

Himmler sent Skorzeny to the Corbières for the last time in early 1944. Not on behalf of Hitler and the Third Reich no doubt, but as an agent and confidante of Himmler himself and his inner circle. This time there was a touch of desperation about the mission, since the Allies had already invaded Italy, and it was an open secret that an invasion of France was coming. Therefore, to find and recover the Corbières treasure would have been a matter of now or never.

What Skorzeny may have found is not known for certain. However, the American Colonel Howard Buechner in his book *Emerald Cup – Ark of Gold*, is quite adamant that Skorzeny discovered part of the treasure that had belonged in turn to the Visigoths, Templars and Cathars. Removed from the Corbières and transported via Toulouse through France to Germany, at least some of the treasure ended up at the unlikely village of Merkers in Thuringen (about 320 km south-west of Berlin). When Merkers fell to the Allied forces on 4 April 1945, a chance encounter by two American military policemen with some local residents, revealed that the nearby Kaiseroda potassium mine had become the repository for the Nazis' stolen treasure. As an officer in the advance party, Buechner was well-placed to know its nature and extent.

But how could Bueckner have known about the Corbières excavations? As far as is known, Buechner never met Skorzeny – and had he done so, it is unlikely that Skorzeny would have volunteered anything useful to someone he would have regarded as his enemy. Furthermore, Walter Birks, in *The Treasure Of Montségur*, points out that the Pog, the mountain on which Montségur had been built, was systematically surveyed and explored by the Société Spéleologique de l'Ariège in 1960. Every cave and opening on the rock was apparently explored and nothing remotely resembling a treasure chamber was discovered. But why then did Skorzeny make several return visits to the region, particularly in 1944 when there was certainly much he could have been doing at a critical time elsewhere? As if to back this up, there is also the arrival in the region in March 1944, of the 2nd SS Panzer Division.

There is no doubt of the staggering size of the plunder held in the Merkers mine. Whilst some of it had been stolen from concentration camp inmates – before or after their deaths – this was a small percentage when compared with what else Buechner claims was there. His claims must be taken seriously, because it is on record that, following the capture of the town, the top Allied commanders, generals Patton, Bradley, and Eisenhower, took time out to go and inspect the treasure themselves. A separate account of this incident can be found in the book *Nazi Gold* by Ian Sayer and Douglas Botting, in which they confirm, from the recollections of General Patton's ADC, Colonel Charles Codman, the staggering amount of wealth, in paper currency, gold, and art treasures, found in the mine. In fact they report that it required thirty-two ten-ton trucks to transport the haul to the Reischbank building in Frankfurt.

The main point of variance between the two reports, is Buechner's assertion that amongst the treasure were 'gold coins, some of which dated back to the early days of the Roman Empire' and items 'believed to have come from the Temple of Solomon'; a singular omission from all other accounts if it is true. Though, given the momentous symbolism of such a treasure and the circumstances of its discovery, perhaps it is not so surprising that steps were taken to maintain secrecy and its existence officially denied.

General Patton's own interest in the esoteric is also documented; he wore a pair of pearl-handled handguns and reputedly saw himself as the reincarnation of ancient heroes such as Julius Caesar and Alexander the Great. Furthermore, he was to acquire the famous Spear of Destiny, and in his poem *Through a Glass Darkly*, curiously posits himself as Longinus in a previous life. He was furious to hear that some of the treasure had been stolen during its transfer from the mines. It is known that he had promised a full enquiry: perhaps he appreciated its deeper significance. A few days later, he was involved in a car crash in circumstances that have never been satisfactorily explained, and died in hospital eleven days later. The mystery surrounding the incident, and the lack of an ensuing official enquiry, do perhaps add weight to the possibility that there was something to be covered up about what had been found in the Merkers mine.

Buechner[4] is amazingly candid and informative in his book. He even relates how Skorzeny found the treasure on 15 March 1944, one day before the 700th anniversary of the fall of Montségur and the burning alive of its Cathar defenders in 1244. Three other incidents add further intrigue to the events of 15 March 1944.

First, Skorzeny[5] was very friendly with Hitler's right-hand man, Martin Bormann[6], and was in fact a key member of his 'Brotherhood'. Bormann escaped after the war and was never found; it seems probable that he was one of the early beneficiaries of the ODESSA escape network. However, Bormann's wife did not escape with him, but was subsequently arrested by the Allies. In her possession were 2241 ancient gold coins.

Second, General Lammerding's 2nd SS Panzer Division was unexpectedly withdrawn from the Eastern Front and moved right down to Toulouse, in March 1944, ostensibly for retraining. It is strange that such a prestigious tank Division with its celebrated commander should be removed so far from the anticipated Allied invasion at Pas de Calais on the Channel coast. Toulouse is, however, the nearest major railhead to Montségur.

The third puzzling incident is the visit of Heinrich Himmler to the 2nd SS Panzer Division in April 1944, so soon after its arrival. With so many priorities at that time – not least the escalating disasters on the Eastern Front and the threat of an Allied invasion – he appears to have taken time out to visit Lammerding and his Division. Surely they were only involved in regrouping and retraining – coupled with routine garrison duty. Of course, what took place at that meeting between Himmler and Lammerding will probably never be known; but this meeting could have led to one of the most tragic incidents in wartime France.

The wanton destruction of the village of Oradour-sur-Glane on the orders of General Lammerding has left a deep scar on the psyche of many French people, especially those whose who lost family or friends in the massacre. But even more, this personal tragedy has also been revealed to be a blow to the French polity, exposing a web of corruption embraced by even the very highest level of government. The roots of this shameful situation can be traced back to the political upheavals throughout Europe following World War I. But in what way was the corruption manifest, who were involved, and what were the actual circumstances that produced it? And how is it that the mysterious past of Rennes-le-Château is found to be woven into this tale of conspiracy and intrigue?

Chapter 10

National Regeneration: A Conflict of Interests

On 22 January 1917 an eventful chapter closed in the chequered history of Rennes-le-Château. The Abbé Saunière had died, having been struck by a heart attack, or stroke, five days earlier[1]. But the relentless cycles of events continued to unfold and others will be drawn into this web of power, greed, and the search for treasure.

At the time of Saunière's passing, Europe was still immersed in the bloodiest conflict ever seen in the history of humanity; the result of a clash of empires, dynasties, and super-powers in the pursuit of expansionism or survival, in a rapidly changing world of industry, education, and social awareness. In a movement that had started with the French Revolution, elite and autocratic regimes were proving no longer sustainable as citizens desired to take more control over their own lives. The outcome of this First World War, and the signing of the Treaty of Versailles in 1919, broke up the German empire and that of the Austro-Hungarian Habsburgs. Yet it failed to bring political stability. Great resentment at losing the war, and demoralisation through the sanctions imposed by the victors, opened the door to a powerful German and Italian nationalism that was to result in another great war, twenty years later.

In Russia, the war had brought more problems to a country whose financial and social condition was already in rapid decline. Ruled by the absolute power of the Tsar, with the support of a small number of nobles, army officers and government officials, together with the Christian Russian Orthodox Church, her people were subjected to living under an oppressive feudal system little changed since the Middle Ages. But in March 1917, revolution brought about the end of the Tsar's rule. Following social principles proposed by the 19th century German philosopher Karl Marx, the Bolshevik leader, Vladimir Lenin, became the first ruler of a new Russia – and was the first country to fully embrace Communism. The ramifications of this were to dramatically affect European and World politics for the next eighty years, with an even further-reaching legacy.

The adoption of Communism by such a large and influential country, and its spread to Russia's immediate neighbours, sent alarm bells ringing in the Vatican, the Church fearful of the spread of an ideology in which there was no place for it. Over the next eighty years the Catholic Church would become involved in secret and subversive activities aimed at bringing about the fall of Communism, including strategies that would rely on the formation of some rather unholy alliances. These of course were tactics that had been adopted throughout the centuries whenever the Church found itself under threat.

The instability of the inter-war years, 1918 to 1939, was to be felt, to some extent, by almost every country in Europe. The resulting social and financial upheavals were to prove fertile for exploitation by extremist interest groups. Italy, in turmoil following defeat in World War I, was the first to fall under the fascist spell. The Italian people had little confidence in their fragmented government; the landowners, industrialists and businessmen were concerned about the communist rumbles in their industries; and economic crisis created huge unemployment and rampant inflation. Into this arena strode Benito Mussolini, a disaffected Socialist. Preaching a doctrine of firm government opposed to Communists and Liberals, his Fascist party was supported by middle-class Italians, businessmen, factory and property owners, and army officers. Initial progress was slow, but after resorting to bullying and other violent tactics, Mussolini finally achieved complete control of government and, from 1924, his unelected dictatorship[2].

The German response to the depression of the 1920s was eventually to follow the Italian model. The government that took over from the displaced Kaiser managed to suppress a Communist revolution, yet Communism continued to be a significant force feared by many people, and disaffection with perceived weakness in government was strong. Adolf Hitler, an Austrian born in 1889, moved to Munich and joined the German army in 1914; he was wounded twice and awarded the Iron Cross. His interest in politics took him into the German Workers Party where his talent for public speaking brought him to the fore. Having taken charge, he changed its name to the National Socialist Workers Party, 'Nazi' for short, and in 1920 launched a new twenty five point programme which included elements of nationalism, socialism and racism – especially against the Jews. Gradually its socialist objectives gave way to a stronger nationalism, and the economic crisis generated by the Wall Street crash gave Hitler a great opportunity to promote his grandiose plans for national regeneration, laying the blame for the country's ills at the feet of the Communists and the Jews.

He came a creditable second to Hindenburg in the 1932 presidential elections, which assisted the Nazi party in increasing its support amongst other right-wing groups, whilst the Socialists and Communists remained divided. Political manoeuvring secured the Chancellorship for Hitler with the endorsement of the commercial and financial sectors who thought they would fare better under Hitler's political stance than under that of the Communists.

Following the death of Hinderburg, Hitler assumed the position of President besides that of Chancellor, and was able to control and manipulate all aspects of German society. Having achieved ultimate power and having collected around him a High Command of dedicated and ruthless Nazis, Hitler was able to initiate his avowed foreign policy of uniting all German-speaking peoples. This soon turned into a relentless drive to occupy every country in mainland Europe. Inevitably this was to provoke opposition especially from Britain and France, but since neither country relished the prospect of another war, they employed every tactic to delay making decisions or to appease Hitler at as little cost to themselves as possible. There were even those in the British Establishment who were somewhat sympathetic to Hitler and admired his efforts at national regeneration after the deprivations of the Treaty of Versailles, and in addition saw the Nazi regime as a solid bulwark against the expansion of Communism. Most of the wealth, land and means of production in Britain at the time resided in the hands of an hereditary aristocracy, or a parallel one of industrial giants, financiers and bankers, many of whom would have felt empathy with (and even envy of) Germany's economic 'miracle'.

The British Royal Family had close ties with its German aristocratic cousins; and although considered to be a democracy, Britain herself did preside over an empire of countries forced to accept a government and a head of state unelected by them. It has been seriously suggested by some historians that Hitler believed Britain, which he admired for its achievements and considered as a natural ally, would eventually form an alliance with him, and that his contact with the abdicated King Edward VIII, the Duke of Windsor, would bring the rest of the British Establishment on side. Weight to this hypothesis is perhaps given by Hitler's personal reluctance to launch a full scale invasion of Britain, despite the failure of Dunkirk and his military superiority at the time.

By this time, the political map of Europe was divided into three major competing power blocs: communism, fascism and liberal democracy. The continuing conflict between these factions drove a number of both open and secret agendas; but crucially, provided an excuse and cover for the pursuit of individual power in the form of idealistic ambitions and the acquisition of personal wealth. As we will see, although absent from public consciousness , the treasure of the Corbières continued to remain in the forefront of the minds of some individuals.

The French reaction to the Nazi militarisation had been to divert a huge amount of public expenditure to the construction of the Maginot Line, a 320 km line of fortifications along its border with Germany that was considered impregnable. On the day that the newly elected British Prime Minister, Winston Churchill, told the House of Commons that he was fully prepared to wage war by land, sea and air, the Germans launched a blitzkrieg attack on Holland, Belgium, and France. Panzer tank divisions rolled straight over Holland and Belgium meeting limited resistance; whilst other divisions skirted the Maginot Line by advancing through the Ardennes rendering the French defences ineffective. The German occupation of France was to expose fundamental divisions in French society that had their roots back in the Revolution but that had been re-asserted in the early 1920s.

Since the Revolution, French politics had been inclined to the Left, espousing democratic Socialist principles much to the continuing dismay of those who favoured the ancien régime – that is, those who still identified with an aristocracy, property owners, the Catholic Church and the many who felt let down by the Republic. Amongst factory workers, a trade union movement in the form of Syndicalism evolved which rejected the normal parliamentary process for resolving disputes and instead advocated direct action of the labour force. Furthermore, they sought worker control and ownership of industry; it was inevitable that, after 1918, Syndicalism should become absorbed by its younger and more virile cousin, Communism.

As in the other major European countries, the Wall Street crash of 1929 had brought about a financial crisis and a loss of confidence in the government; a situation that provided golden opportunities for disaffected groups to bid for power over the next decade. When the Minister of Finance, later briefly Prime Minister, Paul Reynaud, proposed devaluation of the franc to alleviate the economic depression, he was swiftly and viciously denounced as a traitor by the extreme right-wing Catholic traditionalist-monarchist newspaper and movement, *Action Française*. Political instability followed; liberal democratic government was perceived to have failed. Just as in Italy and Germany, this opened the door to the possibility of a strong authoritarian government. Prior to the German invasion of France, the political scene had become polarised, with public and secret organisations at both ends of the spectrum. These were epitomised by the Front Populaire of the Left, initially uniting the Socialists and Communists, and Action Française on the Right, trading in a paranoid fear of Communism. In fact the Front Populaire was denounced by the Conservatives as being a Jewish-Boshevik plot – that familiar battle cry of the right wing.

In 1936, Léon Blum, a French politician who had converted to Socialism in 1899, became the first Jewish and Socialist prime minister of France. The election of a Jew, let alone a Socialist, to the post of prime minister, was like a red rag to a bull for the right-wing traditionalists. Their main standard bearer was the staunch Catholic writer, Charles Maurras, founder of Action Française. Maurras' main enemies were Freemasons, Protestants and Jews; but he also clearly hated all foreigners, the Revolution and the Republic, parliamentary democracy, the proletariat, free education and social justice, and wished to return to the social structure of the 18th century. He maintained an ambiguous relationship with the Church, and despite describing the Gospels as having been written by 'four shabby Jews', and Christianity as 'the religion of the rabble', it continued to support him until the Vatican, in 1926, placed his newspaper on the index of forbidden works. This was however rescinded by Pope Pius XII in 1939.

It was the extremism of Charles Maurras that was to become the blueprint for Vichy policies. Founded in 1908, Action Française expounded the tenet that the Catholic Church and the monarchy were essential to French civilization, exactly the sentiment so dear to the Abbé Saunière and his colleagues. It is tempting to speculate that Saunière may have been well aware of Maurras' organisation, and could have played some part in it.

Charles Maurras was by no means alone in publishing anti-Semitic material. Many endeavoured to foment hostility towards the Jews, claiming that this was the natural attitude of patriotic Frenchmen. One late 19th century protagonist in this was the Catholic novelist Maurice Barrès who, according to the authors of *The Holy Blood and the Holy Grail*, was another who may have been party to the Saunière secret. A friend of Claude Debussy and Victor Hugo, the young Barrès had been involved in the Rose-Croix circle, founded by Péladan, that we encountered in chapter seven. In 1912 he published a novel, *La Colline Inspirée* (The Inspired Hill), which despite containing striking parallels to events at Rennes-le-Château, in fact refers to the hill of Sion-Vaudemont, the ancient pilgrimage site in Lorraine. Yet again the hand of coincidence appears to bring Bérenger Saunière and his little village into contact with the worlds of the occult and European politics, and to connect them with those who saw significance in Sion.

The occupation of France finally provided the Right with the opportunity it had been waiting for, and so brought about the formation of the wartime Vichy government. Since the industrial base of France, which Hitler needed to exploit in order to support his war effort, was in the northern half of the country, an agreement was reached by which the southern half could remain under the control of a French government if it were authorised by the Germans. Unwilling to be party to an armistice, the Prime Minister, Paul Reynaud resigned and his deputy, a hero of the World War I, Marshal Pétain, succeeded him. A virtually unknown protégé of the Reynaud administration, the junior defence minister General de Gaulle departed for England to set up a French National Committee to 'act as the provisional guardian of the national patrimony'. While later highly significant, this went almost unnoticed in France at the time.

The new French government, set up under Pétain in the spa town of Vichy in central France, imitated many of the policies of the Third Reich, including its virulent attitude to the Jews. At the beginning of the war it is estimated that there were about 330,000 Jews in France, some of whose families had been resident for centuries; within two years nearly 76,000 Jews, predominantly those who had fled from the Nazis to France, had been forcibly deported or repatriated to Germany. Despite this, Marshal Pétain, who was himself at the heart of anti-Jewish legislation, received support from the Catholic Church through its representative the Archbishop of Paris, Cardinal Emmanuel Suchard, for his 'National Revolution'. It must also be remembered that the Catholic Church never excommunicated Hitler (who was a Catholic), in spite of his massive abuse of civil rights; according to the Church, he had never broken any Canon Law!

The division of loyalty between the collaborative Vichy government and the exiled resistance organisation de Gaulle set up was to divide the French nation so deeply that, even over sixty years later, the wounds are not fully healed. It also provided an unexpected opportunity for those with no loyalty, except to themselves, to achieve the necessary power or influence to pursue their own agendas. Not surprisingly, this will include those attempting to gain possession of documents concerning the secret of Rennes-le-Château, and ultimately, the treasure itself.

It is often thought that because of its collaboration, the Vichy government was entirely pro-Nazi; but Vichy supporters actually considered themselves true patriots, who sought a renewal in independent Gallic pride, and accepted collaboration as a necessary step towards eventual liberation. The French right wing only mirrored German fascism in some areas. However, in policies such as anti-Semitism, some Vichy ministers were to prove themselves to be even more efficient than their Nazi counterparts. René Bousquet, having been appointed national Chief of Police, demonstrated his ruthless administrative ability by organising the rounding up and deportation of 76,000 Jews to Germany, for which he won great praise from the Nazis, and came to the attention of SS chief Heinrich Himmler. The two men were to meet in Paris in 1943, after which Himmler stated that Bousquet was a precious collaborator, and would possibly play a leading role in French politics. Fiercely anti-Communist, Bousquet had possibly exercised his power against the Jews more as an example to others than as a callous anti-Semite. Interestingly however, Bousquet managed to escape the punishments normally received by collaborators after the war, and was to remain a close friend, until his death, of the later president of France, François Mitterrand – who was himself a one-time member of Vichy.

But it was some 200 km south-east of Vichy, near the city of Grenoble, that one of the collaborationist government's most fascinating and secretive activities was to take shape. Situated in the dramatic and mountainous Rhone-Alpes region, Grenoble is a bustling industrial alpine city; 50 km to its north is the ancient monastery of La Grand Chartreuse, famous for its liqueur. But it was at the impressive Château Bayard[3], with its 12th century foundations, situated east of Grenoble on the high plateau shared by the village of Uriage-les-Bains, that this most ambitious and controversial enterprise unfolded.

Long before the war, the importance of youth education and training had been widely appreciated; even the 'Catholic' scout movement[4] had been manipulated to be militantly patriotic, authoritarian, opposed to materialism, and to liberal and democratic values. Though avowedly non-political, this scout movement was decidedly anti-Republican. At the Château Bayard these sentiments were to form the basis of a curriculum aimed at a 'National Revolution', to be led by an intellectual elite of youths who would replace the old administration and, in the process, purge Jews and Freemasons from positions of influence.

Under the direction of Pierre Dunoyer de Segonzac, a dashing young cavalry officer from staunch Catholic aristocratic roots, this ideological school, called the Ecole Nationale des Cadres d'Uriage, was the flagship of a network designed to prepare a new elite for the control of France following the Liberation. Just like the Catholic scouts, the students were required "to exercise a heroic effort for the renewal of France, the reconstruction stone by stone of a Christendom of Europe", in the words of Father Marcel-Denys Forestier, founder of the Rover scouts – a group within the larger Catholic scout movement.

John Hellman, professor of history at McGill University, has carried out an extremely detailed analysis of the history of this elite school and the counterparts it spawned, published in his book *The Knight-Monks of Vichy France, Uriage 1940-1945*. The second edition contains an appendix in which can be found important new material concerning former president François Mitterrand's little known connections with the Uriage group, and how knowledge of these schools has been largely removed from French public consciousness.

The Uriage enterprise spread to other provincial centres, but by the end of 1942, the Schools, despite their initial success, came under attack from youth groups and others, possibly out of jealousy, but also concerned at their growing influence and lack of accountability. The aims of the Uriage school had shifted to even greater horizons, beyond Vichy and France, to that of a European New Order. However, the war starting to turn against the Germans, the Vichy regime came under closer supervision and began to lose even more of its fragile independence. The administration of Dunoyer de Segonzac was removed from the school at Uriage and replaced by a far more sinister organisation, the Milice[5].

Selected from an organisation founded on the direct orders of Hitler who wanted an auxiliary police to maintain internal order, the Milice instructors were mystical fascists committed to a curious, Catholic-Nazi vision of National Revolution. Added to the curriculum were studies of communist methods, military training focused on guerilla and street combat, and an exhaustive study of the fighting that preceded the advent of National Socialism in Germany. It is very obvious that this military tuition was aimed not at defeating the Germans but at combating subversives – that is, those who would challenge the system of authority, whether French or German. By 1944, the Milice, according to American Intelligence, had become the most formidable pro-fascist political organisation in Vichy France, and had continued to maintain the strong religious tone of Catholic monarchists. Retaining Catholic ritual and tradition, the Milice endorsed national and racial purity, the priority of labour over money, and condemned Gaullism, Communism, Freemasonry, and Judaism, outright.

This frightening and disquieting institution was remarkably successful in its recruitment and it is estimated that during the occupation some 200,000 French citizens actively identified their own interests, and that of France, with Hitler's New Order. It was never systematically purged following the war. One has to ask what influence the former pupils of the Milice may have had on the French post war politics and even the vision of a United Europe. Its influence appears to have extended as far as the presidency of France. The vision of this New Order is also much the same as that adopted by the secret societies found at the heart of the intrigue surrounding the secret treasure of the Corbières. Can it be mere coincidence that some of the same people involved with the core of Vichy policy, especially the youth movements, also surface as those involved in the quest for the hidden treasure?

Having been ousted from his position at Uriage, Dunoyer de Segonzac and his colleagues unobtrusively regrouped at the Château de Montmaur, near Gap, to concentrate more on their spiritual values, in a tightly disciplined and hierarchical community. Developing in time into a more formal Order of Knighthood, with accompanying rites and rituals, the 'Knight-Monks of the Uriage' then moved into the Château de Murinais, above the Isère valley in the French Alps, to accommodate Segonzac's new community in relative security. Divisions between the Order's so-called elite, and those members of the 'Resistance' dedicated to fighting the German occupiers, however, were soon clearly revealed. Members of the Resistance who came into contact with Segonzac were alarmed at his presumption to provide unelected leadership over the French; on the other hand, members of the Order were advised to deal carefully with the Resistance groups, avoiding their possible Masonic and foreign influences. But the Order's existence was proof that any attempt to return, after the anticipated 'Liberation', to a pre-war form of republic would be fiercely opposed. The Order's attitude to Jews was resolute, unambiguously expressed in one Uriage document: 'Israelites were not to be admitted to the Order... we ought not to underestimate the danger of a Jewish revenge (organisation) nor ignore the existence of a Jewish international (Zionism) whose interests are opposed to those of France'. However in some contradiction to this the same document continues: 'Our present attitude remains in the framework of an aid to oppressed Israelites'. By the explicit choice of terminology, it would appear perhaps that a distinction was being drawn between the newly-arrived immigrant Jews, and those of the old resident communities.

The Order, just as the Milice had at Château Bayard, studied rival groups competing for power in a 'liberated' France. These included Freemasons, the Synarchist movement, and the Communist party. In this shadow battle for prospective power, most were to resort to subversive activities, some of which will be seen to continue to the present day. A paranoia even later developed in which more effort was expended hunting down Communists than Germans! Those loyal to Pétain and Vichy were suspicious of the Resistance movement, both for fear of upsetting the status quo but also because they believed it to have been infiltrated by Communists. Perhaps this was indeed so; Henri Frenay, head of the Resistance movement Combat, told Segonzac at the begining of 1944 that although the Communists were courageous 'Resistance' fighters, they seemed to him, more and more, 'to be preparing to take power'.

By the end of summer 1943, the war had swung dramatically in favour of the Allies. A French army had become united under General Giraud, whilst in the political arena General de Gaulle was becoming more prominent. The changing fortunes of war and the increased demands of the German occupiers appeared also to bring about a change of attitude and loyalty in Segonzac towards Vichy. He admitted misgivings about the Pétainist vision, even expressing veiled doubts about Pétain's character. In a complete about face, Segonzac even arranged a meeting with de Gaulle[6], and offered his service to the Free French forces. At the Château de Murinais a subtle transformation was also taking place. While retaining the lofty elements of Knighthood, the agenda was moving closer to a military and political stance more attuned to the changing situation of the war. Still inspired by the sense of belonging to an elite and the spirit of French regeneration, the Uriage pupils now looked to the Resistance to fulfil their destinies and reached out to establish contact with the local Maquis (Resistance activists). It is not surprising that these overtures were met with a great deal of suspicion; and it was only after the Germans attacked and closed down the school at the Château Murinais, that the former Uriage members became more acceptable to the Resistants. In time, with careful rewriting of its recent history, the agendas of the Uriage school and its provincial satellites were sanitised of their extreme pro-fascist leanings, to become more moderate, with a politically transcendental viewpoint.

This new agenda came to terms with the growing power of Charles de Gaulle and his Free French, now the predominant symbol of Liberation and Renewal. Segonzac travelled to Algeria, where the exiled provisional French government had established itself in June 1943, in order to meet de Gaulle. Despite a frosty and mistrustful reception, Segonzac came back with a positive and glowing impression, reporting that 'General de Gaulle has a very strong personality… extraordinary… its sense of grandeur, spirit of independence carried to the extreme, intelligence, energy, taste for command and nobility of style are its principal characteristics'. Evidently seduced by de Gaulle's personality, he concluded that, 'We of the Order and of the Movement ought to support him; he is our best chance'. He further observed that 'the Americans constitute a genuine danger for France. It is a very different danger from that which Germany represents and from what the Russians might eventually pose for us. It is in the economic and moral sphere'.

Yet while Segonzac and his Uriage Order switched their allegiance to de Gaulle, they continued to prepare to fill the political void created by the departure of the occupying forces with an ambitious plan to provide cadres (educated elite) for a 'Revolution of the 20th century'; they would continue to oppose the Communists, modern American culture, old-style Republicans, and any others who might stand in the way of the 'Regeneration of France' by their select elite.

As D-Day approached, Segonzac firmly established himself within the Resistance and gained command over two hundred men of the Maquis; old habits die hard however, and he subjected the group to Catholic and Uriage teachings – much to its amazement, since many were either Protestant or Jewish. However the Uriage members were extremely bright and, throwing off their Pétainist image, established themselves at the very heart of the Resistance, without compromising their former principles integral to their vision of a renewed France. Of all those able to make this astonishing transformation from Vichyite to Resistance supporter, the most important and influential was François Mitterrand, later President of France. His position occupies a critical place in this tangled web.

Parallel to the diverse aspirations of the Vichy government, the Uriage Order, the Communists, the Resistance and the Gaullists, were the aims of a neo-Masonic brotherhood, the Ordre Martiniste[7]. Prominent in the 1930s, such Synarchist groups had demonstrated active involvement in Masonic politics. The OM adopted as aims (besides the Fraternity, Liberty and Equality, sentiments common to all Masonic groups) finance through capitalism, the use of traditional symbols of the past, influence through covert means, a drive for a united Europe and a worldwide association of countries. This was diametrically opposed to the Vichy/Uriage philosophy, and the OM became the subject of persecution. The Nazis, even if they had used secret society methods to gain power themselves, banned such organisations once in power, and the Vichy government was not slow to follow.

An extreme right-wing journalist and anti-Semitic collaborator, Henri Coston, became head of Vichy's Centre d'Action Maconique (Centre of Masonic Action) and authorised the looting and seizure of Masonic archives. This order included all secret societies that the authorities considered a potential threat. In the course of this he came across the Synarchist programme, which outlined a plan to exploit the turmoil in French politics of 1942 to infiltrate the Vichy administration. The Synarchists, in sympathy with the Resistance, had also established close contact with British Intelligence; the British made use of their secret lodge network for intelligence gathering. Faced with the threat of suppression, one Martinist group, the Ordre Martiniste-Synarchique, hastily transferred its HQ to Switzerland. Meanwhile, a parallel branch, the Ordre Martiniste de Lyon, was less fortunate and its Grand Master, Martin Chevillon, was caught and executed, not, as is commonly known by Klaus Barbie, the 'butcher of Lyon', but by the equally ruthless French Milice. Significantly, the Lyon lodge's archives, amassed over two centuries, were carted away.

It is from the acquisition by the Milice of these Martinist documents, that certain members of the Vichy government, their covert allies, and even some rogue elements in British Intelligence, would have been able to gain knowledge of those ancient documents which had belonged to General Dagobert, and those found by the Abbé Saunière, which related to the secret history of Rennes-le-Château. Certainly, individuals from the Vichy government, Martinists-Synarchists, British Intelligence and SOE operatives, were all to become involved, often in opposition to each other, in covert activity centred on the aptly named mystery of Rennes-le-Château.

Chapter 11

Called to Account

There is no more powerful an image of the liberation of Paris than the sight of the Allied forces parading down the Champs-Elysees on 26 August 1944, led, on foot, by a jubilant General de Gaulle. This was both emotional and symbolic: de Gaulle and his provisional government in exile had triumphed over the collaborative government of Marshal Pétain. Formerly condemned to death as a traitor by the Vichy government in absentia, de Gaulle was now warmly received by former collaborators – who by now appeared as confirmed Resistants. Yet great tensions still existed between the two camps, even if to the outside world their differences were hardly apparent now that the war was over. The future president François Mitterrand, who wrote, 'Seen from the camps, Pétain and de Gaulle appeared the same. They were both representatives of official France engaged in battle... Seen from Germany, Pétain and de Gaulle did not represent contradictory policies'. In fact, there are suggestions that both Pétain and de Gaulle[1] were playing in the same murky waters in their quests for a rejuvenated France.

Following the fall of France and the traumatic shock of becoming an occupied country, it had taken some time for organised resistance to develop. One of the first visible signs, in late 1940, was the clandestine publication of a magazine entitled *Combat* by Henri Frenay, and *Liberation* by Robert Lacoste and Christian Pineau, both of which attempted to create a unity amongst the potential Resistants. But a closer look at Frenay and *Combat* illustrates unexpected associations.

Henri Frenay had also been a student at Saint-Cyr military school and was both a classmate and close friend of Pierre Dunoyer de Segonzac, who (as we saw) was head of the Ecoles Nationales d'Uriage. Frenay strongly criticised Pierre Laval and the Vichy government for deporting young French workers to Germany, among other policies, but he stopped short of criticising the Marshal himself. He maintained regular contact and friendship with Segonzac, for whom in 1943, he acted as an intermediary with de Gaulle; and it was Frenay who told Segonzac in 1944 that although they were courageous fighters, the Communists seemed motivated more by the possibility of taking power after the war.

Combat attempted to recruit new Resistants from among prominent Catholic Pétainists, but it also attracted contributions from some influential right-wing writers such as Thierry Maulnier, who expressed views remarkably similar to those of the Ecoles Nationales d'Uriage. Other notable contributors were Drieu la Rochelle, Robert Brasillach, intellectual fascist writers, and François Mitterrand, who admitted to reading the works of these fascist writers long after the war. Mitterrand also contributed to the review *France, Revue d'Etat Nouveau* founded by Gabriel Jeantet, a former President of the Students of Action Française, the extreme right-wing group of Charles Maurras. Jeantet's politics were clearly pro-Pétain and he was virulently anti-Communist, anti-Capitalist, anti-democratic, anti-Nazi and anti-Gaullist. He even claimed that he was an intermediary between Pétain and the circle of German officers plotting against Hitler, and that he later worked as a mediator between de Gaulle and Pétain for reconciliation after the war. Jacques Laurent, a pro-Vichy novelist, affirmed that Mitterrand and Jeantet were very close, though he further added that Jeantet was a great Resistant; this illustrates how confusing the wartime picture has become. Mitterrand, of course, has gone down in history as a Socialist.

Without doubt, the Pétainist Vichy regime received more support than is generally acknowledged today. This is partly explained by its stand against communism, considered worse than rule by Nazi fascists to many sections of society; Nazism also offered a chance for regenerated national pride so damaged in the previous century. It must also have appeared to be the best option in view of the continuing Nazi threat to extend its occupation in France, and the wasteland that fighting Germany in 1914-18 had produced in northern France. Once the war swung in favour of the Allies, and Vichy began to be discredited, many former supporters either claimed to have been secretly active in the Resistance movement or simply denied former affiliation. Inevitably and understandably, a certain mythology has also grown up around the Resistance, encouraged by de Gaulle and his administration. The Resistance episode has thus become sacred, a story both simplified and embellished, from which a new national identity has been built after the traumatic and turbulent experience of the German Occupation.

This is certainly not to deny the actions of true courage performed by many French and other Allied Resistants, and their enormous contribution to the ending of the war. And whatever justification is given for the French collaboration, it is mostly seen as responsible for national and individual shame, hence the sympathetic rewriting of wartime history. However, the confusion this has generated, has been exploited by those with subversive or self-serving agendas, and has acted as a convenient smoke-screen both for those in prominent positions and those who prefer to remain in the shadows[2]: Some of these play key roles in this remarkable story.

It is certainly sometimes legitimate to hide one's true colours – think of the act of resistance itself. But it also creates grey areas; it becomes difficult to pinpoint the true political stance and beliefs of even the most prominent of politicians; and facilitates the concealing of tracks and re-creation of their past. When the politician is also involved in the world of secret or occult societies the situation becomes even more complex. And mirroring the patterns of history, certain major players of the war and post-war years begin to slip surreptitiously between the political, Intelligence and occult worlds in order to further their ambitions, usually a combination of power and wealth.

A key figure in the post-war episode of this saga is no lesser person than François Mitterrand, President of France from 1981 until 1995. Born into a rural Catholic bourgoise family from Jarnac, a village on the River Charante, Mitterrand showed a youthful fascination with politics, and attended rallies and meetings of all shades of the political spectrum. From 1934, he studied at the prestigious Sciences-Po, France's leading school for the political elite. As a product of Jesuit education, it was quite natural that he would eventually drift more towards the right, and despite his later denials, there is abundant evidence that he supported Action Française. It is also said that he attended meetings of La Cagoule, an even more extremist, active and secretive organisation that endorsed violent means to confront its perceived enemies. In fact it was a prominent member of this group, Raphael Alibert, who obtained for Mitterrand a position in the Vichy government. Without doubt, prior to the outbreak of war, Mitterrand had also established friendships, some of which were to last throughout his career, that were firmly on the right-wing of French politics – and even at the extreme end. It is generally accepted that he was a man of many sides, an intelligent but complex personality who liked to keep his entourage guessing. As a natural leader, Mitterrand also adopted the style of an aristocrat, which caused people to regard him later as more of a monarch than a president – an impression he actively encouraged.

In June 1940, he was captured by the German army and brought to the prison camp Stalag IX, near Kassel, in central Germany. According to his memoirs he escaped three times, each attempt more extraordinary than the previous, and he claimed to have joined the Resistance on his return to France. Yet some incontrovertible facts cast doubt on the accuracy of Mitterrand's memoirs. His period of imprisonment was significant in several ways. First, as he himself recalls, it enabled him to discover that he had a great capacity for survival. Second, it appears that the experience of prison culture, the comradeship, sharing and mutual support, made a strong impression on his political philosophy, which was to influence his later career as a Socialist. However, in spite of this apparent enlightenment, Mitterrand's instincts for survival, and political manoeuvring dictated that he would continue in the Pétainist camp for the time being.

It was during his time as a POW that he made contacts that would dramatically affect his future. He met the brilliant young French composer and musician, Olivier Messiaen, whose rhythmically complex works were heavily influenced by religious mysticism. Having a penchant for the esoteric himself, Mitterrand must have been fascinated by the thinking of the young composer. Mitterrand's attraction to the esoteric and the world of occult symbolism[3] is investigated in *Mitterrand, Le Grand Initié* by Nicolas Bonnal. A life-long friendship also developed from his meeting with Roger-Patrice Pelat, who will be shown later to have had a huge influence on his political career; truly a man from the 'shadows', Pelat was later to become involved in suspicious business activities; to some extent he became an embarrassment to Mitterrand. Yet against all advice, he remained loyal to his old friend.

But perhaps in the context of this investigation, his meeting with Antoine Gayraud and Antoine Courrière was to prove most significant. Both of them had been prominent local Socialist politicians in the Department of the Aude. Through them he would have learnt of the story of Saunière, the treasure of Rennes-le-Château, and the activities of the German SS officer, Otto Rahn, who had apparently died only the year before. This information was clearly valuable; Gayraud and Courrière enjoyed successful political careers under the Mitterrand administration. These and the other friendships that he developed throughout his career increasingly involved Mitterrand in the mysterious web that extends from the little village of Rennes-le-Château.

In contrast to the rather heroic and romantic accounts of his escapes from the prison camp, Mitterrand was probably released by the Germans under the terms of the Franco-German armistice, in which French POWs were repatriated. And rather than joining the Resistance, he clearly became an active member of the Vichy government from May 1942 until late 1943, as an official in the Commissariat General for Prisoners of War[4]. During this period he was to add yet more friends to his inner circle who would prove to be instrumental not only in his political career, but in the even darker occult world that he chose to frequent.

Another myth is his alleged welcome into the Resistance and immediate acceptance by de Gaulle. Like Segonzac, Mitterrand was greeted with suspicion, and as de Gaulle confided to the author of his biography (one of his former ministers) Alain Peyrefitte, when he met Mitterrand in Algeria in the winter of 1943, he regarded him as a defector from the Vichy regime, and a likely double agent. His intense dislike for Mitterrand was never to die and, even in 1965 de Gaulle was to refer to him as 'a thug', 'an impostor' and 'the prince of political schemers'. Mitterrand himself always maintained that he was really a Resistance infiltrator and not a true member of the Vichy government, but evidence to the contrary is overwhelming and his denial has never been convincing. However, he did likely eventually work for the Resistance, and Martin Gilbert claims in *The Day the War Ended* that Mitterrand flew to England, in late 1943, from a landing strip near Angers and returned two months later by motor gunboat to begin active Resistance contact with French deportees and POWs.

Some of his former Vichy compatriots also managed for a time to achieve high political posts despite their dubious past, but most, like Maurice Papon, a minister under Giscard d'Estaing, were eventually brought to justice. But Mitterrand had staying power. He was a man well able to perform complex mental gymnastics in recreating a past, and in displaying separate public and private faces, and furthermore very adept at operating in the 'looking glass' world of secret societies and their hidden agendas.

During the period that François Mitterrand was working for the Vichy administration, a newspaper entitled *Vaincre* (Conquer), with the sub-title *Pour une Jeune Chevalerie*, edited in Paris, commenced circulation. In issue No. 1, published on 21 September 1942, its founder is introduced, with a head and shoulders photograph, as Pierre de France. A young man of twenty-two years old, his full name was Pierre Plantard; he had at times also added the rather grandiose 'de Saint-Clair'. This pretentious suffix to his name has often been dismissed as egotism but it is in fact easily explained in light of the teachings of Action Française. They had a fixation on genealogy and many members of Action Française assumed nobility and created false ancestry in order to add a title to their names.

An accurate biography of Pierre Plantard has been difficult to assemble as the various available sources are both meagre and at times contradictory; what follows is a synthesis of the most reliable. Plantard was born on 18 March 1920 in Paris, to Pierre, a wine merchant, and his wife Raulo who died two and a half years later. He was to continue living with his mother until at least 1943. It is claimed he entered university, in 1939, where he excelled in Graeco-Roman archaeology. It was here that he met and developed a life-long friendship with the Marquis Philippe de Chérisey, the son of a minor aristocratic family from the Ardennes. Certainly, he and de Chérisey did form a close friendship, but it is unlikely that Plantard received a university education. The journalist Jean-Luc Chaumeil reveals that Plantard's full name was Pierre Athenasius Marie Plantard, and that he claimed to be a journalist; available evidence only confirms his work for several years as a verger at the church of St.Louis d'Antin, in Paris. He had also tried to establish an anti-Semitic and anti-Masonic organisation, presumably without success as no accounts remain of it, but he did lead a group in the Catholic youth movement[5]. This has been dismissed as insignificant by some researchers, but youth groups were considered to be of great importance to the French National Revival; in this capacity, Plantard may well have already achieved some distinction. In 1940, he is also said to have approached Marshal Pétain and started working for the Vichy government. Little is known of this early period because, as in the case of Mitterrand and many others, association with the Vichy government tended to be forgotten after the war. However, his appearance in *Vaincre* illuminates some remarkable details about the strange world of chivalric and secret societies, and their links to Rennes-le-Château and the Abbé Saunière, given his other activities.

Plantard always claimed that he worked undercover for the Resistance, and that *Vaincre* was in fact a Resistance journal in which the articles carried hidden meanings. A close look at the six issues still obtainable shows this claim to be very difficult to substantiate. Many of the articles are openly supportive of Marshal Pétain and Vichy policies. But there are also indeed some strange anomalies. The company that printed *Vaincre* is indicated as being that of Poirier Murat, described as a former officer in the French Resistance, holder of the Médaille Militaire, and Chevalier of the Légion d'Honneur. And surprisingly, the newspaper is of particularly good production quality, especially when one considers that it was produced under the difficult circumstances of the German occupation with its degree of rationing. Its founder and editor Pierre Plantard must have had quite some influence, even at the young age of twenty-two.

Each edition of *Vaincre* features a crest, next to the title, which clearly belongs to an organisation called Alpha Galates; its statutes are printed in full on page four of the first issue. The aim of the Order of Alpha Galates, as confirmed in many of the other articles, can be summed up as a French National Renewal. The methods outlined in the statutes are remarkably similar to those promoted by the Ecoles Nationales d'Uriage. Thus one cannot escape the conclusion that Plantard and his supporters shared this same vision of a French spiritual and cultural regeneration. The statutes, declared to the Prefecture of Police as required by law, are dated 1937, and show that Pierre de France is the 'Gouverneur Général', at the tender age of eighteen! One of the most prestigious contributors to *Vaincre*, Professor Louis le Fur, a right-wing thinker and writer who occupied a central educational post in the Vichy administration, gives Plantard a ringing endorsement as the new head of Alpha Galates. Professor Le Fur also mentions the retirement from the leadership of Alpha Galates, on 21 september 1942, of his old friend, Le Comte Maurice Moncharville[6], who is described as Professeur de Droit a la Faculte de Strasbourg. Furthermore, Le Fur claims to have been in the Order of Alpha Galates since 1934, and mentions yet another friend, Georges Monti[7], as a man of great competence.

According to the article in *Vaincre*, it was actually Georges Monti who had founded Alpha Galates in 1934. Monti, who assumed the prename 'Israel' (and also adopted the name Marcus Vella for his occult activities), was born in Toulouse in 1880. Abandoned by his parents, he was brought up by the Jesuits. But despite a rigid Catholic education, he developed an interest in the occult and was initiated into the Rose-Croix Catholique by its founder Josephin Péladan, and then into Martinism[8] by Papus – at the very time that the Abbé Saunière had become initiated. It is therefore possible that Monti could have known and associated with Saunière.

Monti then became initiated into the Ordo Templi Orientis by Aleister Crowley, who later worked for British Intelligence, and who was alleged to have been central to the plan to bring the Nazi, Rudolph Hess, to England in 1941. This allegation is given weight by the fact that Monti and Crowley had established contact with the superiors of several German lodges that had been involved with bringing the Nazi party to power. He appeared to delight in danger, working as a spy for the Germans in the First War, then for the Nazis, British Intelligence and even for the Second Bureau of the French Intelligence Service. It is not known for sure whether he was a double agent, and with whom his true loyalties lay. It is perhaps not surprising to learn that he was eventually assassinated, dying in a flat in Paris in 1936, from poisoning. But before all this he had made the acquaintance of the young Pierre Plantard, who, according to an article by Plantard's first wife Anne Lea Hisler, 'was a friend of characters as diverse as; Le Comte Israel Monti, one of the brothers of the Holy Wehme …' The Holy Wehme is said to have been an assassination squad.

It is thus possible that Monti passed on knowledge of the secret of Rennes-le-Château and the deposits of hidden treasure, to Plantard, who was to become the head of Monti's Order, Alpha Galates. This would help to explain the comment made by Professor Le Fur that he had always hoped to penetrate the 'secrets' of the Order; it also explains how Plantard was to become so involved with the area of Rennes-le-Château some years later. But there is another connection (although unsubstantiated) between Pierre Plantard and the Abbé Saunière. It is claimed that Pierre's grandfather, Charles Plantard, a journalist by profession, spent much time at Rennes-les-Bains where he became a close friend of the Abbé Boudet. In a preface to the 1978 reprint of Boudet's *La Vrai Langue Celtique*, Pierre Plantard recalls that his grandfather recorded a description and impression of Saunière and Boudet that he had gained during a visit to Rennes-le-Château, on 6 June 1892. An original copy of the book, allegedly given to Charles Plantard by Boudet, contains a dedication to him, accompanied by Boudet's signature, which has since been verified by the discovery, in the mid-1990s, of a signed letter from Boudet that accompanied a copy of his book sent to the Bodleian Library in Oxford. The evidence presented so far suggests that Pierre Plantard had been aware of the mystery of Rennes-le-Château from an early age and was considered by his elders to have been a quite remarkable character. Indeed, he appears to have been one in which they could place their trust in the troubled times of the Occupation.

An article in the fifth issue of *Vaincre* entitled 'Un Homme Nouveau' ('A New Man') by Professor Le Fur, reveals something of perhaps even greater consequence. In commenting on the succession of Plantard as head of Alpha Galates following the death of the Comte Moncharville, Professor Le

Fur refers to a meeting with Hans Adolf von Moltke, who had been appointed German ambassador to Spain, at which he recalled that this '… grand homme allemand, maitre dans notre Ordre… (great German man, master in our Order)' was very happy that they had found such a worthy young man as Pierre de France to lead the Order. This is all the more significant given that Hans Adolph von Moltke was a cousin of Helmut James Count von Moltke, who with his great friend Peter Count Yorck von Wartenburg, founded the Kreisau Circle[9], named after the Moltke estate, which dedicated itself to planning a reorganisation of Germany following the expected fall of Hitler. This effectively places Plantard not just a passionate advocate of French National Renewal, but a possible associate of German resistance to Hitler and his Nazi party – and, as will be seen, in the formation of a new Christian-based spiritual and moral order for Europe.

Though the long-term aim of the Kreisau Circle was the rebuilding of a European community of nations – almost a blueprint for today's European Union – its most urgent task was the removal of Hitler. On 20 July 1944 at 12.45pm a bomb exploded at one of Hitler's briefing sessions with his high command at Rastenburg, 560km north-east of Berlin. The bomb had been planted by Claus Schenk Graf von Stauffenberg, a cousin of the von Moltke family and member of the Kreisau Circle. Despite the deafening explosion in the confined space of the briefing room, Hitler, though badly wounded, survived. The plotters were hunted down and within a short time more than 200 Germans were executed, including 21 generals, 33 senior officers, 2 ambassadors, and 7 ministers. Yet this tragic event demonstrates the extent of the secret German opposition to this ruthless regime and the desperate hope for a new Europe. However, even though by this time the Allied Forces had secured a firm foothold in northern France, it would be a further ten months before Europe was completely freed from the oppression of the Nazi regime.

The parallels between the political objectives of the Kreisau Circle and those expressed in *Vaincre*, and the individual aspirations outlined in the statutes of Alpha Galates, cannot be dismissed as they form the basis of a European-wide vision shared by many diverse groups that were, and still are, active. What is more, those committed to recovering the lost treasure hidden in the Corbières have also deliberately entangled themselves within this movement for the spiritual and moral regeneration of Europe, especially in the guise of chivalric orders; a convenient and effective cover for their own clandestine activities.

A further review of the extant issues of *Vaincre* reveals the use of some extraordinary, but significant, symbolism. On page three of issue No. 1 is an illustration that depicts a knight on horseback riding along a road towards the setting or rising sun. On the road is printed 'Etats Unis d'Occident' ('United States of the West'); within the 'E' is inscribed 1937; whilst the areas on either side of the road are labelled Bretagne (Brittany) and Bavière (Bavaria). The 'sun' carries the date 1946 with the astrological sign for Aquarius at its centre, possibly representing the 'new age' aspiration of the New Order and its anticipated fulfilment. The mounted knight carries a large standard, with, at its centre, a device entitled the Cross of the South which is surrounded by seven stars (reminiscent of the original European Union flag).

The Cross of the South, which also appears in other issues, is made up of several parts, amongst which is the symbol for Aquarius at the centre of the cross and on the arms of the cross, the French monarchist symbol, the fleur-de-lys. The cross stands upon a heart, at the centre of which is the eastern symbol that represents harmony, the yin and yang. This can also be found carved on the exterior beam of the house in Alet-les-Bains mentioned in a previous chapter, which also carries the carving of the Star of David. Significantly, both these symbols can be found on the dungeon walls of the castles at Chinon and Coudray, etched by the Knights Templar during their captivity. It should be recalled that it was these symbols that were of particular interest to Charbonneau-Lassay, the archaeologist involved with the Hiéron du Val d'Or at Paray-le-Monial. The use of these details in the symbolism of Alpha Galates and *Vaincre* were presumably carefully chosen to represent the philosophy, beliefs or aspirations of the Order, which could be readily understood by those of like mind.

The Cross of the South would thus appear to represent an ideology which was neither Vichy nor Resistance, but was instead Catholic Monarchist, with mystical esoteric elements. The cross standing on a heart is yet another symbol closely associated with the mysterious society, the Hiéron du Val d'Or[10], based at Paray-le-Monial, that had promoted the cult of the Sacred Heart and the restoration of a Catholic empire or kingdom.

Designating the cross to be 'of the South' may refer not just to the southern half of France that had initially remained free from German occupation, but more specifically to the Languedoc-Roussillon region, the ancient Septimania; the exact area in which the Knights Templar had tried to establish an independent state. This, of course, is the region in which is said to be deposited the fabulous treasure of the Visigoths.

By contrast, de Gaulle and his Free French forces adopted the ancient Cross of Lorraine. This symbol was based on an actual relic, housed and protected by the sisters of the Heart of Marie in their chapel at Bauge. Said to be constructed from a fragment of the 'True Cross', this 27cm high double-armed cross was brought from Crete to Anjou in 1244, by a knight named Jean d'Alluye, Lord of Château-Lavallière, who was very possibly a Templar. He donated the cross to the Cistercian Abbey of La Boissière for safekeeping, where it remained until the outbreak of the Hundred Years War, when it was taken to the château at Angers for protection by the Dukes of Anjou. It remained an object of veneration and was adopted into their coat of arms. Following his successful and memorable battle of Nancy in Lorraine, René II, Duke of Anjou, renamed it the 'Cross of Lorraine' in recognition of its power in helping to defeat his enemies. From then on, the Cross of Lorraine became a potent Catholic symbol for the protection of France.

This symbol evidently exercised its magic once again in August 1944, when France was liberated. In November of the following year, General de Gaulle was elected President, and the task of rebuilding and regeneration began. But though the war with Germany was over, new dangers threatened the stability of France and Europe. The Communist Soviet Union, dividing Germany and Berlin and dedicated to expansion, embarked on the Cold War with the democratic West. Meanwhile, France found itself at war with its Indo-Chinese empire and struggled with its troublesome colonies, Algeria and Tunisia.

Once again, circumstances favoured opportunists. Two characters of similar age, who shared a common vision of the spiritual renewal of France, and who were both aware of the secret embodied in the village of Rennes-le-Château, embarked on a quest to attain lofty positions of power and influence in this sort of climate. François Mitterrand was to become President of France, whilst Pierre Plantard was to become the Grand Master of a secret society whose name would become pre-eminent in the world of occult politics.

Chapter 12
Politics and the Priory of Sion

A strong sense of Gallic independence, national identity, and even destiny has long influenced French politics. But the Republic's public political arena has also been powerfully influenced by an almost invisible one, the world of the secret and occult. Under their cloak of secrecy, and as they have throughout history, various groups have sought, or created, opportunities, to pursue their own agendas, often in league with prominent politicians and public figures. The agendas pursued are not necessarily always in the public interest.

The liberation of France and the collapse of the Vichy government left a political vacuum. The new provisional government, the French Committee of National Liberation, based in Algeria, had yet to establish control in metropolitan France, so the door was momentarily wide open for a Communist bid for power. Local Liberation Committees (CDLs) had been set up in towns and villages; of these, Communists formed almost a third of the membership, the remainder Socialists, Christian Democrats or Gaullists. In early September 1944, six representatives of departmental CDLs met at the château of Vizille, near Grenoble – where the French Revolution is said to have started – and within a couple of kilometres of Uriage and the Château Bayard, home to the Order of Knight-Monks of the Uriage. At this meeting, the six groups formed an association with sufficient potential power to be able to dictate terms to the provisional government. History, as so often in this tale of treasure and conspiracies, seems again to have been repeating itself.

Post-war French politics were in almost permanent turmoil, with twenty-four different governments of the Fourth Republic holding office between 1944 and 1957. A number of conditions conspired against a Communist seizure of power, however – not least the American determination to prevent the spread of Communism in Europe. Thus de Gaulle managed to retain his status of saviour, and his position as the man best able to bring about the renewal of France. De Gaulle's idea of a national renewal was of a state with a centralized bureaucracy and a strong presidential regime. He had support within his inner circle; in fact, Michel Debré, working in his private office, argued in a pseudonymous pamphlet that, 'the only chance for French democracy is, if the term may be used, a republican monarch'.

De Gaulle's desire for a more authoritarian regime would not have received popular support, had it been publicly known, especially from those in the Resistance. Having fought against their German occupiers, they looked forward eagerly to participating in a French National Regeneration, but not necessarily on those terms. But de Gaulle was only following an ancient Gallic tradition which believes that France holds a unique position in Europe, a sort of 'chosen land', which needs to be governed, or ruled, by a divinely inspired leader.

It is against this background that one must judge the curious writings of a certain R.P. Martin; one of his articles, heralding the appearance of a book, was indeed entitled *The General de Gaulle awaits the return of the Great Monarch*. One could ask though, whether it would have been more accurate to state that de Gaulle considered himself to be this Great Monarch[1]. In another work *The Book of Secret Companions; the Secret Teaching of General de Gaulle*, Martin (who turns out to be a Father Martin Couderc de Hauteclaire) claims that after the war, de Gaulle had formed a group of forty-five companions. They were dedicated to the promotion of Gaullism, and were obliged to remain anonymous for ten years after his death. It is possible that the choice of the number forty-five was purely symbolic and represented the formation of the group in 1945. But of particular relevance is the implication that there were links between this group of companions, and a secret society in which Jean Cocteau, André Malraux, Marshal Juin and Pierre Plantard are claimed to be prominent members. This secret society, that calls itself Le Prieuré de Sion (the Priory of Sion), is one active at the heart of the Rennes-le-Château intrigue and the search for its ancient treasure.

Martin's article, which was published in the magazine *Nostra*[2] (18 October 1982), is actually signed by the unexplained 'Bayard', which as we have seen, could be a coded reference to Château Bayard, the centre of the Ecole Nationale d'Uriage and its Knight-Monks. This is confirmed by the assertion that the initial CDL group was joined by members of the Ecole Nationale which had been founded by Captain (later to become General) Pierre Dunoyer de Segonzac. The group had adopted the apt motto 'More is in us', which highlights their goal of striving for excellence. The purpose of the Ecole Nationale was revealed as the ideological education of the elite youth of France for future posts in an authoritarian and paternalistic government – very similar to de Gaulle's covert intentions for his post-war government. Whilst there is no evidence that the Priory of Sion is the same as, or linked to, the group of forty-five companions, the article was clearly intended to draw attention to a political philosophy common to de Gaulle, the Ecole Nationale, and the Priory of Sion. In the article, Bayard states plainly that de Gaulle was not actually a member of the Priory of Sion but was privy to their internal affairs and enjoyed a significant influence. Certainly, Pierre Plantard, Governor General of Alpha Galates, was to become a key member of the Priory, and claimed to be instrumental in the politics that returned de Gaulle to power in 1958.

After the death of her priest and life-long companion in 1917, Marie Dénarnaud, then aged forty-nine, continued for a while to live alone in the presbytery which had been leased by Saunière. As was traditional in rural France, she dressed in somewhat sombre clothes but remained smart and alert and, despite living as a virtual recluse, still received the respect of the other villagers. Within a short time, Marie was assailed by various people claiming to be friends of the late priest, but who were likely unknowns hoping to discover the source of his wealth. No doubt taking advantage of Marie's vulnerability, these uninvited guests seem to have been responsible for the disappearance of most of Saunière's books, papers, curios, and ornaments. However, much of his extensive library (the beautifully made bookshelves can still be seen lining the walls of the first floor room in the Tour Magdala) was bought by a dealer in books, called Derain, from Lyon. This would seem to reinforce Saunière's other connections with Lyon; only through some previous personal contact could the dealer have been likely to know of his book collection, hundres of miles away.

Antoine Captier recalls that his father, the grandson of Saunière's bellringer, remembered seeing Marie burning sheaves of papers in the garden in front of the Tour Magdala. Were vital clues to the Saunière mystery accidentally or deliberately destroyed? Captier further confirms that amongst the surviving papers are letters that suggest he had deposited certain sums of money in various French and foreign banks. In 2005, Jean Luc Robin published information that Saunière had had a bank account in Budapest, far removed from the small village of Rennes-le-Château. From magazines that he had received, it appears that Saunière had also speculated in stocks and shares. It is possible that Marie, being of little education, did not appreciate the value of share certificates and destroyed them along with other papers. An alternative explanation might be that after the turmoil of World War I, the shares may have become worthless; indeed the franc had lost over 70 percent of its value at this time. This would explain why, although being the sole inheritor of all Saunière's wealth, Marie was to find herself in financial difficulties.

She appears to have managed only with financial assistance from local priests, who had been close colleagues of her former companion, and was frequently encouraged to sell the domain for a more permanent solution. Either unable or unwilling to take this option, Marie continued to live a simple life for nearly thirty years, whilst the domain fell gradually into neglect.

In July 1946, Noël Corbu and his family arrived at Rennes-le-Château to take up residence in Saunière's domain. As with many other aspects of Rennes, Noël Corbu and his acquisition of the domain have become clouded in mystery. Noel's daughter Claire, married to Antoine Captier and still connected to the village, has revealed some detail in their book *L'Héritage de l'Abbé Saunière*; but possibly because of her young age in 1946, she may not have been fully aware of all the facts. A full and intriguing account is presented in a book by Jean Markale, a professor of philosophy and a specialist in Celtic history. Unfortunately, he doesn't reveal his sources (common in many French books), but as a man of academic integrity, his account has to be given due consideration.

Noël Corbu, living at that time in Perpignan, was an entrepreneur with an interest in several small businesses, and had even published a detective novel. However, for some reason to do with his attitude to the Occupation – possibly through black-market activity – he found himself in some trouble. Leaving Perpignan in 1944, Noel, his wife and two children, went to live in the village of Bugurach, only 10km south-east of Rennes-le-Château, at the foot of the mountain. Noel quickly befriended the local villagers, and it was probably from the primary school teacher that he learned of the story of Saunière and the treasure. On a family outing in 1945 they established contact with the elderly Marie Dénarnaud, who showed them souvenirs from her life with the priest. Determined to acquire the property, Noel made several visits to the village and developed a friendship with Marie, eventually making her an offer to buy the domain. In return he agreed that she could remain in her home where his family would look after her. So, on 22 July 1946, an agreement was drawn up whereby Noël Corbu became the legal inheritor of the estate in the event of Marie's death.

Shortly after, leaving Marie at Rennes-le-Château, Noël Corbu took a group of young villagers to Morocco, where he had an interest in a sugar factory. Problems with this venture meant only short trips back to France, but his daughter recalls that during one of these trips Marie told him, 'don't be so worried, my good Noel, ... one day I will tell you a great secret that will make you a rich man... very rich'.

In January 1953, Marie died, aged 85, without having revealed any secrets she may have shared with the Abbé Saunière. Old age and a minor stroke had by then prevented her from passing on any knowledge, had she been inclined to do so. Convinced that a treasure did exist within the confines of the domain, Noel obtained permission from the local authorities to undertake formal excavations on his property (which was necessary because of a blanket ban on unauthorised excavations in the region). To provide income, he turned the villa into a small hotel and restaurant, hoping to attract visitors by promoting the enchanting story of the Abbé Saunière.

Among the steady trickle of visitors to the twin villages of Rennes-les-Bains and Rennes-le-Château was a man, claiming to be an archaeologist, who seemed to be remarkably interested in certain features. According to Jean Markale, the man was none other than Pierre Plantard, the leading light in the Order of Alpha Galates. Among other things, Plantard is said to have been very interested in two thermal sources known as the Madeleine and the Bains de la Reine, and to have spent time investigating the cliffs which border the valley of Rennes-les-Bains. This is the very area surveyed in the map by Edmond Boudet that appears as page 301 of Henri Boudet's book *La Vrai Langue Celtique*. These visits, and the locals' impressions of Plantard, are confirmed by the objective researches of René Descadeillas, former director of the municipal library at Carcassonne.

That Plantard should have visited the area is not surprising, since he alleges that his journalist grandfather Charles, had come here often – perhaps in pursuit of a story – and was well acquainted with Boudet and Saunière. There is scant evidence that Pierre Plantard ever met Noël Corbu[3], but it is more than likely that, during at least one of his visits to Rennes-le-Château, Plantard would have called in at the domain, if not the restaurant, that now belonged to the Corbu family. Plantard's researches were evidently fruitful; he was later to buy a large amount of land around the area of Blanchefort and Rocco Nègre, the site of the gold-mine where some of the treasure was said to have been deposited[4].

Except for some odd glimpses, other details of Plantard's activities for the decade following the end of the war are at best sketchy, with only some vague references from his first wife Anne Lea Hisler[5], who died in 1970, and, from some of his colleagues. Though independent corroboration of most of the claims – of which some are astonishing – has not been possible, Plantard himself, in subsequent interviews or letters, confirms, or at least fails to deny, the bulk of them.

A key date in this affair is 1956. It was a politically difficult year for Britain and France, as Anglo-French forces, following Israel's initiative, came into conflict with Egypt over the Suez Canal. Rumblings of discontent in Algeria were growing ever louder, whilst the French were still smarting over the Indo-Chinese debacle, not to mention the failure of successive governments to gain the confidence of the electorate. At the same time, final preparations were being made for the signing of the Treaty of Rome, which would bring about the European Economic Community.

It is against the background of this European and national news that, on 12, 13 and 14 January 1956, a series of three sensational articles appeared in the prestigious newspaper *La Dépêche du Midi*. Compiled by a journalist Albert Salamon, and entitled 'La Fabuleuse Découverte du Curé aux Milliards de Rennes-le-Château' (The Fabulous Discovery of the Millionaire Priest of Rennes-le-Château) the articles featured interviews with Noël Corbu, the revelation of the life led by the Abbé Saunière, and his alleged discovery of a great treasure. In comparison with the millions of words written on these subjects since, these articles are remarkably direct. They focus only on the unexplained expenditure of the priest and his building programme; the discovery of parchments written in Latin, found in an ancient altar pillar, that referred to a treasure deposited by the medieval Blanche of Castille; and the pressure put on Saunière, by his bishop, to reveal the source of his wealth. No other conclusions were expressed in the articles, except that the writer claimed that a contemporary of Saunière, from Carcassonne, had said that he had actually seen some gold coins that the priest had found. Noël Corbu had to admit, however, that though his excavations had revealed some interesting artefacts and skeletal remains, no treasure had so far been located.

Five months after these articles appeared, the existence of the Priory of Sion was made public for the first time. In accordance with a law of 1901, that requires all associations to register a copy of their constitutions with the local police authorities, the Priory of Sion lodged a copy of their statutes with the sub-prefecture at the police station in Saint-Julien-en-Genevois. Confirmation of this is found in the 20 July 1956 issue of the official journal in which such registrations are published. It has been remarked by certain researchers that the public exposure of a supposedly secret society is somewhat strange, but to have operated outside the 1901 law (enacted as a result of suspicion of secret societies due to their supposed participation in the French Revolution and later machinations) could have brought unnecessary difficulties for the Priory. The statutes reveal little about the organisation, other than its administration. However, several verifiable details are worthy of note.

The sign of the Priory is stated as being the Cross of the South, and its emblem a White Cock, both of which are identical to those found in *Vaincre*, the publication of the Order of Alpha Galates, in which Plantard had played such a prominent role. The Priory declares itself a Catholic Order of Chivalry in the 'ancient tradition', dedicated to a moral and spiritual regeneration; without doubt, there are echoes here of the elite Ecoles Nationales of the Vichy government. Paragraph (c) of article III of the statutes calls on the members to assist in the founding of a priory as a place for study, meditation, peaceful rest and prayer on the aptly-named Montagne de Sion in the Haute-Savoie. But most intriguing is that the Priory's headquarters is stated as being at Sous-Cassan, evidently near Annemasse, on the outskirts of Geneva and the Swiss border. This address has proved impossible to trace, suggesting a front or a pseudonym. Was this a secret location, intended as a contact point for those trafficking goods or money from France to Switzerland?

This is the explanation that becomes probable in the light of an assertion, confirmed by Plantard, that in 1952 he participated in the transfer of gold ingots worth more than 100 million Francs from France to the Union des Banques Suisse, Switzerland. Such a transaction was not illegal at the time, but later changes in the law would have necessitated the establishment of a border contact point if other similar transactions were required to take place. Plantard's explanation was that the gold had been transferred on the orders of General de Gaulle as part of a special fund for the use of the Committees of Public Safety, of which Plantard was secretary-general. Although unconfirmed, Plantard's admission is not improbable and raises certain questions. Could this episode be why Robin Mackness encountered such intense interest during his arrest and interrogation in December 1982, when he told French customs officials that he was carrying gold to Annemasse? We will see how significant this is in a later chapter.

The connection with Switzerland reappears in a pamphlet by Plantard's wife Anne Lea Hisler, who stated that he had been invited in 1947 by the Swiss Federal Government, to stay for several years in Switzerland near Lake Leman, where a number of other foreign delegates could be found. She doesn't, however, reveal the purpose of her husband's stay, or the nature of the other delegates. In the context of Plantard's initial support for Pétain and his Vichy government, it is unlikely to be a mere coincidence that a number of important collaborators were living in this precise region at that time; a fact that will prove to be highly significant as this research unfolds. If Hisler's report is fabricated, what was the motive for such a statement that wrongly implied her husband was involved with former collaborators?

She further states that her husband, known under the pseudonym of 'Way'[6], was a director, with Andre Malraux and Michel Debré (under the authority of Marshal Juin), of the Secretariat of the Committees of Public Safety in metropolitan France. These remarkable but uncorroborated statements are given some measure of support by a series of articles that appeared in the newspaper *Le Monde*, in June and July 1958. These articles, in referring to the role of the Committees for Public Safety, affirm the authority of General de Gaulle and the prime objective of 'national rehabilitation'; Plantard, under his pseudonym 'Captain Way', is their signatory. Another article published on the 29 July 1958, and reported in *The Messianic Legacy* by Baigent, Leigh and Lincoln, confirms the connection: 'Captain Way', signatory of this communique, has already published, during the month of May, several appeals and declarations in the name of the 'Central Committee of Public Safety for the Paris Region'. As we have already indicated, he is M. Pierre Plantard ... who, together with certain friends, took the initiative of establishing this committee. The 'Movement' which will comprise the successor to the Committee is directed by M. Bonerie-Clarus, a journalist; Its treasurer is M. Robin; M. Pierre Plantard is secretary and in charge of propoganda...'

The Committees of Public Safety were set up to provide support and stability for de Gaulle during the potentially explosive Algerian problem; like those established during the Revolution, they had the potential for great political power. It is possible that Plantard himself sent these articles to

Le Monde, which, if true, would cast doubt on their reliability. That Pierre Plantard claimed to have been appointed to such a prominent position, however, further emphasises his desire and determination, first seen in *Vaincre*, to become involved at the heart of French politics. Plantard is certainly a man who didn't wish to be ignored.

The sub-title of the Priory of Sion is 'Chevalerie d'Institution et Règle Catholique et d'Union Indépendante Traditioniste', known in short as CIRCUIT, which became the title of their newsletter. The statutes – signed by P. Plantard in his capacity as Secretary-General – and the contents of *CIRCUIT*[7], are little less than a manifesto for Catholic traditionalism in the Vichy mode of Charles Maurras and his Action Française, which themselves drew on the philosophy of the Sacred Heart cult of the Hieron du Val d'Or with which Saunière was so closely associated.

This association with the Hieron, and by extension Paul Le Cour, is given more substance by the Priory's choice of yet another symbol. As we saw, Le Cour founded the group and magazine *Atlantis* of which the symbol was 'La Poulpe' (the Octopus). This symbol, in strikingly similar form, is also found on documents almost certainly emanating from the Priory of Sion. The Octopus is a symbol of the primeval tradition, an esoteric spiritual tradition that originated in the legendary Atlantis. According to Le Cour, the aspiration of the Age of Aquarius[8] is a return to this tradition which will be manifest in the return of Christ the King.

Finally, Le Cour calls for the formation of a new Knighthood, 'For more than twenty years we have been calling in *Atlantis* for the formation of a new order of knighthood and indicating the means by which it might be achieved... Jules Romain, in *Le Problème Numéro Un*, published in 1947, wishes, in the face of the current enormous danger, for a spiritual power consisting of a grand order of chivalry.' A similar sentiment will be expressed in his own writings by a board member of *Atlantis*, the French esotericist and collaborator, Raymond Abellio. In a very different guise, Abellio will be seen to be yet another key figure in this tangled tale. In addition to the search for documents and treasure, and the restoration of a monarchy, this call for a new knighthood is thus a common thread found throughout the occult world in which Plantard wished to become a major player.

Chapter 13

Parchments and Publications

The considerable volume of works on the Saunière and Rennes-le-Château mystery that has appeared since 1956 offers an abundance of opinion and information, some factual and some fantastic. These publications fall into two categories: those written by independent researchers and those written by authors involved within the tight circle of the Priory of Sion. In the latter case, there is no doubt that many of the 'revelations' originate from a common source, that appear to be part of a co-ordinated process of information or more probably, disinformation. The actual facts seem to be hidden within a profusion of other truths, half truths and fabrications that have successfully masked the reality behind the mystery. Possibly an objective reality can be deduced; certainly all genuine new findings seem to fit like pieces of a giant jig-saw into the known larger picture. The true agenda of the Priory of Sion, within this overall picture, has been carefully concealed. But 'reading between the lines' of Priory-inspired writings has succeeded in lifting the veil a little.

One glimpse is offered in *Rennes-le-Château: Capitale Secrete et l'Histoire de France* by Deloux and Brétigny who report that: 'On the 1st June 1967, some months before the publication of the work by Gérard de Sède, who relaunched the affair of Rennes, Mgr. Boyer, vicar general, published, in *La Semaine Religieuse de Carcassonne*, an article entitled 'Mise au point et mise en garde'. In this he states; 'One can confirm without hesitation that a treasure is hidden in an ancient necropolis, and that the bishop of Carcassonne knows the existence of this necropolis but refuses to reveal its secret.'

The reference to treasure and tombs is unsurprising when viewed against local tradition. The implication of the Catholic Church, through the agency of the Bishop of Carcassonne, in this affair is a new element. Nobody, however, either from within or outside of the Church, has come forward to deny this assertion. Is the Catholic Church therefore more involved in this strange affair than it would care to acknowledge?

Much of the published material about the Priory has been based on a series of publications known collectively as the Dossiers Secrets, which have appeared periodically in a variety of printed forms since 1956. These documents have been given considerable status by the authors of *The Holy Blood and the Holy Grail*. Indeed, they underpin the main thrust of their thesis. Although a great deal of the contents of the Dossiers Secrets is highly speculative, often dubious and even obviously fabricated, there are some aspects that do deserve closer attention. The central allegation in the Dossiers is that the Priory, founded in the Middle Ages after the Christian conquest of Jerusalem, was formed as a secret chivalric Order, with authority over the Knights Templar, dedicated to protecting the blood-line of the Merovingian kings, and to their eventual restoration to the throne of France. Despite the dissolution of the Templars, the Priory of Sion is said to have continued to operate throughout the centuries, adopting various pseudonyms and strategies to attain political influence and control. Even claiming one of their more effective guises was the Compagnie du Saint-Sacrement, also known as the Children of Solomon.

Another Priory assertion is that the descendants of the Merovingian King Dagobert II were descended from Benjamin, an ancient tribe of Israel, exiled from the Holy Land. In fact a tradition exists in France that informs that their ancient monarchs were of Jewish descent, and that the descendants of Benjamin, as those of their neighbouring tribe, Judah, are the true inheritors of the biblical nation of Jews; a fact that is significant when considering legitimacy for possession of the lost treasure of Jerusalem. Much space in the Dossiers Secrets is also devoted to revealing genealogies confirming the survival of the Merovingian dynasty through the descendants of a few aristocratic families, notably the Lords of Rennes. In addition, there is a genealogy compiled in 1939, by the Abbé Pierre Plantard, Vicar of the Basilica Saint Clotilde in Paris (a relative of Pierre), in which the Plantard family itself is shown to be of Merovingian descent. Of very dubious authenticity, this would appear to be no more than a naive, or devious, attempt to establish a claim to a share in the legendary treasure of the Corbières – that symbolic treasure the present Priory of Sion, as self-appointed hereditary guardians, are pledged to locate and protect.

According to the Dossiers Secrets, the Priory has been guided by a succession of Grand Masters, referred to as 'Nautonniers' (Helmsmen) in their statutes. A varied collection of twenty-six eminent historical characters, these include René d'Anjou, Leonardo da Vinci, Nicolas Flamel, and Issac Newton. The antiquity of the Priory, and the authenticity of this list of its alleged Grand Masters[1], is certainly dubious. The last four on this list, however, who are said to have presided over the Priory since the French

Revolution, share a most interesting and illuminating connection. It suggests that they were chosen, neither at random, nor even to endorse the Merovingian claim, but rather as a symbol of a social and political ideology. Charles Nodier, Victor Hugo, Claude Debussy and Jean Cocteau, said to have been Grand Masters from 1804 to 1963, can be shown to have had a profound influence on the literary, artistic, philosophical and occult circles in Paris during the 19th and early 20th centuries. Is it merely a coincidence that these were the very same circles, in the late 19th century, with which the Abbé Saunière had become associated through his involvement with Martinism?

But the next step through the maze of the Dossiers Secrets is to pick up the trail of the archives and documents that were said to be acquired by Saunière and his contemporaries. In view of the unique nature of the archives, documents and parchments, the trail has had to be pieced together from a number of sources, some able to be confirmed, and some more reliable than others. The account rendered here is a 'most probable' scenario that fits the known facts, and offers a measure of explanation for the subsequent activities of those involved with the Rennes affair.

As we have seen, the archives themselves have originated from more than one source. There are the documents of General Dagobert, collected during his tenure as proprietor of goldmines in the eastern Corbières, which probably relate to the mines and their legendary deposits of treasure. These documents were given to his Masonic brothers of the Grand Orient prior to his departure for military service in the Army of the Eastern Pyrenees. After his mysterious and untimely death in 1794, the archives were acquired by the Marquis de Chefdebien, founder of the Masonic lodge, the Philadelphes, and kept in his family archives.

A century later, Alfred Saunière, a Jesuit priest, was employed as a tutor and chaplain to the family of the Marquis de Chefdebien at their home in Narbonne. He was caught rifling through their family papers, and dismissed. Alfred's action was not as surprising as it may seem since it was considered a mission by some Jesuit priests to infiltrate aristocratic and influential families to 'keep an eye on them'. Documents, apparently stolen by Alfred, were then passed on to his brother, Bérenger, parish priest at Rennes-le-Château who like his brother, was dedicated to the restoration of the monarchy.

Of course, other parchments are said to have been discovered by Bérenger Saunière during the initial restoration of his ancient church and the replacement of its 9th century altar. They were reportedly rolled up in wooden tubes secreted in the hollow altar support pillar[2], having been hidden there by the Abbé Bigou before 1789. The find, apparently witnessed by Elie Bot, Saunière's clerk of works, and two of his workers, is said to have comprised ancient genealogies of the families who had become guardians of the Merovingian bloodline and the fabulous treasure. More recent researches have, however, cast considerable doubt on this account. But it is known that Saunière did make a discovery of documents during the restoration of his church. Due to his sharp-eyed bellringer, Antoine Captier, who had found the little glass vial, containing a small parchment, that had been hidden in a recess in a wooden balluster, Saunière gained access to the hidden crypt[3], in which had been deposited the Hautpoul archives and heirlooms.

In spite of his training in classical languages, Saunière was unable to make sense of two of the parchments. Apparently familiar texts from the New Testament written in Latin, they were composed in such a way as to imply a concealed message. As the story goes, it appears that, having made copies of his find, he obtained permission from his bishop to go to the church and seminary of St. Sulpice in Paris, where some priests had gained a reputation for an expertise in deciphering ancient and esoteric documents. Evidence of this trip has not been confirmed and certain researchers do not accept that it ever took place; though Claire Corbu, the daughter of Noel, is convinced of its authenticity.

According to Deloux and Brétigny, Saunière stayed in Paris for five days, staying at the home of a M. Ane, nephew of the Abbé Bieil, director of St. Sulpice. M. Ane owned a factory that manufactured religious art and statuary, from which Saunière purchased a set of Stations of the Cross for his church. It was through Ane that Saunière was introduced to Émile Hoffet, the trainee priest who had already acquired a reputation for knowledge of Masonic and esoteric subjects. Hoffet had begun his training at the juniorate of Sion[4] (Meurthe-et-Moselle) before being ordained in 1897, and went on to have a not undistinguished career during which he wrote articles on pontifical theology for a journal that openly supported a restoration of the monarchy in favour of the Count of Chambord. He was also closely involved with the centre for the devotion of the Sacred Heart at Paray-le-Monial, where he would have undoubtedly made contact with the archaeologist and historian, Louis Charbonneau-Lassay. Certainly, Émile Hoffet later frequented the Parisian occult circles that had become so fashionable at this time. But at this early point in his training it is hard to believe the claim that, through him, Saunière was introduced to Claude Debussy and Emma Calvé. There is, however, another more credible possibility. Saunière's involvement with Martinism and its prime movers, Papus and Péladan, both members of the Parisian occult circles, could equally have brought him into contact with Debussy, himself a great supporter of Péladan, and Emma Calvé. So here we have just one example of how a simple fact has been re-worked into the Saunière story, by Priory insiders, for their own purposes.

One can only guess what role the parchments and archives played in the last twenty years of Saunière's life. The ostentatious lifestyle and his obstinate refusal, not only to reveal the source of his wealth but also to accept a posting away from Rennes-le-Château, still remain at the heart of this enigma. Subjected to the full wrath and sanctions of his bishop, Saunière resorted to all possible tactics to hold his ground. Unquestionably, he had an extremely strong reason to maintain his silence and to remain in his little village.

According to the exhaustive researches of Roger-René Dagobert, a descendant of the family of General Dagobert, Saunière confided the precious parchments and archives in January 1917 to his old friend Dr. Paul Courrent, who stayed with him during the last days of his life. Twelve years later, Dr. Courrent retired to a large house at Embres-le-Castelmaure, a little village close to Cascastel, the home of the Pailhoux family of General Dagobert's wife. The archives were then carefully concealed in the doctor's extensive library.

In 1939, the elderly Marquis de Chefdebien, descendent of the founder of the Philalephes, loaned his remaining archives, including some of the documents of General Dagobert, to the Archaeological and Historical Society of Narbonne for further study. By a remarkable coincidence, these were then passed on to their most eminent member, Dr. Courrent, who now had possession of all the documents found by Saunière and those collected by General Dagobert.

Evidence for this deposit of documents can be found in a report of the Commission Archeologique de Narbonne, Volume XVI, 1943, which states: 'At a meeting on Monday 16/12/1940, the Secretary read a note relating to the archives of Chefdebien, given to the Commission by the heirs of Marie-Louise de Chefdebien, who died in Narbonne in 1939. Our eminent correspondent has been able to examine a part of these noble archives (including those of Pailhoux and Dagobert). The extreme value draws attention to the importance of confiding them to a specialist archivist for study and the complete classification of this collection which contains particularly rare and precious manuscripts.'

It was in the following year that the Germans occupied France, and along with many others, that François Mitterrand was sent to Germany as a POW. During this spell of imprisonment, Mitterrand was to meet Antoine Gayraud and Antoine Courrière, both prominent local politicians from the Aude, from whom he was to learn the fascinating history of Rennes-le-Château and the activities of Otto Rahn. He was also to meet a person, later alleged to be a Grand Master of the Priory of Sion, Roger-Patrice Pelat, who would continue after the war to play a key role in Mitterrand's political career.

Dr. Courrent died in 1952 and his papers disappeared. Once again evidence of this can be found within the archives of the Commission Archeologique de Narbonne: 'At a meeting of 3/02/1954, the Secretary indicated that the Chefdebien family had sought to reclaim the family archives bequeathed by Marie-Louise, who died at Narbonne in May 1939. The Commission was embarrassed since the precious archives had disappeared shortly after the death of Dr. Courrent to whom they had been confided.'

Furthermore, in the course of his researches, Roger-René Dagobert learned from the great-nephews of Dr. Courrent that the archives had been stolen by some people 'who were aware that these documents could fetch a great deal of money'. It is tempting to speculate that these are the same documents that so interested the International League of Antiquarian Booksellers.

The following year, 1953, saw the death of Marie Dénarnaud, and it is three years later, in 1956 that the *Dépêche du Midi* articles and *Le Livre des Constitutions* appeared, concerning the history and aims of the Priory of Sion; that year they also registered their Statutes with the authorities. *Le Livre des Constitutions*, the first book to mention the Priory, was also published in Geneva by Editions des Commanderies de Genève. Despite efforts by researchers, the existence of this publisher has never been traced, further adding to the mystery that surrounds the Priory. This association with Switzerland is repeated in certain parts of the Dossiers Secrets, purported to originate from the Grande Loge Alpina (the Swiss equivalent of the United Grand Lodge of English Freemasonry). Another more tangible link with Grande Loge Alpina comes in the person of a fervent esotericist, Robert Amadou. A Martinist and an official in the Grande Loge Alpina, Amadou admits meeting Pierre Plantard whilst being initiated into Alpha Galates, in 1942. In fact, he contributed an article entitled 'Situation de la Chevalerie', published in the second edition of Plantard's newspaper *Vaincre*. In a private letter from Philippe de Chérisey to Pierre Plantard in 1985, there is a reference to the wartime period when Plantard met, amongst others, Robert Amadou (a former schoolfriend of de Chérisey), Louis Le Fur, and Adolphe von Moltke.

In 1966, Gérard de Sède claimed to acquire part of the archives of the Abbé Émile Hoffet, who was known to have amassed an extensive and impressive library of books and documents, including many on occult and secret societies. Among these was a dossier that the cleric had compiled on the enigmatic Georges 'Israel' Monti, with whom he claimed to have been personally acquainted. Within a year, de Sède published *Le Trésor Maudit de Rennes-le-Château*, in which he revealed the extraordinary history of the village and the mystery of the two encoded parchments that refer to the Merovingian king, Dagobert II, and to the legendary treasure of Sion. This book has been the foundation for many of the subsequent books on Rennes-le-Château; it is almost certainly the result of access to some unpublished archives. It was also in 1966 that M. Marius Fatin, owner of the castle at Rennes, and himself an archaeologist and ardent Freemason, received a letter from the so-called International League of Antiquarian Booksellers in London informing him of the antiquity of his castle and its illustrious past.

More light is thrown on the fate of some of the parchments in a document given to the authors of *The Messianic Legacy* by Pierre Plantard, at a meeting in May 1983. The document, officially notarised, contained a request to the French Consulate in London by Viscount Leathers, Major Hugh Murchison Clowes and Captain Roland Stansmore Nutting[5] for permission to export three parchments from France. The text states: '... three parchments whose value cannot be calculated, confided to us, for purposes of historical research, by Madame James, resident in France at Montazels (Aude).

She came into legal possession of these items by virtue of a legacy from her uncle, the Abbe Saunière, curé of Rennes-le-Château (Aude)'.

This is not the only written reference to the parchments. In his *L'Enigme de Rennes*, the Marquis Philippe de Chérisey[6] makes an even more detailed revelation: 'Saunière found it – and never parted with it. His niece, Madame James of Montazels, inherited it in February 1917. In 1965, she sold it to the International League of Antiquarian Booksellers. She was not to know that one of the two respectable lawyers was Captain Ronald Stansmore of the British Intelligence Service and the other was Sir Thomas Frazer, the 'eminence grise' of Buckingham. The parchments of Blanche of Castille are presently in a strongbox of Lloyds Bank Europe Limited. Since the article in the *Daily Express*, a paper with a circulation of 3,000,000, nobody in Britain is unaware of the demand for the recognition of Merovingian rights made in 1955 and 1956 by Sir Alexander Aikman, Sir John Montague Brocklebank, Major Hugh Murchison Clowes and nineteen other men in the office of P.F.J. Freeman, Notary by Royal Appointment.'

Finally, a press release on 22 January 1981 concerning the Priory of Sion and announcing Plantard's election to Grand Master, contains the following reference: 'the parchments of Queen Blanche of Castille, discovered by the priest Saunière in his church at Rennes-le-Château (Aude) in 1891. These documents sold by the niece of this priest in 1955 to Captain Ronald Stansmore and to Sir Thomas Frazer were deposited in a strong-box of Lloyds Bank Europe Limited in London.'

These three sources, whilst concurring with the basic details of the sale of the parchments, do reveal some inconsistencies. First, there is the difference in the date given for the sale of the parchments, which can possibly be put down to a genuine misprint – 1965 for 1955. Second, though one of the versions states that the parchments were only loaned for the purpose of research, the others report their actual sale. Attempts to trace the alleged niece of Saunière, Madame James (actually Jammes) have revealed that she was indeed the daughter of Saunière's younger sister Bathilde (or Mathilde), who married a Jean Oscar Pages; Bertha Pages married Louis Jammes thus becoming Madame Bertha Jammes. But Madame Jammes would have been only nineteen years old in 1917; would her uncle have bequeathed her such a legacy?

She was reportedly upset with her inheritance, unable to appreciate its value. If all these accounts were fabricated at the same source – as is claimed by the sceptics – one would not expect to see the differences. It is actually more likely that these are genuine reports with accidental errors. However, from the British names quoted here (all genuine characters who were involved with wartime Intelligence activities), and from other documents concerning the export of the parchments, these reports certainly draw attention to a connection with British Intelligence, which along with the Special Operations Executive (SOE), was very active in France during the war and for some time afterwards. If these reports were deliberately falsified, it is hard to understand the motive. How could the inclusion of British Intelligence and SOE in the story of Rennes-le-Château benefit the perpetrators? How did they know of these various British characters and their connections?

By some coincidence, another Madame James appears in a different context elsewhere in this story. In the book *Operation Orth* by Jean Robin, Madame James is mentioned as someone associated with the literary contributions of Abbé Hoffet, René Guenon and Charbonneau-Lassay to the magazine *Regnabit*, circulated in the 1920s, and its successor, *Le Rayonnement Intellectual*, which published a curious mix of ultra-traditional Catholic views with those of esoteric-occultists. In fact, Madame James wrote that certain circles desired to: 'to reduce the order into chaos, in working for a new kingdom affirming the spiritual over the temporal or, more graphically, of spirit over matter'. This statement clearly echoes the concept of the Grand Monarch, a theme that is common to this version of occult politics.

Here we have confirmation of the thread that runs alongside that of the parchments, and that of the secret of the Visigothic-Merovingian treasure: one of occult politics – a vision of the future of France held by the Priory of Sion but unacceptable in modern mainstream politics, tacitly encouraged by the traditionalist wing of the Catholic Church, and subconsciously inherent in French public life over several centuries. As we shall see, this continues into the present era through the presidency of François Mitterrand, who delighted in being perceived as a man of mystery. *The Death of Politics* by John Laughland is a remarkable and revealing analysis not only of his political career, but also the unseen influences of his close circle of old friends. Always something of an anomaly as a Socialist, he was considered by many of his contemporaries as a monarch rather than a president.

This chapter has preoccupied itself more with the politics of secret societies, especially the Priory of Sion, and the ownership of documents, than the location and control of the treasure we have been tracing; however, it is within the activities of the secretive hierarchy of French government that the thread of politics will be found woven around the trail of the gold. Gold that is not only believed to be deposited deep in the Pyrenean foothills but also that stolen, or reclaimed, from the Nazis who themselves had pillaged most of Europe.

Chapter 14
Mitterrand's Inner Circle

In 1881, John Emirate Acton, Fist Baron Acton, coined the adage that 'power corrupts and absolute power corrupts absolutely'. In the context of this story, it would be more applicable to say that treasure, wealth and hard currency are the most corrupting influences. Sadly for the French people, this adage can be accurately applied to at least one former president of the Republic and his circle of close friends.

Elected in 1981, François Mitterrand became the first Socialist president of France. In pursuing what was, in effect, a continuation of the cause of a French national renewal, Mitterrand appeared to avoid any specific ideology and pursued whatever policies would maintain him and his regime in power; a strategy that worked well for a previous president, General de Gaulle. The new French administration acted in striking contrast to its neighbour across the Channel. The British Conservative government of the time showed little interest in conserving Britain's European-based heritage, preferring instead to look to America as a model. Mitterrand, on the other hand, was attracted to a model of French culture that had more in common with pre-Revolutionary tradition than a modern liberal-democratic Republic, and, like most other French politicians, viewed with alarm the encroachment of American capitalistic culture. This substantial difference in attitude and loyalties has contributed to a general political mistrust, by the French and other members of the European Union, that Britain is little more than an agent for the United States.

Initially promising a radical change of life for French citizens, Mitterrand's presidency also talked of the power of a 'tranquil force' which came to mean little more than stagnation for most areas of French life, but also attracted the accusation of creating a climate in which opportunism, corruption and favouritism could flourish. Certainly, Mitterrand assumed a persona that was far less of a dynamic, modernising and determined politician, but more of a calculating, conservative and complacent monarch.

His experience in a POW camp was significant in several ways; first, as he himself recalls, it enabled him to discover that he had a great capacity for survival. Second, he affirmed that the experience of prison culture, the comradeship, sharing and mutual support, made a strong impression on his political philosophy, which was to influence his later career as a Socialist. So, initially attracted by extreme right-wing doctrines, exemplified by those of Marshal Pétain and the Vichy government[1], he gradually appeared to move towards the Socialist left. But despite his Socialist stance and public condemnation of unfettered capitalism, his close friends and colleagues, all remnants from his past, prospered under his administration – some are even alleged to have been involved in the most blatant financial scandals. Taking little account of the political embarrassment of maintaining some of these old friendships, Mitterrand not only remained loyal, but used various strategies within his power to protect them from disgrace or even prosecution. The French public had long accepted that corruption was rife amongst their politicians, but the activities of some within the Mitterrand regime exceeded even this pessimistic view of their leaders. What motivated such loyalty by the President to these shadowy friends?

René Bousquet, a member of the Pétainist Vichy government, appeared to be a most curious choice of friend for a man claiming a Resistance past and affirming Socialist values. Born in south-west France, at Montauban, where his father was a barrister, he went on to study law in Paris, before making his mark in the Vichy administration. Resolutely anti-Semitic and anti-Marxist, his enthusiastic support for Pétain gained him the Légion d'Honneur at the age of twenty-one and later, during the Battle of France, the Croix de Guerre. Appointed Chief of Police, Bousquet excelled himself in rounding up and deporting 76,000 immigrant Jews to Germany, earning the praise of the Nazi high command in the process. On 22 July 1942, he went to meet General Oberg and other SS officers and concluded an agreement to allow the Vichy government to continue to take responsibility for law and order in France in exchange for the continued harassment and deportation of foreign Jews. Considered a cultured and brilliant professional, the resolute nationalist Bousquet faced up to the Germans; even Himmler, after a five hour meeting in August 1943, recognised that Bousquet was a 'precious collaborator' and 'would play a leading role in French policy'. Accused of war crimes, he was brought to trial in June 1949, but Mitterrand, who was then Minister for Information, proposed an amnesty for all collaborators just two days into Bousquet's trial. According to Paul Webster in his book *Pétain's Crime*, the British were said to have intervened in the lifting of the nominal sentence of 'five years national disgrace' given to Bousquet because of his alleged work for the British Intelligence service.

Unable to resume a political career after the war, he enlisted the help of former associates and entered the world of merchant banking. He achieved the position of second-in-command in the Bank of Indochina and was appointed to the boards of numerous companies. Bousquet was thus able to provide financial support for Mitterrand's electorial campaign against Charles de Gaulle in 1965. At that time, Bousquet controlled the influential newspaper *La Dépêche du Midi*, which had been the first to reveal the strange story of the Abbé Saunière. Once again accused of war crimes, this time by the Nazi-hunter Serge Klarsfed, Bousquet was due to attend a trial in June 1993; two days before, however, he was assassinated. This gave rise to much speculation. It was said to be almost impossible to 'shoot' him with a camera, let alone gain access to his apartment and shoot him in cold blood. Klarsfeld later remarked that he believed Mitterrand had ensured Bousquet never came to trial; yet once Bousquet was dead, Klarsfeld dropped all investigations. What was it that Bousquet held over Mitterrand that had bought his protection? Was it Mitterrand's ambiguous wartime career, or was it some other deeper secret that they shared?

Mitterrand's role in the Vichy government appears relatively minor, but the nature and source of his political funding could have been embarrassing. Did these ex-collaborators believe that, despite his public Socialist stance, he would help them to profit themselves and achieve their particular vision for France, the blueprint for which can be found in that of the old Vichy government? Were they also party to a secret concerning looted Nazi wealth and even possibly the lost treasure of the Corbières? Events will show how credible this assessment is.

In 1992, Mitterrand reluctantly appointed Pierre Bérégovoy, one of his Socialist ministers, as Prime Minister in order to quell the growing public storm over corruption within governmental circles. Bérégovoy, one of the only politicians to have retained an untainted public image, announced that after a probing investigation he would reveal the names of the guilty politicians. Never having been admitted to the inner circle, Bérégovoy had already tasted the ruthlessness of Mitterrand when, in 1981, the president removed him from a prestigious 'grace and favour' apartment which had been his right as Secretary-General of the Elysée Palace. The apartment was then granted to François Durand de Grossouvre[2], a close friend and advisor. Bérégovoy innocently accepted a loan of 1 million Francs, in 1986, from Roger-Patrice Pelat, one of Mitterrand's closest friends, to purchase a new apartment. This decision would come back to haunt him; it is most likely that the loan was deliberately set up as a means of future embarrassment. It was obvious that Bérégovoy's appointment as Prime Minister was only a public relations exercise; he was never going to be allowed to penetrate the secrets held by Mitterrand's inner circle. On 1 May 1993, Pierre Bérégovoy apparently committed suicide. He was found on the bank of a rural canal, shot in the head and barely alive. In spite of adverse weather conditions, a decision was taken to transport him by helicopter, not to the local hospital nearby, but to the Val-de-Grace in Paris. Initial reports were that he had died outright; the later official version account claimed that he passed away in the helicopter.

Almost a year later, on 7 April 1994, François Durand de Grossouvre, an eminence grise during Mitterrand's presidency, was found dead with a gun in his hand, shot in the head at his office in the Elysée Palace. A former Vichy collaborator before entering the Resistance in 1943, Grossouvre had been closely involved in the financing of Mitterrand's election campaigns. However, his later verbal attacks against others of Mitterrand's inner circle brought about his fall from grace; it must be asked whether his inside knowledge had indeed become a dangerous liability. In fact he had repeatedly warned two journalists that he was in danger of being killed. Of particular note is that he had become head of the French stay-behind network, Arc-en-ciel, set up by NATO and part of the Europe-wide, anti-Communist, Operation Gladio. We will encounter Gladio again in a later chapter.

One of those who would certainly have been exposed by Bérégovoy was another of Mitterrand's lifelong colleagues from his war years. Though he had died in 1989, at the height of a financial scandal of insider trading called the Péchiney affair, Roger-Patrice Pelat continued to cast a long shadow over Mitterrand's presidency. Accused of having been at the heart of a number of irregular financial dealings involving illegal share trading, secret Swiss bank accounts and shell companies, telephone tapping and payments to people close to the president, Pelat appears to have manipulated, controlled and financed Mitterrand's political career. In September 1993, an extensive article in the popular newspaper *Minute*, was dedicated to investigating the theft of Pelat's papers. Somewhat inconclusive, the article raises a number of complex issues that may never be fully penetrated, but certainly involve the highest level of government; the exact nature of the papers has never been revealed.

But the allegations laid against Pelat were not confined to financial impropriety. During his time as a POW with Mitterrand and the two politicians from the Aude, Pelat also learned of the curious history of Rennes-le-Château. He was to later accompany Mitterrand on his election campaign visits to the village, where on one occasion in March 1981, they were photographed on top of Saunière's Tour Magdala. Furthermore, in an internal circular of the Priory of Sion, distributed in 1989, it is alleged that Pelat had been its Grand Master and had resigned only one month before his death on 7 March that year.

This allegation was examined, in 1993, by Judge Thierry Jean-Pierre, who was leading an investigation into Pelat's financial scandal. When questioned under oath, Pierre Plantard admitted that there was no truth that Pelat was involved with the Priory of Sion. Whether he was telling the truth or not, a fundamental question remains. Why would Plantard have wished to associate his Priory of Sion, at the highest level, with such a notorious character; especially one who was under investigation for serious financial irregularities?

The letter also refers to Pelat 'as an honest and just man who was tricked by certain American initiates'; this was a direct reference to the Péchiney affair, which involved the New York Securities Exchange Commission investigation of insider trading of shares, by Pelat and others, of an American company called Triangle. This becomes even more plausible in the light of the claim that the Priory of Sion is said to have infiltrated key positions in the financial worlds of New York and London, and that since the early 1980s a split had occurred between the American and European factions of the Priory. In February 1984, at the restaurant La Tipia in Paris, the authors of *The Messianic Legacy* met with Pierre Plantard. Amongst other matters, Plantard referred to a degree of friction within the ranks of the Priory brought about by the 'Anglo-American contingent', who 'wished to move in a different direction from their Continental brethren'. It is entirely possible that Plantard's Priory had been infiltrated by people with a very different agenda from that of its founder. It also appears that from the publication of *The Holy Blood and the Holy Grail* in 1982, and the unexpected exposure of the Priory of Sion to the English-speaking world and beyond, Plantard was gradually losing control of his foundation.

These links between François Mitterrand, Plantard, and Rennes-le-Château, and the claimed affiliation of one of his oldest friends to the Priory of Sion are, at the very least, remarkable coincidences; more probably, they

During the 1980 French presidential elections, Francois Mitterrand visited Rennes-le-Château and the enigmatic domain of Bérenger Saunière

Bérenger Saunière

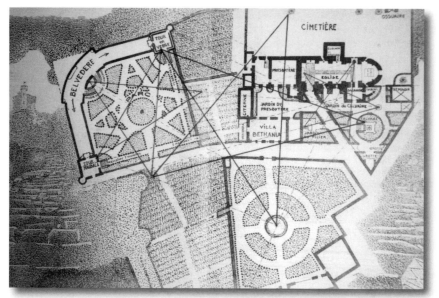

Plan of Saunière's church and domain, showing the pentagonal layout (original drawing by Alain Feral)

The village of Rennes-le-Château

Montségur. Site of Cathar massacre in 1244. Site of SS Colonel Skorzeny's excavations in 1944.

Ring of ancient castles (Visigothic foundations) surrounding the area containing the treasure deposits.

Barn at Chaillac (nr St Junien) where local Resistants were said to have met regularly – and possible planned the gold theft of 10 June 1944.

The ancient cathedral of Sion, Switzerland. Seat of the bishop and county of Sion in the Merovingian epoch

The forge and mine buildings of General Dagobert at Padern.

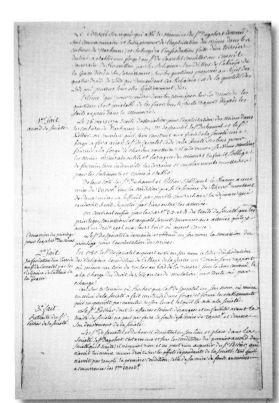

First page of the act of 1785 giving permission to re-open the mines of the Corbières. Granted to General Dagobert and his colleagues by the monastery of Lagrasse.

The medieval city of Carcassonne

The Hautpoul castle in Rennes-le-Château

The castle of Arginy

Remains of the castle of Auriac

The parish church of St. Laurent-de-la-Cabrerisse, home of Émile-François Cayron

Remains of the castle of Bézu

are part of a greater conspiracy. It is hardly credible that someone of the make-up of Roger-Patrice Pelat, once made aware of the great secret of the treasure, would not have taken steps to pursue it.

It is possible that amongst his missing papers were some of the ancient Dagobert/Saunière/Chefdebien documents that referred to the treasure deposits in the Corbières. If he had attained some influence within the Priory of Sion, he could have acquired these from the other members who had managed to pillage the library of Doctor Paul Courrent, who had died at Embres-le-Castelmaure in 1952. Due to the cloak of secrecy that shrouds these matters, it is not known for certain what actions the Priory has taken since acquiring the archives. However, the enterprises and fortunes of its most prominent member, Pierre Plantard, were to include both the buying up of several significant parcels of land near Rennes-les-Bains, on which could be found the ancient gold-mines, and an alleged transfer of a large quantity of gold to Switzerland in 1952. This may well have been just the tip of the iceberg.

Yet another surprising name is mentioned, as a senior member, in Priory documents, that of the Corsican, André Guelfi. Nicknamed Dédé la Sardine, Guelfi became a millionaire from building specialist boats for the sardine industry. In 1975, he moved to Lausanne on the bank of Lake Geneva, the favoured area for ex-collaborators. He was implicated in the high-profile French petrol giant ELF scandal, and admitted acting as an intermediary in the transfer of $40 million, through his Liechenstein bank, to Helmut Kohl's Christian Democratic Party in Germany, on behalf of François Mitterrand.

The Elf investigation was particularly explosive because it revealed a rarely visible side of French culture[3]: the 'reseaux', or secret networks of power that subtly connect top government and business officials with shadowy intermediaries and secretive circles, such as the Corsican underworld and France's still-potent Freemasons. Mr. Le Floch-Prigent and other former ELF executives have said that they were merely continuing long-standing ELF practices — often with explicit endorsement from France's then-president, François Mitterrand. Once again, we must ask why the Priory would wish to be associated with such characters and events.

As we have seen, two of Pelat's associates, Antoine Gayraud, the old mayor of Carcassonne, and Antoine Courrière, met Mitterrand during his spell as a POW. Having initiated him into the curious secret history of Rennes-le-Château, both were to be rewarded with successful political careers. But these were not Mitterrand's only contacts with the secret of Rennes-le-Château and the Priory of Sion, for at the very centre of his entourage was André Rousselet, who had been the Chef de Cabinet des Prefets de L'Ariège et L'Aude in 1944. That is, he was a chief administrator of the very region in question. Often accompanying Mitterrand on his journeys, Rousselet remained close to his old friend until the end; so it was not unexpected to find him named as the executor of Mitterrand's will. More surprising is his family relationship to Pierre Plantard. André Rousselet had adopted a daughter named Chantal, who in April 1964 married Jean Maurice Marie (known as Yannick) Plantard, the son of François Plantard, an engineer at Aéro-Spatiale and a cousin of Pierre. Chantal and Jean had a son Christophe Plantard, who works at Canal Plus, the broadcasting company founded in 1984 by his father-in-law, André Rousselet. In 1998 Marcel Plantard, who owns a photographic shop in Nantes, confirmed that his cousin Pierre had remained in regular contact with the rest of his family.

But there is a more sinister dimension to these associations that has its roots in the war. Prior to their arrival in Limoges in 1943, the Dagobert family had lived in St. Nazaire at the mouth of the Loire, until forced to move to avoid the massive Allied bombing of the Naval dockyard. As manager of the local undertakers, and as a member of a Masonic lodge Libre Pensée, Roger-René's father was well acquainted with many other locals, including those who worked in the dockyard. Employed as engineers at St. Nazaire were François Plantard and Eugène Deloncle, both members of the Société Anonyme des Chantiers et Ateliers de St. Nazaire-Penhoet. François Plantard, as we have seen, was the father of Yannick who married the adopted daughter of Mitterrand's friend, André Rousselet. Eugène Deloncle ran the extremely militant right-wing group La Cagoule, to which Mitterrand is said to have belonged before the war. Furthermore, one of Deloncle's nieces was to marry François Mitterrand's brother, Robert. Another prominent member of La Cagoule was Jean Filiol, the same Milice chief that will be seen to be implicated in the tragic Oradour affair. Jean Filiol and François Mitterrand, both born at Jarnac, were close friends.

Further confirmation of these disturbing relationships can be found in Carmen Callil's *Bad Faith : A Forgotten History of Family and Fatherland*, published in 2006. Many of the extreme right leaders had close connections with bankers and industrialists, an unusually large number coming from the cosmetics industry. François Coty funded the paramilitary Croix de Feu, launched in 1928. Eugène Schueller, founder of the beauty empire L'Oréal, was also a major source of funds for nationalist and fascist groups. After the war, L'Oréal became 'a factory to recycle the extreme right' into safety, in particular two key members of the Cagoule; Jacques Correze, Deloncle's adopted son and deputy in the Cagoule, ran L'Oréal's American subsidiary until the 1990s, and Jean Filliol, Deloncle's top assassin, escaped justice and managed a subsidiary in Spain. François Mitterrand's brother married Deloncle's niece, and his sister Jo became the mistress of Jean Bouvyer, another cagoulard. Furthermore, Mitterrand himself worked for L'Oréal after the war, and was working for Schueller when he fought his first election campaign in 1946.

We can see in this labyrinthine world of power politics, driven by ambition, greed and political vision, the key ingredients of money, information and secrecy. Just as in the scandals of successive French governments, these same ingredients lie at the heart of the Priory of Sion agenda and the strange mystery of Rennes-le-Château with which the Priory has become entwined. The choice of key references within the Priory's publications appears to be motivated by the desire to draw attention to a specific political ideology. Plantard wished to associate himself and the Priory unashamedly with the pro-Vichy vision of many ex-collaborators. Priory writings appear to contain symbols, archetypes and coded messages designed to appeal to, or even attract, these former collaborators. The links between Mitterrand's inner circle, Plantard's family, and the Priory of Sion, are at the very least surprising. We will see how these links encompass the thread of the gold and extend to the present day.

Chapter 15

The Gold of Oradour

Since his death in 1995, Mitterrand's memory has been tainted by the suspicion of financial scandals involving his inner circle of close friends; some are still subject to judicial enquiry. There is, however, one particularly dark shadow that hangs over the highest level of French government that concerns us in this investigation; the true events that led to the destruction of the village of Oradour-sur-Glane, and the massacre of its inhabitants by the Nazis, on 10 June 1944. Although some of the details remain unconfirmed, and many of those alleged to have been involved remain silent, sufficient information has come to light to reveal an extraordinary cover-up over this tragic incident.

Oradour-sur-Glane lies 21km north-west of the town of Limoges, capital of the Haute-Vienne department. Straddling the River Vienne, Limoges is a lively commercial town and a major railway intersection on the mainline from Toulouse 250km away in the south, Angoulême and Bordeaux in the west, and from Clermont-Ferrand and Switzerland in the east. The rail network was used extensively by the Nazis for military purposes. But it was also not uncommon for them to use it to transport gold and other valuables, plundered from occupied territories, normally to Germany or Switzerland. Subjected to frequent attacks by the Resistance – or those who masqueraded as such – these treasure trains offered what could be conveniently considered to be 'spoils of war' by their new owners.

The trail of events that led to the destruction of Oradour-sur-Glane originated at Montauban, near Toulouse, with the activities of General Lammerding, commander of the 2nd SS Panzer Division Das Reich. According to Col. Howard Buechner, the Division was visited in April 1944 by the SS Reichsfuhrer Himmler, and was involved in the transportation of gold and treasure recovered from the mines and caves of Montségur, the Ariège and the Corbières.

Many SS officers are known to have acquired substantial personal wealth through wartime activities, and to have stockpiled their gains in Switzerland or other safe areas. In fact, it was reported in the *Daily Telegraph* that Himmler himself maintained an account (No. 54941) at the Zurich branch of Crédit Suisse. It appears that General Lammerding was no exception and had managed to acquire a large quantity of gold for himself during his Division's three-month stay at Montauban.

Within hours of the Allied landing in Normandy on 6 June 1944, General Lammerding and his mighty tank division was ordered to travel north to the Normandy beaches in support of the defence against the Allied invasion. The 750km journey by rail, expected to take about three days, actually took over three weeks due to highly successful Resistance activity that dogged their progress. As a result of the ingenious sabotage of the flat-bed railway cars, necessary for transporting the tanks, the Division was obliged to travel by road. This necessitated the huge force to be divided into three sections, each taking a different route north. Accompanying the 300 tanks, hundreds of supporting vehicles and 15,000 men, was a small separate convoy consisting of a car carrying the senior officer Lieutenant Walter, an armoured half-track with ten SS soldiers, and a large truck. Ostensibly carrying the regimental records, the truck was later said to have been transporting a treasure that included at least 600kg in gold ingots.

The activities of General Lammerding and Das Reich had been closely monitored by British Intelligence and local agents, who advised SOE operatives, Resistance units and Maquisards (Resistance activists) as to what actions should be taken to sabotage their movements. It is thus possible that the possession of treasures and gold bullion by Lammerding and his officers was known by at least some local Resistants.

On Friday 9 June the convoy arrived at the small town of St. Junien, some 30km west of Limoges along the River Vienne. The town was buzzing with activity since the first battalion of the Regiment Der Führer (of the Division Das Reich) had already arrived. The regiment was regrouping under the command of Major Dickmann[1], who had established his HQ at the Hôtel de la Gare having arrived at 10.30 am that day. The deaths of two German soldiers, the sabotage of the railway-bridge over the Vienne, and the knowledge that there were possibly 1800 Maquisards in the town, created added tension. As senior officer, Major Dickmann was responsible for the security of the convoy and its precious cargo, and would quite naturally have ensured it was properly guarded, but without attracting undue attention.

Most of what took place in St Junien during the rest of the day has been pieced together from eyewitness accounts, but with one significant omission; the fate of the truck and its cargo. In stark contrast, the tragic events that took place the next day at Oradour-sur-Glane, have been vividly recorded by M. Robert Hébras, the only surviving resident of the village.

At 2pm, a detachment of about a 120 SS soldiers from St. Junien, on the orders of Major Dickmann, arrived at the village. The senior officer Captain Kahn, demanded that all the inhabitants should assemble in the main square. On the pretext of looking for 'prohibited merchandise', Khan briefly questioned the Mayor and several individuals. The 648 villagers were then divided into groups. The soldiers first led the women and children to the church; then the men, split into six groups, were led to various stone barns within the village. Having ordered his soldiers to shoot the men in the legs, Major Dickmann interrogated each wounded man in turn; obviously without success. He then ordered a complete search of the village, before the systematic demolition of all the buildings. Within two hours the village had been destroyed, all but five men and one woman had been shot, and the church and barns set on fire. The Germans went away empty-handed.

The motive for this atrocity has been generally accepted as a reprisal for local Resistance activity, such as the death of the two soldiers at St. Junien. But this explanation doesn't answer at least two questions. Why was the backwater village of Oradour selected by the Nazis? And why did they take so much trouble to search and demolish all the buildings in such a systematic manner?

The first hint that there may indeed have been an alternative motive came to light in 1988 with the publication of *Oradour: Massacre and Aftermath*. In this book, Robin Mackness describes his extraordinary and dramatic experience while engaged as a freelance investment manager to a bank[2] in Switzerland. In 1982 – the year after Mitterrand's election – Mackness was stopped by French customs officials on the autoroute outside Lyon, and arrested for being in possession of twenty 1kg gold bars; some of these were stamped with the Nazi initials RB – Reichsbank.

He had been asked by the Swiss bank to contact a client in Toulouse, who wished to deposit some gold bars. Due to the client's nervousness, Mackness was requested to transport the gold personally to Evian, from where it would be taken illegally across the lake by another agent, into Switzerland. During a two-hour meeting, the client, whom Mackness renamed Raoul[3] to protect his identity, had related the story of how he came to possess the gold and the events that led to the massacre at Oradour.

Having trained as a Resistance activist[4], Raoul was ordered to execute acts of sabotage designed to delay the progress of the SS Panzer Division Das Reich on its journey north to Normandy. Following the Division from Toulouse, Raoul eventually arrived south-west of Limoges, where he was given charge of six young Maquisards. They were ordered to travel as fast as possible to the village of Chaillac, situated on the opposite bank of the river Vienne facing St. Junien. He was told that just outside the village of Chaillac they would find a barn, owned by the foreman of a local glove factory, in which they could shelter safely and where they would receive further instructions.

His orders were to sabotage a railway bridge near the village of Nieul, north of Limoges. At nightfall on 9 June, Raoul and his colleagues left the barn to carry out their mission. To avoid the intense Nazi activity at St. Junien they crossed the river at St. Victurnien, then cycled north on the road leading towards Oradour-sur-Glane. At some point along this road, he claimed to have encountered the small convoy that had left St. Junien at midnight, travelling under cover of darkness. A fierce fight ensued in which all but Raoul, and a German, who somehow managed to run away, were killed.

It was when he looked into the back of the truck that Raoul discovered the gold ingots, packed in thirty small wooden boxes. Each about the size of a shoe-box, they contained a total of around 600kg of gold. After some reflection, he decided to bury the gold just inside a field by the side of the road. Having completed the task, he doused the wrecked vehicles and all the corpses, both French and German, in petrol and set them alight. He then cycled away, determined to return to recover the gold once the war was over.

Finding that the gold had been hijacked, Major Dickmann immediately called a crisis meeting with his senior officers. Noting that Oradour-sur-Glane was the nearest village to the place of ambush, they naturally concluded that the gold may well have been concealed somewhere in the vicinity. It was thus that the detachment of SS soldiers arrived at the village on the afternoon of 10 June looking for it.

Research by Mackness for his book confirmed certain key parts of this account, but all aspects of the gold hijack itself rely totally on Raoul's testimony. For whatever purposes, it appears that Raoul may have been somewhat economical with the truth; there is the matter of his true identity, the name by which he introduced himself to Mackness would obviously have been a pseudonym. But from whom did he wish to remain anonymous?

Roger-René Dagobert recalls that, at the age of fifteen, he had watched the armoured vehicles of Das Reich drive past his father's house in Limoges. His father, René, the director of the local undertakers, was given the job of removing and burying the bodies after the massacre at Oradour. In the course of this unpleasant task, he noticed that all the men had been shot in the legs, leading him to conclude that they had been tortured before being killed. But why would they have been?

Despite a reluctance to speak publicly, some locals do acknowledge that theft of gold may be at the heart of the Oradour mystery. But Raoul's version of events is problematic: not one local inhabitant ever found evidence of a burned out convoy on any road in the area. Certainly, there would have been extensive wreckage; the road surface and verges would have been unmistakably marked and deformed as a result of the heat of the fire. Even a well-equipped clear-up unit would not have been able to remove all traces. Nobody in the area detected the smoke and pungent smell generated by the burning wreckage, tyres and corpses – and this in a rural area where people habitually rise early, especially in June. One must therefore conclude that a hijack of the gold was executed at a location and in a manner that left no traces.

But if a hijack did not take place as Raoul reported, then why did the SS carry out the destruction of Oradour? Roger-René Dagobert offers another solution. He suggests that the hijack of the lorry and the theft of the gold were far from spontaneous actions, but had instead been carefully planned. There were many independent 'rogue' Maquis units, loosely connected to de Gaulle's Secret Army, whose actions, sometimes motivated more by self-interest than patriotism, were often overlooked provided they continued to harass the Germans. Raoul may well have belonged to one of these. It is likely that they stole the gold either in St. Junien, or whilst in transit on the southern approach road that passes by Chaillac, and took it to the barn for safe-keeping.

Whichever account one accepts, the theft must have been accomplished without drawing immediate attention from the Germans or their response would have taken a different course. By midday of 9 June, Major Dickmann had ordered the whole population of St. Junien to produce their identity papers for inspection at the Town Hall. Meanwhile, Gestapo officers – assisted by Jean Filiol, head of the Limoges Milice – were investigating the Resistance activity of the previous days. The next morning, it appears that two local informers told the Gestapo that they should move their search for partisans to Oradour, evidently to draw attention away from St. Junien. Shortly afterwards, Major Dickmann sent a company of specialist sappers to Oradour with orders to look for 'prohibited merchandise'.

Confirmation that others, besides Raoul, knew of the gold comes from Roger-René Dagobert himself. The Gourt brothers, who owned the glove factory at St. Junien and the barn at Chaillac, had told him confidentially, in 1962, that the Oradour massacre was connected to the theft of Nazi gold. This was some twenty years before Raoul related his story to Robin Mackness. The manager of the information department of Chaillac's Mairie confirmed, in 1998, that Resistance activists had indeed used the barn in June 1944. Since the Gourt brothers owned the barn, it is most likely that they were fully aware of Raoul's plan, if not actually involved in it. There have even been hints that it was the Gourts who informed the Gestapo about Oradour, no doubt to protect themselves.

Pierre and René Gourt moved from St. Junien in 1946, evidently with some new and unexplained wealth. Settling in Nantes, they bought and refurbished two shops (of which Roger-René Dagobert was the architect) and later became a major outlet for ready-to-wear clothes supplied by the prestigious Yves St. Laurent. Intriguingly, the managing director of Yves St. Laurent was Pierre Bergé[5], a close friend of André Rousselet and François Mitterrand.

Yet another of Mitterrand's inner circle had connections with Limoges and the Oradour incident. Roland Dumas, alleged to have profited from clandestine Resistance activities, was to become an important government minister (President of the Constitutional Council) and a close confidante of Mitterrand. His father Georges, a financial administrator at the Limoges town hall, was also responsible for the local Resistance. On 3 March 1944, denounced by a Gestapo collaborator, George was arrested and shot for Resistance activities. However, it is suggested in *Les Puissance du Mal* by Jean-Edern Hallier, that he was actually shot for acts of brigandage in the Haute-Vienne, where trains carrying gold were frequently attacked. Hallier's version may receive some support from an article published in *Le Monde* on 18 June 1998. It reported that during a recent judicial enquiry in which he was a witness, Roland Dumas informed the judge that the five gold ingots, which he had sold in 1992, had previously belonged to his mother. It is difficult not to believe that these were actually part of the 'spoils of war' acquired from the Nazis by his father.

But Jean-Edern Hallier further reveals that during the war the Dumas family gave shelter to the Felderbaums, a Jewish family that had originally fled from Austria. According to former Capitain Paul Barril in his *Guerres Secrètes à l'Elysée*, Joachim Felderbaum formed a lifelong friendship with his contemporary, Roland Dumas. After the war, Joachim adopted the name Jean-Pierre-François, and became a very wealthy financier in Switzerland. It has been reported in the French press that he had been involved in a number of financial scandals, though he has always been quick to refute these accusations. In one lawsuit brought about by two associates of the Bank Romande, he confided his defence to two lawyers, Georges Dayan and François Mitterrand. Another lawyer, Roland Dumas, appeared as a character witness. Despite his dubious reputation, Jean-Pierre was later said by investigating journalists to have exerted a strong influence in government circles and to have acted as Mitterrand's personal financial advisor. In the next chapter, we will examine how Jean-Pierre's network of contacts, power and influence has spread throughout several areas of this investigation, from the financing of François Mitterrand to the creation of the European political union, and the mystery surrounding and associated with Rennes-le-Château.

With such close links to those directly or indirectly involved with the tragedy of Oradour and the mystery of the missing gold, it is not surprising that Mitterrand should have taken steps to ensure that the truth was never made public. He was a major signatory to an amnesty granted, in 1952, to Alsatian conscripted soldiers who had taken part in the Oradour massacre. Despite provoking outrage amongst those who lost relatives and friends at Oradour, the amnesty decision was ostensibly taken in the interest of French unity. (Alsace had been temporarily annexed by the Germans, in 1940, but the Alsatians had always considered themselves to be more French than German.) But it is just as probable that the French authorities did not want to risk any incriminating details about Oradour to be revealed. Mitterrand and his friends were always to maintain a wall of silence about this period, refusing adamantly to respond to requests to reveal the truth.

The arrest of Robin Mackness, in possession of gold ingots, presented the French authorities with a long-awaited opportunity to try to track down Raoul – and of course the whereabouts of the remaining stolen gold. His incarceration and continued interrogation must have been authorised at a high level; the customs contrived to prolong his eighteen-month sentence to twenty-one months. The great interest shown by his interrogators when Mackness innocently revealed that he was en-route to Annemasse suggests that they were well aware of the transferring of gold to Switzerland, an activity in which Plantard admitted to being involved some thirty years before.

But there is yet another twist in this tragic tale. In his book *Le Fil et la Pelote*, Roland Dumas reports that on 10 November 1942 he joined the Group No. 1, Maréchal Pétain, of the Chantiers de Jeunesse located in the forest of Troncais[6] in the Allier. To escape recruitment into the STO (Service du Travail Obligatoire), he returned to Limoges where he stayed for a few weeks before finding accommodation at a farm in the region of Dorat, in the north of the Vienne department. His friend, Joachim Felderbaum, remained in Lyon under the protection of the Abbé Sage.

Researchers Gilles de Luce and Christian Guérin have confirmed that the farm was La Borderie at the château of Lussac-les-Eglises. The proprietor of the château was Bertrand Cressac de la Bachelerie[7], a collaborator in contact with the Ahnenerbe[8] of the SS well before the war. In a pamphlet about his castle's history, he relates some extraordinary events that took place in 1944. He reports that, at nightfall on 23 May of that year, three armed and masked maquis broke into the castle. Having seriously assaulted his parents, the intruders escaped with 300,000Fr. The leader was apparently identified as a refugee Alsatian who had been welcomed at the castle a short time ago as part of a group of refugees. A month later, they returned and pillaged the castle, taking away a truck-load of 'various souvenirs'. The Alsatian leader was apparently shot in mid-July whilst in possession of a small fortune. Significantly, this episode occurred during the period of the Oradour incident; other sources maintain, however, that very different activities were taking place at the château.

Gilles de Luce and Christian Guerin add yet more detail. One of Lammerding's officers, Lt. Gerlach, and his chauffeur, had been kidnapped by the Maquis, the day before the alleged gold theft and Oradour massacre. Lammerding assumed that the lorry carrying the division's records and the gold had suffered the same fate as his officers and had fallen into the hands of the Maquis. He had arranged that the gold would be taken to the château of Lussac-les-Eglises to be stored until it could be shared out between Lammerding and his two accomplices, presumably at a more convenient time. Major Dickmann appears to have been unaware of the secret arrangements that had been made between Lammerding and Bertrand Cressac. Unable to contact Cressac, Lammerding feared the worst until he could visit the castle for confirmation. Meanwhile, Dickmann was to carry out the most brutal of operations in the search for the apparently stolen gold.

The story is taken up by the present owners of the castle. On Monday 12 June 1944, accompanied by a select group of his senior officers, General Lammerding returned to the château of Bertrand Cressac to find out whether everything had gone well. Following this meeting, Lammerding and his officers were observed celebrating in the local restaurant by villagers surprised to see Germans in their village. To conceal their activities, the Germans claimed unconvincingly to have arrived at the village unexpectedly having confused it with Lussac-les-Châteaux in the Vienne[9]. Lammerding's jovial mood was evidently caused by relief that the gold had arrived safely at the castle. But General Lammerding was never able to enjoy his ill-gotten gains; the Allied offensive on D-day marked a decisive change in fortune for the Germans. The post-war trials ensured that Lammerding was never able to return to France after the war.

So what happened to the gold? Was it taken by Raoul following the ambush, as related to Mackness; or did Bertrand Cressac de la Bachelerie profit from the Nazi defeat and become sole possessor of the gold; or was it, as Cressac claimed, stolen from the Château by rogue Alsatian Maquis? With such a confused picture, probably we will never know for sure. What we do know is that Mackness was arrested for illegal possession of twenty 1kg gold bars and that he was told a remarkable account of their history, many aspects of which have been confirmed, but key elements of which remain suspect. Was Raoul's story manufactured to hide the reality of the theft and to maintain anonymity for the perpetrators? More crucially, what was the real identity of Raoul? Was he just the spokesman for a group? Without doubt there were others aware of the truth, or at least parts of it, but for whatever reason have chosen to remain silent. The role of Alsatian troops in both the massacre and the alleged theft from the castle could well be a significant factor. We will also encounter the name of Cressac de la Bachelerie again, but in different circumstances. As with so much of this tangled story, many key characters can be seen to appear in very different threads.

With established links to those directly or indirectly involved with the tragedy of Oradour and the mystery of the missing gold, it is not surprising that Mitterrand should have welcomed the opportunity to obscure the truth. He was after all a major signatory to an amnesty granted, in 1952, to Alsatian conscripted soldiers who had taken part in the Oradour massacre. Despite provoking outrage amongst those who lost relatives and friends at Oradour, the amnesty decision was ostensibly taken in the interest of French unity. Although the Alsace had been temporarily annexed by the Germans, the Alsatians always considered themselves to be more French than German. But it is just as probable that the French authorities did not want to risk any incriminating details about Oradour to be revealed. Mitterrand and his friends were always to maintain a wall of silence about this period, refusing adamantly to respond to requests to discuss it.

Despite the evidence to the contrary from both Robin Mackness and Roger-René Dagobert, many Oradour locals deny that the massacre of the village had anything to do with the gold. The trauma of the Oradour tragedy lives on in family and friends, and their views must be respected. Others, however, are equally convinced that the Germans were looking for something. But the spoils of war are not confined to France. As we have seen in the Mackness affair, there are those in the Swiss banking system who have been happy to profit from such opportunities.

Chapter 16

The Shadow Men

Although there is no evidence to connect him with the theft or fate of Nazi gold, the biography of Jaochim Felderbraum[1] reveals some very interesting and surprising connections that deserve closer examination. We will also see from a digest of his extensive business and banking career, how he became involved, by accident or design, in a world that appears as background to this investigation. This is the secret world of right-wing synarchist politics, especially that of French collaborators and monarchists.

Born in Vienna, in 1922, he was adopted by Simon Felderbaum, who married Joachim's natural mother. In 1936, he discovered that he was actually the son of Baron Hamilkar Nikolia Von Wassilko, a banker and monarchist aristocrat close to the Habsburgs. Aware of Hitler's intentions, the family decided to emigrate; after a brief spell in Paris, they settled in Limoges where they were befriended by the family of Roland Dumas. This would be the start of a life-long friendship.

As a result of the Occupation of France, in 1940, Joachim and Roland went to study at Lyon University. They met Abbé Sage, a teacher at the affiliated Catholic faculty, who helped Joachim acquire certain papers (including a Baptism Certificate) to create a more French identity with the name Jean Fèvre. In 1941, they joined the local Resistance, organised by Abbé Sage, a member of the communist inspired 'Front National', as cycle couriers. During this time their conversations included political subjects and Joachim/Jean later claimed to have been inspired by the 'Pan-Europa' ideas of Coudenheve-Kalegi and Otto von Habsburg – a vision of a European Union. The following year, Roland Dumas was obliged to join the Chantiers de Jeunesse in the forest of Trocais in the Allier, and Joachim moved in to a flat with his girlfriend, Tita, who assumed the guise of his sister. When the Nazis invaded the Free Zone, Joachim claimed to have worked for the Resistance as a guide between Collonges, Lyon and Annemasse.

Following the Liberation of France, in late summer 1944, Joachim had a chance meeting with Antoine Berger, head of Berger Sucres, who proposed that he could work for him with his son-in-law, François de Grossouvre. He declined the offer but decided to establish a firmer French identity, so again with the help of Abbé Sage and Cardinal Gerlier, he created another fictitious past with supporting documentation in the name of Jean-Pierre François (JPF). Six months after their marriage, in December 1945, he and Tita moved to Switzerland, where he obtained a job with a family firm, Société Natural-le-Coultre. The Le Coultre family had made a lot of money during the war. Demonstrating exceptional ability, JPF was promoted to director of a section and installed in an office over-looking Lake Léman. This was the area favoured by ex-collaborators and where, from 1947, Plantard was said to have spent several years.

On a business trip, JPF met the Corsican, Jean Caneri, who was involved with Pakistani nationalists preparing for conflict in pursuit of independence from British Partition. They formed an association to supply the Pakistanis with arms; with the profits of this trade, JPF was able to purchase the Le Coultre business. In recognition of their assistance to the Pakistani nationalists, JPF and Caneri were granted lucrative contracts to help in the development of the new Pakistan state, created in 1947.

Following an unsuccessful business deal, JPF returned to trading with the Pakistanis and created a new company called 'Transhipping'. He and Caneri sought the most capable individuals to run the new enterprise. Among these were the cousins, Christian and Jean Dehollain, who introduced an old friend, a civil engineer called Georges Soules, better known in esoteric circles as Raymond Abellio. Accused of collaboration, and condemned to ten years hard labour, in 1948, Abellio had fled from France to Lausanne, where he stayed in the flat of an old friend. Bringing an impressive range of technical abilities, Abellio joined the Transhipping team as a contracts and financial supervisor in the buying and selling of military equipment.

We will return later to the significant role played by Abellio, a key figure linking aspects of the mystery of Rennes-le-Château, collaborationist activities, and the financial and political world of François Mitterrand. In the meantime we will continue to trace the evermore influential career of Jean-Pierre François.

In June 1951, his wife Tita tragically died of cancer. Some months later JPF commenced a relationship with a twenty-year old Iranian girl whom he was later to marry. Her father was a retired high-level financier and JPF set up an office in Teheran to assist his ventures in Pakistan. He was, however, about to embark on a different path, that of commercial banking. But more specifically, this would bring him into close contact with the financial world of former French collaborators and that of Opus Dei.

The first step occurred when Abellio introduced Jean-Pierre François to Hippolyte Worms, President of Banque Worms, who had been imprisoned after the Liberation of France, for collaboration. Furthermore, Hippolyte Worms and his associates, Jacques Barnaud, and Gabriel Leroy-Ladurie, had been the synarchist financial power behind the Vichy government[2]. Hippolyte and JPF decided to work together to form an international bank to finance Third World projects, and a European bank. This latter initiative was encouraged by Jean Monnet, regarded by many as the architect for European Unity; although Monnet was probably not aware of JPF's financial association with former collaborators. They then established a relationship with Union des Mines, an exclusive and aristocratic financial establishment. Georges Albertini, an old friend of Abellio, was brought in as a strategic adviser. Albertini had collaborated closely with the Germans during the Occupation, but it was rumoured that being a Freemason of high rank helped him escape prosecution after the war. JPF also opened relations with the bank Lehideux, yet another bank that had belonged to this financial network supporting Vichy. The head of the family, François Lehideux, had been one of Pétain's ministers. The bank continued to retain intimate contact with ex-Vichyites that had exiled themselves in Madrid. We should recall that, at this time, Otto Skorzeny was running a clandestine business empire from Madrid with finance arranged through Swiss banks. It would be surprising if JPF had not been aware of the murky history of his various business colleagues and allies. One must also question the motives of the banks and individuals with which JPF came to be associated. In the context of this investigation, it is very possible that they were all, in some way, involved in the trafficking of Nazi gold.

Another chapter began when JPF was approached by Alberto Ullastre, a lawyer and eminent member of Opus Dei, to open a bank in Andorra. Impressed by the record of the traditional Catholic Bank Lehideux, Ullastre persisted and, in 1952, JPF founded Le Credito Andorra. Whether JPF was aware of it at the time, Credito Andorra would become a major cog in the Opus Dei financial empire. In order to facilitate the expansion of their business and financial dealings and to conceal the ownership of property, Opus Dei needed some innovative corporate structures. The most important of these was 'Esfina', created by Ullastre, in the mid-1950s. Esfina acquired or founded various businesses useful to Opus and financially dependent on it. In 1955, Esfina moved into the banking sector and, amongst others, bought Credito Andorra, the largest and most active commercial bank in the principality. Within a few years, Spain was financing almost half of Opus Dei's global operations. Andorra, with its relaxed banking laws, acted as an intermediary for exported funds. The centre of several financial scandals, a court investigation concluded that money went from Andorra to Switzerland. Despite the lack of evidence, it is tempting to believe that JPF and his associates were fully aware of, and profited from, these huge transfers of funds.

One of the first and major scandals involved a technical support company for the textile industry, called Matesa[3]. Founded in 1956, the company was founded by Juan Vila Reyes, one of the first graduates of IESE, Opus Dei's prestigious business school. Realising the potential value of technology, Reyes exploited this sector to create the illusion that his company offered high-tech solutions. With his established network of business contacts, Reyes quickly accelerated Matesa's development. He had acquired the services of a multilingual lawyer, Jose Villar Palasi, who, though not himself a member, worked closely with Opus Dei. In 1962, Alberto Ullastres, then Spanish Minister of Commerce, appointed Reyes as his under-secretary. For the following six years Matesa enjoyed rapid expansion, building an assembly plant, establishing a research centre that employed hundreds of technicians. Reyes set up a maze of foreign shell companies through which he was able to channel the public and private funds that he had been able to obtain.

The Spanish Minister of Finance, appointed in 1956, was Espinosa San Martin, a member of Opus Dei. Espinosa had close contacts with the Giscard d'Estaing family and with Prince Jean de Broglie, a co-founder of the Giscardian Independent Republican Party. A minister under General de Gaulle, Giscard d'Estaing was later to become president of France. Prince Jean de Broglie was a successful financier with extensive contacts in the right-wing pan-European movement. On a mission to Madrid on behalf of Giscard d'Estaing, Broglie met Reyes. As a result of this meeting, Broglie established a holding company for Matesa, based in Luxembourg, with a capital injection of 1 million French francs. By June 1968, Matesa had established itself as a showcase Spanish multi-national company. But this reputation was largely based on fraud, deception, and creative accounting. Opponents of Matesa saw an opportunity to discredit it and to break the hold that Opus Dei had achieved over certain government departments. By 1969, news of the company's true nature became public and Spain's dictator, Franco, disturbed by all the negative publicity, had Reyes and his brother arrested. This was followed by an extensive government ministerial reshuffle and a commission of enquiry into Matesa's affairs.

It discovered that much of the missing cash had been transferred abroad; some had been donated to IESE, and there were rumours that payments had been made to Opus Dei through its 'auxiliary societies', though these were to be denied. A special court found Reyes and one of his employees guilty of illegally transporting $2.5 million in cash by car to Andorra, where it was deposited with Credito Andorra before being transferred to Switzerland. Prince Jean de Broglie, unable to meet a payment of compensation for missing funds, was shot in a Paris street. The general manager of another bank implicated in the scandal and forced into liquidation, was found drowned in Lake Leman; his widow continues to maintain that he had been murdered.

One of the lawyers brought in to examine l'Affaire Broglie, was Mitterrand's and Jean-Pierre François' close friend, Roland Dumas. Dumas told a French journalist, 'A more probing investigation would have shown that Matesa was an instrument of Opus Dei, whose tentacles stretch everywhere in western Europe'. No investigation of this connection was undertaken in the criminal information (against Matesa's management) opened in Madrid or Luxemburg. The reason no doubt resides in the evident links that exist between Opus Dei and the political party of the Independent Republicans whose principal leaders were the friends of Prince de Broglie.' These friends, of course, included the future president of France, Giscard d'Estaing.

In 1955, JPF had to face a new problem, that of his true identity. A SDECE agent, Jean-Pierre Lenoir, who had been part of a secret group that had helped establish the anti-Communist Gladio network, sent a dossier of JPF's identity to the Minister of the Interior. JPF was forced to return to Paris where he was again successfully defended, in court, by his old friend, Roland Dumas.

But scandals seem to hover over the career of JPF like dark clouds. In 1958, he took over the running of Banque Romande (he eventually bought the bank in 1972) that had become embroiled in a scandal concerning missing Canadian funds. He brought in a new team, including colleagues from Transhipping, to take control. The bank had a modest client base but a huge deficit in funds, the result of false accounting practices. JPF determined to track the source of the scandal; a judicial enquiry suggested the presence of the Mafia behind the Canadian and American businessmen involved. The Swiss banking system, embarrassed by the activities of a stranger in exposing a scandal, sought to bring about the closure of Banque Romande. They employed the services of a renowned lawyer, Raymond Nicolet, to lead the case against JPF. He was once again successfully defended by Roland Dumas, and by François Mitterrand who he had first met in 1956.

Banque Romande flourished and JPF became an advisor on international finance. As well as managing Banque Romande, he became deputy head of Compagnie Bancaire at Geneva, member of the bank Troillet et Cie in Martigny, President of Credit Immobilier pour l'etranger (CIPE), and bought the Swiss branch of AGEFI, an agency specialising in economic and financial information. But JPF wanted to retire, in 1972, aged 50. He decided to reduce his business commitments and become more involved with his political interests. For this, he was to be encouraged by his old friend Raymond Abellio to look towards the conservative Right-wing.

At this point it is instructive to look closely at the early career of Raymond Abellio, pseudonym of Georges Soules, who was born in Toulouse in 1907. His parents came from Ax-les-Thermes, in the Ariège valley, only 16km from the ancient Cathar castle at Montségur and a little over 40km from Rennes-le-Château. The Ariège was also part of the region later administered by André Rousselet, confidante of François Mitterrand. Soules was a brilliant student, and during his engineering studies, discovered an interest in politics and converted to Marxism. He joined the Étudiants Socialist of the XIV arrondissement of Paris, affiliated to the French Socialist party (SFIO). Here he befriended the celebrated political philosopher, Claude Lévi-Strausse. Amongst his tutors was Marcel Deat, the politician and philosopher who formed his own party, the Parti Socialiste de France, under the motto 'Order, Authority and Nation'. Soules played an active part and contributed articles to various Left-wing reviews.

In 1931, at the age of 24, he joined the Centre Polytechnicien d'Études Économiques, popularly known as X-Crise. The aim of the group was to study the political and economic consequences of the 1929 Wall Street crash. One of the results of this study was the adoption of 'Planisme', a political philosophy that embraced centralised control of the economy and key services, such as power and transport. It appears that Planist approach offered the best route to a French national renewal and a change in France's economic fortune. Their belief in the need for such a 'strong state', however, was at odds with Socialist thinking and partly explains how far-left Socialists metamorphosed into extreme fascists. Furthermore, this in part explains the enthusiasm for the undemocratic, un-socialist European Union among so many principled, 'Socialist', former followers of Henri de Man, initiator of Planisme.

Amongst Soules' friends at this time was a prominent Planist, Jean Coutrot, said to be one of the founders of the enigmatic organisation, Synarchie. A year later, he joined the adult branch of the Socialist party and became more deeply involved in politics, but still continued his work with X-Crise. He was appointed to a government post under Leon Blum, in recognition of his abilities, eventually moved to the Ministry of National Economy, headed by a Planist, Charles Spinasse, where he was engaged in the control of industrial pricing. In 1938, he joined the Revolutionaire constructive movement where he was to meet one of its chiefs, Georges Albertini, who he would later introduce to Jean-Pierre François.

When war broke out in 1939, he joined the army with the rank of Lieu-tenant and took part in military actions in Holland and Belgium. He was taken prisoner, in 1940, and sent to a camp in Silesia where he attracted some top Pétainist officers interested in his political philosophy. He was freed the following year and returned to Versailles, as an engineer.

Shortly after his return, Soules became a director of Rassemblement National Populaire (RNP), created by Marcel Déat, one of his former tutors. Here he met L'Oréal's owner, Eugene Schueller, who invited him to join the Mouvement Social Révolutionaire (MSR). This group had evolved out of the sinister Comité Secret d'Action Revolutionaire (CSAR), also known as the Cagoule. Soules was now to become acquainted with Eugene Deloncle, head of the political wing, dedicated to secret, direct, and violent action. Deloncle was a maritime engineer who had studied at the Ecole Polytech-nique. At the heart of this college was an inner circle known as the Grand Taupe de France[5] (The Great Mole of France) that had the appearance of a philosophical group with Freemasonic influences. Its aims were to re-cruit talented pupils, of an elitist philosophy, and place them in positions of power and influence. One of these recruits was Jean Coutrot, who we have already encountered. He was to experience a sudden and mysterious death in 1941, believed by some to be suicide but by others to have been an assassination related to his Synarchist activities. Several others close to Coutrot died within a few weeks of each other, adding weight to the conspiracy allegation.

To extend his political ambitions, Soules helped form the Front Revolutionaire National with Marcel Déat. He also frequently returned to Vichy where he became a cabinet minister of Pétain. With the defeat of the Nazis, life became difficult for collaborators and Soules took refuge in a Benedictine monastery and then with some friends at Loiret. It is here that he started to write his first book. Moving to Paris, he joined a theatre, and for security adopted a pseudonym, Raymond Abellio. In February 1947, he crossed into Switzerland assisted by an industrialist who owed him a favour. He eventually settled at Chexbres, between Lausanne and Vevey, an area popular amongst other former collaborators. One of these was Jean Jardin, another Vichy minister, who arranged funding from secret Vichy sources. Abellio became a tutor to Jardin's dyslexic son, Pascal, who became a celebrated author. Following the success of his first book (he won a literary prize), he managed to obtain a contract for three more. He was sentenced in France to ten years hard labour for collaboration, but due to his anti-Communist activities, the Swiss authorities allowed him to stay in Switzerland[6]. He moved from Chexbres to Lausanne where, as we have seen, he was to meet Jean-Pierre François.

So here we have a Socialist turned Fascist, deeply involved in political movements, who actively collaborated with the Vichy government. In the course of his political activities, he was to work closely with Eugene Deloncle, who, as we saw, was closely acquainted with a fellow engineer, François Plantard, and whose niece married Mitterrand's brother, Robert. Abellio was also at the heart of a circle of ex-collaborators employed by Eugene Shueller in his L'Oréal empire. His wartime connections extended to Georges Albertini, former head of Marcel Déat's office and post-war advisor to the Synarchist Banque Worms, whom he introduced to Jean-Pierre François.

With such a record, it is perhaps surprising to find that Abellio had a successful, parallel, career in esoteric and occult political literature. Even more surprising is to discover that he was on the board of the *Atlantis* magazine founded, in 1926, by Paul Le Cour. Le Cour, as we saw, inherited the tradition and leadership of the Hiéron du Val d'Or, and was to be an inspiration for Pierre Plantard's political and esoteric philosophy. Furthermore, it is claimed that Abellio was involved with Bélisane publishing[7], founded in 1973. In his book, *Arktos*, Joscelyn Godwin refers to Raymond Abellio as another 'Bélisane' pseudonym. Bélisane, a specialist in a variety of esoteric subjects, has been a major publisher of books concerning all aspects of the mystery of Rennes-le-Château. Throughout his works, Abellio's views are typical of an extreme right-wing esotericism, the aim of which is to 'renew the tradition of the West'. He wanted to replace the famous Republican slogan, 'Liberty, Equality, Fraternity', with 'Prayer, War, Work', to represent a new society built on an absolute hierarchy led by a king-priest.

The theme of a New or Golden Age is a major thread that, parallel to that of treasure and Nazi gold, runs through this investigation. More specifically, this is a wishful re-discovery of Europe's mythical Golden Age, a world in which spirituality, tradition and symbolism, play a dominant part. Although very different in its manifestation, this ideal, or aspiration, was shared by groups as diverse as the Nazis, the Vichy government, the Hiéron du Val d'Or, Martinists, Atlanticists, and many occult societies including Plantard's Priory of Sion. But there is one group that has emerged from the shadows of occult politics to pursue its long term aim, that of a united Europe. Once again we will find the presence of financiers, aristocrats, ex-collaborators, Intelligence agencies, and idealists, as they sought to create an opportunity for the promotion of self-interest.

It was through Raymond Abellio, and his old Vichy friend, Jean Jardin, that Jean-Pierre François was introduced to Antoine Pinay, former French Prime Minister, and several members of the Pinay Circle, most of whom, at that time, had been collaborators.

The Pinay Circle[8], also known as the Cercle Violet (after Jean Violet a co-founder), established in 1969, was an international right-wing propaganda group which brought together serving or retired intelligence officers of a right-wing persuasion from most countries of Europe and America. The Circle's prime mission was to support prominent politicians and governments that promoted deregulation and which believed in minimal constraint on international business. It is generally believed that, to achieve their aims, the Circle was involved in tactics to destabilise non-compliant governments, leading to their removal from office.

But the roots of the Pinay Circle are to be found nearly 50 years earlier in the activities of another co-founder, the Archduke Otto von Habsburg.

In 1922, Count Richard Coudenhove-Kalergi founded the Pan-European Union (PEU) that, as we saw, was an inspiration to the young JPF and his friend Roland Dumas. Looking for support amongst important political figures, he attracted the interest of the Archduke Otto. The PEU was followed, in 1949, by the Centre Éuropean de Documentation Internationale (CEDI), founded by Archduke Otto and Alfredo Sanchez Bella, a Minister under Franco, later member of the Pinay Circle, and devotee of Opus Dei. Although these groups were outwardly committed to the political and economic union of European countries, they were comprised of mainly right-wing and conservative members determined to create a bulwark against Communism. In fact, the objective of CEDI was the creation of a federation of Christian states, united around a Spanish Bourbon monarch, dedicated to anti-Communism. It is perhaps not surprising to find that CEDI was considered to be an auxiliary operation of Opus Dei, and that Archduke Otto was alleged to be a treasured Opus member.

Membership of the PEU, CEDI and the Pinay Circle, included prominent politicians, aristocrats, intelligence officers, financiers, and representatives of the Roman Catholic Church, who were actively engaged in secret activities to not only break up the Soviet Union but to establish a right-wing governed European Union based on the principle of Free-Market Capitalism. Some of the members, however, were to see opportunities within this secretive network for criminal activity in the sphere of financial fraud.

In 1964, on the instigation of Franz Josef Strauss, German Defence Minister, Jean Violet (acting for Antoine Pinay) presented the German Finance Ministry with an enormous claim for war reparations; specifically, for supplying metals to the Germans during the occupation of France. Strauss advised the German government to settle the claim, but on closer examination, the documentation was found to be faked, and the swindle was exposed.

Five years later, the 'sniffer plane' affair was launched. An Italian professor, Aldo Bonassoli, and a Belgian engineer, Count Alain de Villegas, claimed to have developed a technology that would allow the detection of underground liquid deposits from the air. De Villegas was a member of the Pan-European Union and had met Antoine Pinay. The Pinay Circle hierarchy quickly saw the financial potential of such an invention in a world becoming increasingly short of oil and water. Using connections within the Pinay Circle, they sought funds for the development and sale of this revolutionary technology. Various ministers, politicians, industrialists and financiers, were drawn into the affair and some agreed to finance testing of the equipment. The initial focus on water exploration failed, so taking advantage of the newly elevated oil price, Violet suggested switching to the oil industry. It does appear strange that despite the project lacking any serious technology, so many companies were conned into supporting it at various stages. The scam lasted for over six years and even ELF was duped into paying $200 million. Within the network of banks acting as a conduit for the flow of funds was a subsidiary of Banco Ambrosiano which we will see was also implicated in a major scandal involving the Vatican Bank. Eventually, Giscard d'Estaing sensed the fraud, and the affair was exposed. Some of the money was recovered but the bulk had disappeared into various hands, including, it is said, that of Opus Dei. Despite the involvement of some of its members, the Pinay Circle was to continue completely unaffected.

So we have seen how, prior to the fall of the Berlin Wall, defence against Communism provided a convenient cloak for those with an extreme right-wing agenda to pursue their aims unhindered. Parallel to the activities of wartime collaborators, these clandestine activities have proved to be fertile ground for those with self-interest or criminal intent. Networks of ex-collaborators and right-wing sympathisers can be found at the heart of the early movement for European Unity. Funding for such networks has come from sympathetic banks such as Lazard and Worms, and industries controlled by Nazi sympathisers who escaped justice after the war. There is also a 'black' secret economy based on plundered Nazi gold, and precious art and artefacts that do not normally see the light of day. The Mackness affair represents a mere glimpse of this hidden world. Power, especially in the political world, and wealth are the prime objectives of these individuals and groups, and we will see, in the next chapter, how easily the worlds of politicians, financiers, church leaders, intelligence services, and criminals can become intertwined in the pursuit of common aims and personal gain.

Chapter 17

Inside the Occult Web

At the heart of the 'Rennes-le-Château Affair' is the Priory of Sion; its self-appointed role as guardian of the legendary treasure of the Temple of Jerusalem and the secret survival of a Merovingian bloodline is intertwined with goals that are common throughout the world of occult politics. Rejecting the public democratic forum of mainstream politics that they find inappropriate, a loose network of occult and esoteric societies, within which can be found the Priory of Sion, perpetuate their largely right-wing stance through internal publications, rituals and teachings, and social interaction amongst members. Potential members are often carefully selected, groomed and initiated to ensure a continuity of thought within the group. The culture of secrecy and hierarchy greatly contribute to the success of such groups and help to avoid embarrassing criticism or interference from non-members. A few of the more extreme societies are actively pursuing a variety of right-wing orientated agendas. As we will see, however, there are instances where the hierarchy may be pursuing a more sinister agenda of which the general membership is completely unaware. The financial standing or social status of a member can dramatically increase their society's influence on the wider community. It is for this reason that politicians, local or national, financiers, businessmen, representatives of the police and legal system, and even church leaders, are targeted for recruitment – a criticism often levelled against mainstream Freemasonry.

The Priory presents an innocuous and mystical, even possibly naive, public face designed to divert attention away from their true aims. We have seen how they have gone to extraordinary lengths to create a mythological heritage, claiming that the Priory was founded early in the 12th century to protect a dynasty that carried a specific royal bloodline with biblical associations. The fabricated genealogies show a bloodline that was shared by the Merovingian kings and their successors, the Counts of Razès. The original Priory, founded in 1956, has undergone great changes and has received considerable promotion through the publication, in 1982, of *the Holy Blood and the Holy Grail* by Lincoln, Baigent and Leigh and more recently by Dan Brown's *The Da Vinci Code*.

Since the early 1980s, the Priory has succumbed to internal dissent, division, and infiltration, so it is difficult to trace what has remained of the original. More recent publications, following the death, in 2000, of their founder, Pierre Plantard, reveal an attempt to rewrite their history. Their literature does continue to claim an association with the 17th century Compagnie du Saint-Sacrement, and the 19th century Hiéron du Val d'Or. It is logical to suppose that the Priory, the Compagnie, and the Hiéron, had something in common. They have each created an air of secrecy around their activities. Although their individual circumstances varied, they did share some of the same aims. These include the infiltration of the political establishment to gain influence, the maintenance of an aristocratic elite, and the restoration of a popular constitutional monarchy under the religious authority of a French-controlled Catholic Church – in effect the establishment of a Gallican (French) Holy Roman Empire.

Interestingly, the Compagnie du Saint-Sacrement actually worked in opposition to both Louis XIII and XIV, and to the French statesman Cardinal Mazarin, the Vatican's representative in France. Born in Italy, Jules Mazarin was created a cardinal in 1641 on the recommendation of Louis XIII, despite having never been ordained a priest. Appointed Minister of State in 1653, he wielded enormous political power. The hostility of the Compagnie was rooted in two convictions. First, they rejected the legitimacy of the Bourbons to rule France, especially Louis XIV, the Sun King, who was almost certainly not the natural son of Louis XIII, who it was claimed by many at the time (including his personal physician) was impotent. Second, Cardinal Mazarin represented the reigning papacy, which was perceived to be corrupt and not a worthy successor of Christ's mission. There were also close links between the Compagnie and the Jansenist Catholic Church. Championed by Nicolas Pavillon at Alet-les-Bains, French Jansenism appears to have been founded on a mutual desire to reform the Catholic Church in a spirit of traditional strict observance, in which France would supplant Rome as the world's spiritual centre in Christian terms.

Since the days of the Compagnie, the political, cultural and economic composition of European countries has obviously changed dramatically. This change has necessitated an evolution in the policies adopted by its political successors. But the underlying philosophy of its heirs has continued to embrace the powerful vision, archetypes, and symbols, of the so-called chivalric age, largely rooted in the high Middle Ages. This explains why the symbols and references to Knighthood, Templars, and esoteric wisdom are so dominant in the later publications of the Order of Alpha Galates, the immediate precursor of the Priory of Sion. This symbolism, shared also by the Nazi SS, the Pétainist Vichy government, and many of those with leanings towards the political right wing, has proved to have an enormous appeal, evidenced in the proliferation of Masonic societies, neo-Templar, and other neo-Chivalric Orders in the 19th and 20th centuries.

Four years before the emergence of the Priory of Sion in 1956, a group of occultists, among which were a famous alchemist, an industrialist, and a film director, met at Arginy castle. They believed that Arginy, situated on the plains between the river Saône and Beaujolais, north of Lyon, had been the secret meeting place of the nine founding members of the Knights Templars. They also believed that part of the Templar treasure had been removed in 1307 from the Paris Temple, for safekeeping. It was taken to Arginy, along with artefacts and documents, and concealed in an underground vault, safe from the avaricious intentions of the French king, Philippe le Bel. This isolated castle became the birthplace, in 1952, of a secret chivalric society whose descendent was to experience a much publicised and extraordinary tragedy some forty years later.

French researcher and former architect, André Douzet, having conducted a comprehensive investigation into the strange history and activities surrounding Arginy, has published his findings, which provide a firm basis for this account. Under the leadership of the occult writer Jacques Breyer, who was residing at the old château owned from 1914 by the noble Marquis d'Uxeloup de Chambrun, Comte de Rosemont, this occult group constituted the new Ordre Souverain du Temple Solaire ('Sovereign Order of the Solar Temple'). In 1950, the Marquis had turned down an offer of 100 million French francs, made by an anonymous English Colonel, to purchase the estate. A parallel can be drawn perhaps with the mysterious International League of Antiquarian Booksellers who showed such interest in the castle at Rennes-le-Château and its ancient parchments.

Having participated in elaborate occult rituals, the group claimed to have made contact with the spirits of the deceased Templars who then conferred on them the authority to continue their spiritual mission. As at Rennes-le-Château some years later, this heady mix of buried treasure, ancient wisdom and spiritual questing made Arginy the focal point for Freemasons, Rosicrucians and many others drawn to the occult and esoteric. Breyer, continuing his alchemical research for a further seven years, stayed on at the château, of which the oldest part was the circular Tower of the Eight Beatitudes, also known as the Tower of Alchemy due to the alchemical graffiti that covered its interior walls. Of those attracted to Arginy, in 1959, was the head of the French Secret Service, Constantin Melnik, who reportedly participated in the night-time ceremonies. Shortly after, reports appeared in the French press associating Melnik with a group of Catholic, monarchist, synarchist anti-Communists that called themselves Templars. Despite denials from Melnik of this involvement, the allegations have persisted and do appear credible when viewed against the overall picture.

What Breyer achieved in the course of his researches, which to the general public might seem to be at best naive, is unknown; it is nevertheless remarkable that at the same time, in the United States, a similar group of occultists were peforming identical rituals. Interestingly, Lynn Picknett and Clive Prince reveal, in *The Stargate Conspiracy*, details of this American network, which, like the French, involved several leading industrialists and which equally tried to manipulate domestic politics, in this case, those of the White House.

Despite a possibly inevitable, scepticism from non-believers, the founding of the Sovereign Order of the Solar Temple was a genuine attempt to re-awaken the powerful chivalric archetype of the Templars. Rituals are known to have been practised at Arginy, until 1973, though some nine years before, Jacques Breyer and three of his founding colleagues resigned (other evidence suggests however, that they remained closely connected to the Order). In June 1966, the group elected a new Grand Master entitled 'Jean' – by coincidence the same sub-title applied to the Grand Masters of the Priory of Sion. Publicly launched at the mountain retreat of Sainte-Odile in Alsace, the twin to that at Sion-Vaudemont made famous by Maurice Barrès in *La Colline Inspirée*, the Sovereign Order of the Solar Temple was officially recognised by Prince Rainier of Monaco. The headquarters of the Order became established in the Principality, and came to have a profound and traumatic effect on the oldest ruling dynasty in Europe, the House of Grimaldi.

The founding of the Ordre Temple Solaire ('Order of the Solar Temple' or OTS), in about 1981, was to cause a great deal of confusion with the original Sovereign Order of Jacques Breyer. This confusion was fully exploited by the OTS leadership. The OTS evolved out of several other neo-chivalric and secret societies, all of which have connections with the early 19th century neo-Templar Order, L'Ordre Souverain et Militaire du Temple de Jerusalem ('The Sovereign and Military Order of the Temple of Jerusalem').

This had surfaced under the control of Bernard Raymond Fabré Palaprat in the 19th century, as recounted in chapter 6. For safe-keeping during World War II, the leadership and archives of this Templar Order were entrusted to a Portugese diplomat, the self-styled Count Antonio Campello Pinto Pereira de Sousa Fontes, on the understanding that he would step aside if the membership were to vote for a new Grand Master or Regent. At a meeting in Paris in September 1970, Count Antonio nominated his son to succeed him as Grand Master. Rejected by the member knights – who elected a French-Pole, General Count Antoine Daniel Zdrojewski – the defeated Princeps Regens Count Fernando withdrew to Portugal and renamed the Order, The Supreme Military Order of the Temple of Jerusalem.

The split allowed the extreme right wing to forge alliances with, and even infiltrate, the Order. This allowed them to operate under the cover of an ostensibly harmless chivalric organisation. The Order was covertly linked, from the late 1950s, with the Service d'Action Civique (SAC), a private Intelligence service founded by General de Gaulle, when France was threatened with civil war, and after the General had survived an assassination attempt by Organisation de l'Armée Secrète (OAS) terrorists during the Algerian crisis. The OAS had been formed from dissident soldiers and political extremists who supported the struggle for a French Algeria, and who accused de Gaulle and the politicians of treachery in promoting Algerian Independence. However, the SAC later became an extremist right-wing subversive group that established links with fascist and criminal organisations, including highly profitable drug-trafficking networks. In the 1970s, the Grand Master elect of the Sovereign and Military Order of the Templars, Count Zdrojewski, was in contact with Charly Lascorz, the former head of the SAC – not surprising, since the SAC had gained control of this Templar Order by this time.

Yet another dissident group broke away from the Sovereign and Military Order of the Templars, and established itself as an independent Order in Switzerland. Within a short time a faction led by Anton Zapelli, alleged to have been involved in financial irregularities concerning the Order, broke away from the main branch and formed the new Grand Prieuré de Suisse. He directed his recruitment campaign towards Masons, so it is not surprising that he drew some of his new members from the very secretive Masonic Grand Loge Alpina[1], which itself appears to have connections with the Priory of Sion and the Rennes-le-Château affair. Zapelli based his headquarters, perhaps symbolically, at the ancient town of Sion, in Switzerland

and in an internal circular for members outlined two principal themes of the Grand Priory. There was a strong emphasis on banking and international finance, in which Zapelli's organisation is said to have played an active part. The objective of a united Europe was also high on their agenda, with the assertion that the Grand Priory was dedicated to the fulfilment of an avowed mission of the original Templars – to unify Europe. Attempts to discover direct connections between Anton Zapelli and the other Chivalric Orders, Masonic groups, political parties or criminal organisations have been unsuccessful. However, it is hard to believe that a person of his character, position and interests was not fully aware of the activities of all the other groups, and did not form alliances when expedient to do so.

Meanwhile, a metamorphosis of the Sovereign Order of the Solar Temple was gradually taking place. Though the detail and exact chronology are unclear, certain events and the involvement of certain individuals are indisputable. A key figure was Julien Origas, a French former Nazi sympathiser who, having worked for the SS and the Gestapo at Brest in Occupied France, was arrested after the war and sentenced to five years in prison. Originally a Martinist and a member, under the Grand Master Zapelli, of the OSMTJ, Origas joined the Sovereign Order of the Solar Temple in 1965. Seven years later, having become Grand Master of an off-shoot, called the Ordre Renovée Temple[2] ('Order of the Renovated Temple'), he established links with the European-wide fascist network and other extreme right-wing organisations. At the wedding of Origas' daughter Catherine, in 1977, amongst the wedding guests were Jacques Breyer, Alfred Zapelli, and Joseph di Mambro who would later become a major influence in the Order of the Solar Temple. Di Mambro and Origas were friends and apparently made frequent and regular visits to Italy, where they maintained contact with the rogue Masonic lodge, P2. Some researchers have suggested that Di Mambro had connections with high finance, the international business world and even the Mafia. Both Origas and di Mambro had also belonged to AMORC, the Ancient and Mystical Order of the Rosae Crucis – a Rosicrucian organisation that despite offering legitimate 'occult and spiritual' teachings to genuine adherents has also attracted those with more right-wing views.

In 1979, Joseph di Mambro met the Belgian, Luc Jouret, who was a charismatic figure lecturing on alternative medicine in the New Age circles of Europe and America. Their collaboration was to result in their taking control of the Order of the Solar Temple after the death, in 1983, of Julien Origas.

A British television documentary, screened on 29 December 1997, made the most incredible revelation concerning the Order of the Solar Temple. The Order had already received extensive press coverage three years before due to a series of mass suicides. But the programme revealed that the 'fairytale princess' Grace Kelly, the wife of Prince Rainier III of Monaco since 1956, had been an active but unsuspecting member of the the Sovereign Order of the Solar Temple, the parent organisation from which the Order of the Solar Temple evolved.

Born in 1929, Grace Kelly had been a very successful Hollywood film star before her life in Monaco. Yet the experiences of living in the rather detached and unreal worlds of both Hollywood and Monaco may well have had a psychological impact on her; she was alleged to have suffered from depression. Having had a strict Catholic upbringing, she later found herself in conflict with her faith, and looked for a new purpose in life. These factors appear to have made her vulnerable and susceptible to the overtures of those offering a new brand of spiritual nourishment.

A close friend and advisor of Prince Rainier, Jean-Louis Marsan, interested in esoteric ideas, was encouraged by Jacques Breyer to set up a branch of the Sovereign Order of the Solar Temple at his villa in Monaco, and to become Grand Master. Here members could participate in a spiritual quest. Marsan convinced his followers that they were a spiritual elite whose secret knowledge, gained through the Order, could save the world. Similarly, from 1981, under the influence of Luc Jouret, the members of his offshoot order were subjected to subtle and sophisticated techniques, including the use of holograms, intended to convince them that they were really contacting spirits and seeing sacred objects and symbols – including the Holy Grail.

According to the singer Colette de Réal, an old friend of Princess Grace, she and the Princess attended strange, sexually orientated ceremonies at the Solar Temple centre at Villié-Morgon; her statement has been confirmed by other former members, who note that Princess Grace was present at some of these ceremonies. Situated close to Arginy, this old manor/farmhouse at Villié-Morgon was later bought, in 1983, by a group of Franciscan Friars who discovered a number of artefacts and pieces of unusual furniture there. These were remnants of the rites and rituals of the Order, which appeared to have been a blend of Christian and the occult.

Later, Princess Grace was asked by Joseph di Mambro to donate 20 million Swiss francs to his Order; whether this was for self-enrichment or to be funnelled into a European fascist underground in which he was engaged is not known. What is known is that soon after, on 13 September 1982, the Princess was involved in a fatal car crash on the road leading to Monaco near the point of Cap d'Ail. A cloud of suspicion still hangs over this tragic event, and several details have never been adequately explained.

In 1994, the Order of the Solar Temple achieved world press attention following a series of mass suicides in Canada and Switzerland, and the following year, in France. Amongst the dead were successful professionals, businessmen, and businesswomen – including two millionaires – and astonishingly, the two corrupt leaders di Mambro and Jouret. Even more surprisingly, the dead also included two men said to be members of the French Secret Service. Circumstances at the sites and examination of the charred bodies cast many doubts over the suicide theory; the Canadian deaths were accepted as being murdered, whereas most Swiss victims all suffered several bullet wounds, though these were said to be part of a complex suicide plot. Without doubt other forces were at work, not least to set the buildings on fire after the deaths. Yet another case where speculation will continue to be prolific but, despite a number of tantalising details and a series of high profile trials in French courts, the actual facts will probably never be known[3]. Some investigators claim that there is no link between the original Sovereign Order of the Solar Temple, founded by Jacques Breyer and his associates in 1952, and the Order of the Solar Temple whose members died such tragic deaths. Outwardly, the objectives and practices of the two groups became quite different. However, it is clear that the OSTS leadership was in effect infiltrated over a period of years by those with far right-wing political agendas, as well as those looking for personal financial gain.

But there is another thread to the Templar treasure story. In 1980, Alfred Weysen published *Ile des Veilleurs*, an investigation into the lost treasure of the Knights Templar. Weysen, whose father was a member of the Belgian SS Walloon division headed by Leon Degrelle, and was part of a Nazi group researching and cataloguing castles in the south of France. He concluded that the treasure was to be found in or around two such castles, Soleil and Valcros, in the Gorges de Verdon. In 1972, Robert Spatz founded a Buddhist centre at Château Soleil. At this time the castle was jointly owned by Spatz and his father, also a Nazi collaborator and member of the SS

Walloon division. Endorsed by a group of Tibetan monks who conferred on him the title of lay-Lama, Spatz, and his wife ran a community dedicated to a Buddhist way of life. The subject of several investigations, he was eventually brought before a Belgian Board of Enquiry accused of a range of improprieties that included irregular financial dealings. After a lengthy investigation in the 1990s, he was acquitted. As a result of his inherited properties and financial dealings, Spatz was estimated to be worth at least 50 million French francs.

Meanwhile, in Château Valcros[4], another search was undertaken for the Templar treasure. In 1915, Georges Marcollis, a Pole living in Russia, discovered an ancient parchment lodged in a bible in his family library. Apparently, the parchment had been left by an 18th century monk, Dom Pernety who believed that the lost Templar treasure could be found buried in a cave network near a castle in the Vallée de Croix, in the south of France. Following years of research, in 1955, he located and purchased the ruined Château Valcros. Marcollis was to carry out an extensive search for the elusive treasure until his death in 1967, with no confirmed results. For many years, Weysen assisted in this search for the lost physical treasure; he then changed his focus to the more esoteric. In *Ile des Veilleurs* he reveals his belief that the treasure was actually a giant 6000 year-old zodiac in the landscape of the valley. In an interview with Jean-Luc Chaumeil, he stated that the Belgian Marquis Philippe de Chérisey had met Weysen and had given him an ancient map stolen from Marius Fatin, owner of the castle at Rennes-le-Château. It is said that this map, drawn by the Templars, enabled Weysen[5] to make his discovery.

It is beyond coincidence that the same people crop up in a variety of Orders and neo Masonic organisations, and that many of these have provable right-wing connections. Once initiated, these people normally attain high grades or positions that give them significant influence. But due to the various Orders' similar administrative structures, they remain largely unaccountable to the membership – a potentially dangerous situation. An accurate assessment of the aims and effectiveness of any one of these groups is difficult to undertake due to the secrecy surrounding their meetings and activities. In addition, the aims, frequently found in the realm of the esoteric are often less defined than those of mainstream pragmatic political parties. The Priory of Sion appears to fall into this category. Despite extensive research and publicity, the ultimate agenda and objective of the Priory has never been adequately revealed. Members, former members, critics, journalists, and so-called independent researchers, invariably come to different conclusions ranging from a sophisticated hoax, through delusions of grandeur, to an ancient, powerful organisation in possession of a great secret. The conclusion in this investigation is that the Priory, though certainly not ancient, is not a hoax and is more complex to understand than has been suggested. Without doubt, the views of Plantard, clearly expressed in the wartime journal *Vaincre* form the basis of a philosophy that has driven the Priory at least while Plantard was in control. Whatever they may have said publicly to the contrary, Plantard's known associates must have shared in his views and vision at the time of their involvement, and must have believed that the Priory had a serious basis.

Furthermore, we find that the higher level personnel of the principal esoteric societies belong to more than one group. This is found particularly in Martinism, the Order of the Solar Temple, AMORC, the Sovereign and Military Order of the Temple of Jerusalem (Knights Templar), as well several other neo-Masonic and neo-Chivalric groups. In fact, attempts have been made to bring such groups together, such as the Federatio Universalis Dirigens Ordines Societatesque Initiationis (FUDOSI)[6]. Founded in 1934, its aim was to protect the sacred liturgies, rites and doctrines of the traditional initiatory Orders from being appropriated and profaned by clandestine organisations. The FUDOSI, which dissolved in 1955, was not in itself an Order, but a universal federation of esoteric and autonomous Orders and Societies. More recently, in 1990, the Groupe de Thebes[7] was formed to bring together the heads of various occult groups in secret. The fifteen founder members included a selection of characters immersed in the varied worlds of esoteric studies, Masonry, neo-fascism, traditional Catholicism, Luciferian rites, and far-right politics. Is it a coincidence that many of the members of Thebes are found to play prominent roles in various aspects of this investigation, or have close contacts with those that have? Moreover, many appear to be well aware of the activities of the Priory of Sion and are even in possession of Priory documents.

It has been suggested, without confirmation, that one of the aims of Thebes was the resurrection of the Groupe d'Ur. Founded by Giulio Evola[8], in Italy in 1941, the Groupe was encouraged by the SS to collect documentation and bring together esoteric societies. Ur was disbanded in 1947 and their archives dispersed. It is said that some documents were inherited by the Order of Myriam, which had been founded in 1896 by Giuliano Kremmez. The main aim of the Groupe d'Ur was the foundation of the 'Orden', a synarchic and hidden elite order that would govern a new empire, in opposition to the Nazi SS and its leadership.

The agendas of FUDOSI and Thebes were probably quite innocent, but their culture of secrecy can draw criticism and undue speculation. We will see in the next chapter, however, that the cross-fertilisation of some of these esoteric and occult groups has resulted in activities that are at best sinister and at worst, criminal.

Chapter 18

Intelligence Matters

Although the mystery of Rennes-le-Château springs from the activities and unexplained wealth of parish priest Bérenger Saunière a century ago, it also involves more recent political and financial aspects that are intertwined. We have seen that many secret societies, including the Priory of Sion, have had connections with the financial, business or banking circles, often at international level. Though the extent and result of these contacts is not always fully known, it must be acknowledged that money can buy power and influence, and that political control can be abused to create personal wealth. This combination has attracted many people throughout the centuries with less than honourable intentions; in fact, it is a symptom of occult politics. The extraordinary and sinister activities within the Italian Masonic lodge, P2 (with which Julien Origas and Joseph di Mambro, leaders of the Solar Temple, maintained regular contact) are a case in point.

On 17 June 1982, Roberto Calvi[1], an Italian banker, was found hanging from scaffolding under Blackfriars Bridge, crossing London's River Thames. In the jacket pockets and trousers of his suit were found some half-bricks and large stones, a forged Italian passport, and a wallet with £7000 in various currencies. Initially thought to be a suicide, rumours soon circulated that he had been murdered in order to prevent him from revealing the scandal linking the Vatican Bank to international Freemasonry. These rumours were fuelled by the revelation that the manner of Calvi's death displayed elements of Masonic symbolism, and that his briefcase, known to contain sensitive documents concerning the scandalous dealings between the Vatican Bank, the lodge P2, and the suspect Banco Ambrosiano, had vanished.

In his book *In God's Name*, David Yallop shows that Calvi's death was just the tip of an enormous conspiracy that collided with the political world of Italy and undermined the integrity of the Catholic Church. The lodge Propaganda Due (P2) was not a Masonic lodge in the strict sense of the word, but a secret group of influential and prominent figures formed in order to take power, by a military coup d'état, if the Italian government were to be defeated by the Communists. In the face of a perceived threat of Communist expansion, the business and banking sectors, the Roman Catholic Church and right-wing political groups had supported the formation of extreme anti-Communist secret societies.

In 1981, a huge amount of secret documents pertaining to P2 were seized by the police; they revealed a membership list of over 1000, but later Italian Military Intelligence investigations put the figure nearer to 2000. Amongst the members are said to have been 300 of the most influential men in what was dubbed the 'Free World' – some of which were also connected with the Sovereign and Military Order of the Temple.

P2 was one of three specific groups; the P1 lodge was set up in France, P2 in Italy and P3 in Madrid. The Italian lodge was founded in the late 1960s, allegedly at the instigation of Giordano Gamberini, a Grand Master of the Masonic Grand Orient of Italy, who was a friend of Giulio Andreotti[2], the Christian Democrat politician. Andreotti headed seven post-war governments from 1972 onwards, and was formally charged with corruption and using his position to protect Mafia leaders from justice. Gamberini was also close to Francesco Cosentino who had strong connections with Vatican circles. To set up the lodge, Gamberini chose a successful Tuscan businessman and Master Mason called Licio Gelli[3], but it was persistently maintained by Roberto Calvi that the true head was Andreotti, despite the politician's denials. The real inspiration behind the whole concept, however, was no less than the CIA (itself dedicated to combating Communism), and Opus Dei, an extreme right-wing faction of the Catholic Church which had established itself as the major influence in the Vatican.

Born in 1919, Gelli had acquired a hatred for Communism by the age of seventeen and had fought for Franco in Spain. During World War II, he fought in Albania before serving the Nazi SS in Italy after which he worked as a double agent for the Nazis and partisan Communists. After the war he fled to South America where he became a close friend of the Argentinian dictator General Juan Peron. Following the defeat of Peron in 1956, he continued to expand his power base throughout much of South America. Having become a Master Mason, Gelli was encouraged by Gamberini to conceive a new lodge of important people, and so, under the cloak of Freemasonry, the new lodge, Raggruppamento Gelli (popularly known as P2), was born. One of Gelli's most intimate P2 associates was an Italian lawyer, Umberto Ortolani, who, from his Military Intelligence experiences during WWII, had learned the value of acquiring and storing secret information. As a Catholic he also realised that the true centre of power in his country lay within the walls of Vatican City, and so he set out to penetrate its long and twisting corridors of power. Manipulating his way into the politics of the election of Cardinal Montini as Pope Paul I, Ortolani soon became the recipient of papal awards and honours and extended his sphere of influence to helping his colleagues in P2. He even managed to get Licio Gelli, a non-Catholic, affiliated to the very Catholic but secretive Knights of Malta, and to obtain unrivalled access to the very heart of the Vatican.

Another prominent figure to join P2 was Michele Sindona. A Sicilian lawyer who had profited from black-market trading during the war, he had become an expert in Italian tax laws, thus attracting the interest of the Mafia. Employed by the mighty Gambino Mafia family to launder a huge amount of illegally gained income, he was not slow in developing his own interests and became the director of a number of companies. In 1959, he agreed to help the Archbishop of Milan raise money for an old people's home. In raising the full amount of 2.4 million dollars he attracted the attention of Cardinal Montini, to whom he gave advice on a number of investments. What Montini may not have known was that Sindona had raised the money almost exclusively from the Mafia and the CIA. Covert financial support for the social activities of the Catholic Church was often given by the CIA in the hope that this would help deter the Italian electors from voting for Communism.

Sindona then teamed up with his equally suspect colleague in P2, Calvi, head of a financial empire. Within a relatively short time this shady, ambitious, Mafia-connected individual had become a key financial advisor to the Vatican, even acquiring a bank in Switzerland that still had 29 percent Vatican ownership. Sindona's contacts became prolific and soon ranged from Mafia families, to his old friend Cardinal Montini, now Pope Paul VI, his Cardinals Guerri and Caprio, and the head of Vatican finances, Bishop Paul Marcinkus. Contacts in the political field included heavyweights such as Andreotti and President Nixon, and through his P2 membership, he maintained close links with the dictators that ruled many of the South American countries. Finally, he was able to establish intimate links with some of the world's most powerful financial institutions, Hambros of London, the Vatican Bank, Rothschilds of Paris, and Continental of Chicago. Those involved with P2 turned a blind eye to these and later illegal financial machinations, since the proceeds were thought to be used to support the anti-Communist mission of the lodge. The truth has since been revealed to be somewhat different, and involved the Vatican Bank not only in the loss of millions of dollars but also its financial and ethical integrity.

Sindona and Gelli were now at the centre of an extremely powerful web of politics, finance, and crime.

By mid-1973, through an incredibly complex network of financial institutions and banks, Sindona had skilfully managed to swindle, launder and effectively steal vast amounts of money. At the same time he drew praise for his astute commercial enterprises – not least from the Vatican, for which he seemed to be a most accomplished financial advisor. But time was running out as the huge holes in his own banks, caused by the need to furnish returns for his clients, had reached titanic proportions, becoming increasingly difficult to conceal.

This massive shortfall was the result of siphoning out funds from his depositors accounts into those of his associates, amongst which were P2, the Vatican, the Christian Democrats and right-wing South American governments. A series of financial crises in the USA and Italy exposed the weaknesses of Sindona's empire, and prompted the authorities to begin an investigation. By October 1974, an arrest warrant had been issued. Having taken out Swiss nationality some years before, Sindona fled to Geneva to be safe from prosecution. Within a year his whole empire had collapsed with many banks owned or connected with him, including the Vatican Bank, either collapsing or losing enormous sums; the estimated damage totalled around 1.3 billion dollars. For nealy a decade Sindona devoted his life to avoiding arrest and bancruptcy – resorting extensively to blackmail. Finally, by 1984, Sindona was imprisoned in Otisville prison in the United States sentenced for fraudulent financial activities. He was extradicted to Italy and held in Voghera prison near Milan. On 18 March 1986, he was sentenced to twenty-five years in prison for murder, in 1979, of Giorgio Ambrosoli. Two days later he drank a cup of coffee laced with cyanide. He called his guards shouting, "They have poisoned me!" He died two days later; the official verdict was suicide.

The removal of Michele Sindona from the scene didn't stop his two P2 colleagues, Gelli and Calvi, from continuing business as usual; though by this time both feared the discovery of their criminal activities and went to great lengths to obtain protection. But the net was tightening and Gelli, lured to Switzerland on secret banking business in September 1982, was arrested and imprisoned awaiting extradition. Much to the embarrassment of the Swiss, he escaped almost a year later and was spirited away via Monte Carlo to the relative safety of Uruguay.

A major factor in the collapse of the Sindona-Gelli-Calvi empire was the election in August 1978 of Pope John Paul I. The modernising reforms initiated by John XXIII (Vatican Councill II, 1962–5) had struck a deep chord with a large section of the Church, which was disappointed when many of these never came to fulfilment. The death of Paul VI offered an opportunity to elect a pope who would continue the reforming work of Vatican II. The election of Albino Luciani, Patriarch of Venice, was a triumph for those opposed to the Conservative-dominated Curia and held out the prospect of a Church more in touch with the needs of its almost one billion members – many of which were poor and under-privileged.

Affectionately called 'the smiling pope' for his evident sense of humour and relaxed manner, the truly socialist Luciani took the name John Paul I and set about transforming the papacy. His more liberal attitude to birth control, abortion, divorce and homosexuality was sufficient to draw severe opposition from Opus Dei and other right-wing members of the Curia. But it was his determination to confront the corruption, entrenched within the Vatican, which made him an expendable liability.

Evidently suspicious of the activities of P2, and its connection to certain members of the Curia, the new pope ordered a report – which as we have seen included the state of Vatican finances. Such a report would have revealed the criminal acts of Gelli, Sindona and Calvi, and their involvement with the head of the Vatican Bank, Bishop Marcinkus; it might also have uncovered the hidden hand of Opus Dei pulling the strings. A mere thirty-three days after his election, this fit, energetic and smiling pope was dead. Officially, he was said to have died of a heart attack; but the prior revelation of the scandal of the neo-Masonic lodge P2 added much fuel to the rumours of a suspicious death[4].

The election of Pope John Paul II, by contrast, effectively brought down the shutters on this scandalous affair, with an official denial by the Vatican of any liability. Sindona's former intermediary Paul Marcinkus, responsible for Vatican finances, was recalled to Rome in 1981, where he was promoted to Archbishop and made governor of the Vatican City State. Suffering the indignity of virtual house arrest within the Vatican until his return to the USA in 1990; he risked prosecution in Italy for irregular financial dealings should he have left the sanctuary of the Holy City. He returned to the Archdiocese of Chicago before retiring to Arizona where he lived as a parish priest, refusing to discuss his role at the Vatican. Marcinkus died in

Sun City, Arizona, in 2006, aged 84, of undisclosed causes. Marcinkus vehemently claimed to be innocent and that he had been duped by a friend, others are less charitable and maintain that he was at the heart of the Sindona-Gelli-Calvi conspiracy.

The astounding and illegal activities perpetrated by Sindona, Gelli and Calvi within the shelter of P2 reveals a secret society out of control; a perfect example of how the inherent secrecy found in a lodge, and its network of influential people, can be readily exploited. In this instance, certain organisations, from which one would have expected greater integrity, wantonly assisted the three main conspirators. Justification for the suspect enterprises of P2 was the pursuit of self-interest of the Catholic Church hierarchy and an almost paranoid fear of Communist expansion in Europe. The latter justification claimed by all those in the political and financial sectors that supported Hitler, before and during the war.

An anti-Communist stance had also been a mainstay of Vichy politics and as such had drawn support from the Catholic Church and others, all wishing to advance their own interests. With the war turning in favour of the Allies, many Vichy supporters joined the anti-Nazi Resistance and were sought out by British Intelligence and the Special Operations Executive (SOE) to co-operate in the campaign to disrupt the German occupation of France. Having worked with the Nazis earlier in the war, ex-Vichy Resistants were recognised as having specialised knowledge of the German military, administrative and commercial structures. Naturally, these Resistants had strong fascist or right-wing leanings, but since a large percentage of other Resistance activists was composed of disaffected Communists hoping to achieve power after the war, British Intelligence was naturally wary in its recruitment policy. So by default, the more right-wing elements obtained positions of authority in the Resistance and continued to exercise influence in post-war politics. This trend is confirmed by the exposure of the people associated with the P2 scandal, the Priory of Sion, and other neo-Chivalric organisations operating in Europe and America in the Rennes-le-Château affair.

The end of the war and the defeat of Hitler did not bring an end to the British and American Intelligence activities in Europe. In fact, the perceived Communist threat loomed larger than ever with the partitioning of Berlin. Of particular assistance to the Intelligence services was the extensive network of parish priests throughout Europe, with the help of the Vatican through its own Intelligence service.

The Knights of Malta, formerly the Catholic Knights Hospitaller of St. John, today have their headquarters at the Palazzo Malta on the Via Condotti in Rome. Utilising its worldwide network of over 9000 full Knights and many thousands of lower-grade members, the Order has in effect become the Vatican's Intelligence service. Many prestigious names from other Intelligence agencies known to have had close links with the Vatican – especially from the CIA – have been made Knights[5]. Other prominent individuals from many fields, including politics, the media, and entertainment, have been admitted to the order as a reward for their contribution to supporting and promoting the Catholic faith. Without doubt, the Knight's major role has always been political and until the fall of the Iron Curtain was directed to maintaining a defence against Communism.

British Intelligence (MI6) and the American Office of Strategic Services (OSS), forerunner of the CIA, with the co-operation of the host countries, established so-called 'stay-behind' operations code-named Gladio[6] in Italy and Glaive in France. These were dedicated to a defence against Communism, though not so much an external Communist threat, as the possibility of Communist governments – or even extreme Left-wing – becoming elected in Western Europe. As with the Masonic lodges, the cloak of secrecy and the relative anonymity of members were exploited by agents with their own agendas. It was also not unusual for Intelligence operatives living in the twilight world of deception and unreality to be attracted to the occult, unable to properly discriminate between the worlds of fact and fiction. The teasing mystery of Rennes-le-Château, with its lure of a fabulous treasure, was evidently irresistible to some former Resistants and Intelligence agents; their presence lurks in the shadows of this story.

An extensive investigation of the International League of Antiquarian Booksellers and its supposed traffic in ancient French parchments was undertaken by, Baigent, Leigh, and Lincoln, in their thought-provoking book, *The Messianic Legacy*, the follow-up to *the Holy Blood and the Holy Grail*. Their examination revealed that all the people involved in this unusual incident had connections with the City of London, specifically with the Guardian Assurance Company. It was quite normal during the war that many Intelligence operatives were recruited from insurance companies, their professional expertise considered to be invaluable in planning and executing sabotage missions. Furthermore, Lord Selborne, who is stated to be a central figure in the application to export the ancient parchments in 1956, was overall head of the SOE, whose headquarters at 64 Baker Street was only a stone's throw from the secret London headquarters of the Free French operatives. In a personal interview with Lord Selborne's daughter, his passion for maintaining the integrity of the British Empire and interest in the restoration of other European monarchies was revealed. She also mentioned that he had a great interest in genealogies, and had often enjoyed holidays around the Pyrenees.

Several members of the British-based Rennes-le-Château Research Group have been in contact with former members of British Intelligence, each of whom had an interest in, and a wide knowledge of, the Rennes mystery. These agents also confirmed that many of their colleagues had been members of various occult, Masonic or chivalric societies. It is significant that the fabrication of the Dossiers Secrets and the disclosure of the incident concerning the export of the ancient Rennes-le-Château parchments are typical of almost any Intelligence Service's disinformation techniques. Furthermore, in 1998, a former British Intelligence officer told a Rennes researcher that he had personally seen a room within the Ministry of Defence in the 1970s dedicated to surveillance of the region of Rennes-le-Château. Yet another former Intelligence officer (better known as a highly successful comedian), the late Michael Bentine, warned members of the Rennes Research Group on several occasions that investigation into the affair of Rennes-le-Château could be dangerous. What did he know?

A further fingerprint of Intelligence involvement may be detected in the claim that Pierre Plantard operated under the pseudonym of 'Captain Way' (as we saw previously) during the Algerian crisis of the mid-1950s. Though detail is sparse, it was inevitable that the stay-behind networks would have viewed the deepening crisis with great alarm as France tottered towards civil war. The vacuum left by such political and social upheaval would have provided an ideal opportunity for both the right-wing and the Communists to launch a bid for power. It is therefore not inconceivable that Plantard, with his known right-wing contacts and the political and social zeal displayed during his Vichy affiliation, desired to play some part in controlling this potentially explosive situation. The selection of Annemasse as the headquarters of the Priory of Sion in 1956, of which Plantard was then General Secretary, appears again remarkably coincidental, since Annemasse is reported as being a centre for the anti-Communist 'stay-behind' operations of European Intelligence.

Furthermore as we have seen many times before in this mystery of tangled threads, key individuals appear up at different and apparently unrelated places; this often stretches the bounds of coincidence too far. For example, Herr Wolff who we encountered in the Ariège shadowing the activities of Otto Rahn in his Grail quest, was probably the young newly-enrolled SS officer. Following rapid promotion, Wolff was to become Himmler's Chief of Staff by 1933. Himmler was obsessed with the occult, especially the Grail legends and went to great lengths to acquire artefacts of this nature. It was Himmler who ordered 'Hitler's Commando', Otto Skorzeny, to undertake clandestine excavations at Montségur early in 1944. As a trusted member of Himmler's personal staff who had been involved in Rahn's recruitment into the SS, Wolff was evidently acting as an agent for his superior in his search for the Grail.

In February 1943, Wolff, now a full SS general, was appointed as Military Governor and Supreme SS and Police Leader of northern Italy. The following May, he flew to Switzerland to negotiate the surrender of the German forces in Italy. His contact was Allen Dulles, station chief of the Office of Strategic Services (OSS) in Bern. This series of secret talks, known as Operation Sunrise or Crossword, was carried out between the Nazis, Britain, and the United States. The Soviet Union was deliberately excluded and kept in the dark; an action that was to cause considerable friction. In 1953, Allen Dulles became the first civilian head of the newly-created Central Intelligence Agency (CIA). During his term of duty in Switzerland, Dulles was said to have maintained close contact with the German Resistance to Hitler and to have amassed a great deal of sensitive information on the Nazis. Despite only meagre evidence, it has been said that, even before the war, Dulles was involved with German companies involved in Nazi war preparations, and that he even helped establish the 'ratlines' by which Nazi's could escape to South America. These 'ratlines', in which the Vatican played a vital role, ensured safety for around 30,000 Nazi's, many of which possessed essential skills or knowledge that could be exploited by the British and Americans in their war against Communism.

General Wolff only served a minimum term of imprisonment for his war crimes, allegedly due to his co-operation with the Allies. However, since all negotiations were shrouded in secrecy, we can only speculate on what priceless information he may have gained, and passed on, as a top SS officer and from his pre-war experiences in the Ariège.

There is yet another more surprising relationship that involves the Priory of Sion and US Intelligence. One of the principal architects of the Priory and its mythology was the Belgian Marquis Philippe de Chérisey. De Chérisey married Gloria and, in the 1970s, they had a son Gaspar. Gaspar's godfather was a US Air Force Colonel John Driscoll said to been involved with NATO Intelligence. Also known as Sean O'Driscoll, he was a member of the chivalric Order of Lazarus and after retirement purchased Castle Matrix in Ireland. These facts have been confirmed by Geoffrey Basil-Smith (who corresponded regularly with De Chérisey from 1982 until his death) from a conversation with Liz O'Driscoll, the late Colonel's widow. The connection between de Chérisey and a NATO officer is all the more interesting when we learn that the NATO Commandery of the Templar Order, OSMTJ, whose head was the Portugese Sousa de Fontes, was particularly active in the movement in the 1980s. One has to question why high ranking military officers (US and British) would want to join an organisation with such a dubious history, and, as we saw earlier, even more sinister connections?

Finally, Priory of Sion internal publications reveal that it was run between 1963 and 1981 by a Triumvirate consisting of Pierre Plantard, Gaylord Freeman, and Antonio Merzagora. As with all Priory publications, the veracity of their contents is often dubious and impossible to confirm. Gaylord Freeman, a Chicago banker, was not particularly well known, but according to the *New York Times* biography he was frequently called on by Washington for advice and assistance. When contacted, he denied membership of the Priory and stated that he had never met Plantard. So how did the Priory leadership become aware of Freeman and decide to write him into their mythology?

Even more revealing is the mention of the name Merzagora. Thus far it has not been possible to establish the identity of Antonio Merzagora, or that he actually existed. However, can it be a mere coincidence that at that time Cesare Merzagora was a prominent Italian politician? He was a right-wing Christian democrat, who in 1964 stood in line to assume executive authority of a new Italian government following the assassination of the Prime Minister, Aldo Moro. One of Italy's longest serving prime ministers, Moro had presided over a coalition of Socialists and Christian Democrats before his kidnapping and death at the hands of the extreme left-wing Red Brigade. It has been suggested that right-wing opposition politicians took advantage of this terrorist act and did little to save him. The planned coup, which had the endorsement of the President of Italy, Antonio Segni, was called off and Merzagora never took power, although he did remain President of the Italian Senate until 1967.

Finally, the cover design of Philippe de Chérisey's novel, *Circuit*, published in 1968, clearly shows a Gladius – a short Roman sword – located along the centre line of a hexagon superimposed on a map of France. Gladius is the root of the word Gladio, the name chosen for the 'stay-behind operations' found at the heart of anti-Communist strategy. So once again it is not to believe that the Priory was aware of the political battles in Europe and wished to be associated with a very specific agenda, that of the anti-Communists and the extreme right-wing. In common with other groups of this nature, they attempted to pursue their agenda in the secretive, symbolic, and idealistic world of occult politics.

Chapter 19

Portent and Power

This may be the final chapter of the book, but it is by no means the end of the story; it merely describes a point in time of the continual evolution of Europe's history. Trying to tease out and present the various strands of this tangled web of deception, political intrigue, search for treasure, and drive for power has been at times a tortuous task, made even more difficult by the secretive nature of occult politics. Although the extent of influence exerted by overt religious and political organisations cannot be underestimated, history has been shaped by the activities of unseen forces, although mainstream academia is less inclined to acknowledge them. These underground forces in the political arena, ebb and flow, like tectonic plates occasionally colliding, producing times of stress and conflict. We have seen how the lines between idealism, political opportunism, and criminal deception have become blurred when, in Machiavellian style, the ends are used to justify the means.

In an attempt to unravel the web, we will first review the thread of gold. The lure of gold is timeless, as a symbol of power and wealth, and as a means of achieving them. We have seen in this investigation that gold and treasure have been both the means and the ends. Treasure legends abound throughout the world, but none has attracted as much sustained interest as what remains of the lost treasure of the Temple of Jerusalem, last recorded in the south-west of France nearly 1500 years ago. Commentaries collected from various sources, the works of writers and researchers throughout the centuries suggest that the treasure is probably still deposited in the region of the village of Rennes-le-Château.

Over the centuries, established and proven facts have added weight to the legends, sufficient to convince many of the reality of ancient deposits. But the bulk of the treasure, including that of the Temple, appears never to have been found. In more recent times, treasure-hunters have been seen more openly surveying the region with specialist equipment, including infra-red photography and metal-detectors. The majority of seekers operating under a cloak of secrecy take the necessary precautions to remain anonymous.

Many readers will have had a brief introduction to this story from the publicity arising out of the strange events that occurred a century ago, at the village of Rennes-le-Château. Some have suggested that Bérenger Saunière, the priest of Rennes-le-Château, attained his wealth by the discovery of this particular treasure; it is more likely that he had only discovered the heirlooms that had belonged to the aristocratic Hautpoul family, who had lived in the castle adjacent to his church. But in addition to the family's treasures, hidden a hundred years earlier by Saunière's predecessor Abbé Bigou, were family archives and parchments, the nature of which remains unknown, although the reports arising from their theft from Dr Courrent's library suggests their value. As we have seen, the search for secret precious documents recurs throughout this investigation. In fact, it is a common feature of occult and esoteric societies that they believe each has hidden knowledge: indeed, even the Vatican is alleged to possess true knowledge of the story of Jesus that could undermine its own teachings. It is this belief in secret knowledge deliberately withheld from public view that so effectively fuels conspiracy theories.

Of all the glimpses of events connected to the treasure, some of the most significant are from the dark period of the Nazi occupation of Europe and its aftermath, especially within French and Swiss politics. Obsessed by the alleged power of the Holy Grail, and driven by a vision of a world directed by a modern equivalent of the medieval Teutonic Knights[1], the Nazi leaders Himmler and Rosenberg initiated a search for the lost treasure. For this they employed the specialist services of Nazi SS officers Otto Rahn, Karl Wolff and Otto Skorzeny. The report of Colonel Howard Buechner of the US Army Medical Corps, concerning the actual finds made by the Nazis, cannot be substantiated. But other sources do confirm that the Nazis did acquire a certain quantity of gold, of which some was transported through Central France in 1944, on the orders of General Lammerding. Gold which then fell into the hands of the self-described Resistance activist 'Raoul', in the course of the chance night raid that was to provoke a previously unexplained reaction from the Nazis; the destruction of the village of Oradour and the brutal massacre of its 642 inhabitants.

We have seen how recent findings indicate that the gold theft was actually part of a more widespread web of intrigue than Raoul acting alone. As can be seen from the experiences of Robin Mackness in 1981, the Oradour incident has had repercussions that have continued long after the war. Indeed, it can be claimed that François Mitterrand was aware of the actual truth behind the massacre and the theft of gold, from which those of his 'inner circle' of friends are said to have profited, substantially. These serious and sensitive issues have been investigated by the French justice system, an investigation that unearthed corruption at the highest levels of government. The gold in question is only a small fraction of the wealth amassed by the Nazis from all over Europe throughout the war, much of which was spirited overseas. This so-called 'black' gold[2] is the currency of the murky financial underworld in which governments, dictators, multi-national financial and commercial organisations, and organised crime, participate freely in nefarious dealings.

But within the tragedy of World War II we find other distasteful activities driven by financial expediency and an apparent disregard for ethics, such as the Bank of International Settlements. Established in 1930 from a plan conceived by Hjalmar Schacht (Nazi Minister of Economics from 1933) to handle German reparations settlements from World War I, the bank brought together financial representatives from both the Allied and Axis powers. Whilst the war raged throughout Europe, representatives from the central banks of both sides met, in the most comfortable surroundings of a Swiss castle, to discuss a plan for the economic reconstruction of Europe after the war – irrespective of which side won. Moreover, Montagu Norman, then Governor of the Bank of England, maintained close contact with his old friend Hjalmar Schacht, the man responsible for arranging the financing of Germany's military might. It is quite clear that in the banking world, economic considerations take precedence over human rights.

We have found that Swiss banking secrecy, whilst being highly attractive to investors and depositors, has made it especially vulnerable to accusations of unethical, and at times criminal, dealings. This vulnerability was exposed in the scandal involving the pseudo-Masonic lodge P2 and the Vatican Bank. The superiors of P2 were able to milk the Vatican bank of vast funds, passing them through shell companies and privately owned banks. Swiss banking laws proved to be only too convenient for this gigantic fraud.

The conspiracies and financial irregularities surrounding P2 also revealed the hypocrisy of some of the Vatican hierarchy; this is, however, not unique to this affair, for the Vatican has indeed a long record of unholy activities. Indeed, as one of the world's most powerful political players, the Catholic Church has become embroiled in situations and events in which it has acted in direct opposition to the teachings of its claimed founder, Jesus

Christ. The record of individual indiscretions of popes, cardinals, bishops, and priests is both long and appalling, but in many instances only reflects human frailties. But as an institution, the Catholic Church has to carry the burden of guilt for endorsing policies that have put its own position above that of individual human rights. The support given to fascist dictators; the silence and lack of condemnation for Nazi atrocities, especially to the Jews; the active involvement in subversive occult politics, and its established links with organised crime, do not sit well with fundamental Christian principles. The full involvement of the Vatican in Nazi affairs, including the post-war Ratlines, has extended far beyond a passive, silent acceptance of deplorable activities.

In 1938, Pope Pius XI commissioned an encyclical condemning racism and anti-Semitism, but in 1939, his successor Pope Pius XII refused to publish it – evidently in the hope of appeasing Hitler. Even more damning though, was the complicity of the Catholic Church in the plot to establish escape routes for Nazi officers after the war, of which one was Hitler's right-hand man, the infamous Martin Bormann.

Having engineered his way to the very heart of Hitler's inner circle by 1943, Martin Bormann took effective control of the Nazi administration, by which he was able to amass an enormous quantity of wealth. By the middle of 1944, Bormann, with the help of Otto Skorzeny, his most trusted and able acolyte, had established a network of escape routes out of Germany to Italy, Spain, Egypt, and South America; all countries sympathetic to Nazi ambitions. These escape routes, which often utilised Catholic houses and monasteries, were used not only for the transfer of Nazi officers, but also for the huge amount of wealth they had acquired.

Martin Bormann's wife and family took advantage of an escape route that used a network of priests, known as the Vatican Escape Line, which looked after them until after the war. Unable to escape justice, Bormann's wife was eventually arrested by the Allies, at which time she was found to be in possession of a considerable quantity of foreign coins. Some of these were said to be very ancient – possibly of Visigoth provenance. Bormann, who was never caught, had put himself under the protection of a Franciscan monastery in Genoa and sometime late in 1947, met Bishop Alois Hudal who suggested two avenues of escape; either to join Otto Skorzeny in Spain or to follow Adolf Eichmann to Argentina. Eichmann was the Nazi responsible for conceiving the evil Final Solution – the deportation of Jews to death camps. It cannot surely be just coincidence that Otto Skorzeny, the officer entrusted by Bormann to stockpile wealth and to establish escape routes, was also the officer charged by Himmler in 1944, to find the legendary Holy Grail in the South West of France?

Another thread that has played a major role in the mystery of Rennes-le-Château is the so-called Bloodline. The Bloodline theory arises from the belief that Jesus, besides being the spiritual Christ, had a human nature and married Mary Magdalene, with whom he had children. A reference to a marriage can be found in a 13th century Cathar document, although there is no mention of children. Furthermore, the legend that Mary Magdalene, in the company of her brother, sister, and friends, came to the south of France, has been recognised by both the Catholic Church and the gypsy community at Les Saintes-Maries-de-la-Mer in the Camargue. Despite the lack of any hard evidence, this belief has received widespread support in recent years, spawning a number of books and films[3], becoming inter-twined with the mysterious story of the priest Bérenger Saunière and the mythology of the Priory of Sion.

The mention of Jesus does bring us to another thread, that of the Grand Monarch or Lost King. In the occult world, the Grand Monarch, referred to by Nostradamus[4], represents a ruler, in both the temporal and spiritual sense, who will preside over the end of the current era and the dawn of a new Golden Age. Although the central theme is common to all, details vary between groups, some believing that this leader already exists, ruling over the underground kingdom of Agartha situated in the Himalayas. The theme of the Grand Monarch is given some prominence in the various publications of Pierre Plantard and his Priory of Sion. In fact, Plantard grandiosely refers to himself in this role, although it is hard to believe that he took it seriously. Researchers have even been able to show that some of the events and language of the Priory of Sion were in fact carefully cho-sen to relate to prophecies by Nostradamus, suggesting that Plantard and his allies appreciated the power of Nostradamus prophecies in the occult world. Although Plantard later attempted to distance himself from the ge-nealogy of the Merovingian kings and the role of the Grand Monarch, his early publications clearly demonstrate his self-belief as a political saviour of France.

For some Christians, the Grand Monarch refers to the Second Coming of Jesus. They believe that the Christian Church has become corrupted and is in the hands of the Antichrist; some are even convinced that the pope himself is the Antichrist. The prophecies of the 12th century monk, St Malachy, suggest that the present pope may be the penultimate before the Second Coming, at which Satan and his followers will be cast from the Earth and the Faithful will be saved. Messages received from the Virgin Mary at La Sallette, and the writings of the Hiéron du Val d'Or, also refer to the advent of Christ the King who will sweep away the alleged corruption in the Catholic Church and bring about a spiritual renaissance.

Various Jewish groups are also awaiting a return of a spiritual leader, but this belief also contains a dramatic political dimension that, if fulfilled, could have cataclysmic consequences.

The ancient treasure pillaged from the Temple of Jerusalem has a value far in excess of its material worth. The seven-branched candlestick, the Menorah, and its other religious items have enormous symbolic value for all Jews, especially the Orthodox, their value exceeded only by that of the Ark of the Covenant itself. Should any of these items be found and made public, the effect on the Jewish communities in Jerusalem, and elsewhere, would be dramatic, almost certainly resulting in a call from the Orthodox to rebuild the great Temple of Herod from the ruins that can be seen today.

In fact, Rabbi Ariel Bar Tzadok, an expert in the Torah and cabalistic prophecy, reported in 1997, that a cornerstone for the future third temple had already been laid less than fifty metres from the Mosque at the centre of the Temple Mount. According to Old Testament prophesy, the rebuilding of the Temple and the return of Jews to Israel will herald the return of the 'true' messiah. There can be no doubt that many religious Jews are eagerly awaiting a 'divine' signal to commence this rebuilding.

Such a move would reopen one of the biggest wounds perceived and endured by the State of Israel, the presence of the Islamic shrine known as the Dome of the Rock constructed at the very heart of what was the ancient Jewish Temple. Erected in the 7th century, over the rock from which, according to Muslim tradition, Mohammed ascended into heaven, the resplendent golden Dome, one of the holiest Islamic shrines, is visited annually by millions of Muslims. It is inconceivable that the Muslim authorities would permit the removal of their precious and sacred Mosque to facilitate the building of a new Temple of Jerusalem.

But Jerusalem and the Second Coming has received attention from other quarters. *The Daily Telegraph* reported on 14 October 1998, that 5000 Christians marched through Jerusalem in support of the State of Israel. The marchers were fundamentalists, calling themselves Christian Zionists, who believe that the State of Israel is part of God's plan for the world. A growing political force, especially in the United States, their foundation could well have been a reaction to the appearance of another fundamentalist sect, the Nation of Islam. Under the leadership of Louis Farrakhan (banned from entering Britain for his anti-Semitic speeches), the Nation of Islam has grown to an estimated one million supporters worldwide. According to the media, the Nation of Islam is overtly racist, anti-Semitic, homophobic, and is often compared with white supremacy groups. Dedicated to the establishment of an independent Black state, the Nation encourages Blacks to adopt the Islamic faith for solidarity.

We have also seen that the rebuilding of the Temple of Jerusalem is the aspiration of British Israelites, who believe that the British Empire was the fulfilment of the promises given by God to Abraham. A rebuilt Temple of Solomon would be a physical symbol and focus for a new universal Masonic religion that could unite Christians, Jews and Muslims. One of the aims of British Israelites and their supporters is said to be the restoration of the Jewish biblical treasures, including the fabled Ark of the Covenant. In the light of this, it is perhaps less surprising that so many Masonic rites are based on episodes from the Old Testament. It is clear that the hope for a new age heralded by the return of the Grand Monarch is one in which spiritual considerations take precedence over the more mundane practical politics. There are groups, however, that whilst calling for a spiritual reformation of society, are in reality pursuing an agenda of elitism and authoritarianism. It can be seen that the genesis of many of these groups lies in the wartime arenas of Nazism and Fascism.

In many ways, this final thread in the web of power is inseparable from the others. It is the primary driving force for evolution and change at both the public and covert levels. Political ambition requires power and wealth in order to achieve influence, especially true in the world of occult politics. This thread is itself comprised of several strands including those of domestic, regional, and global politics.

Since the Romans, the history of Europe and the world is largely a commentary of imperial ambition pursued, in the main, by military might.

European monarchs, aristocracies, and political leaders, driven by a voracious appetite for power and wealth, colonised other continents in order to exploit their natural resources. The tragedy of World War I effectively sounded a death knell to these old empires. Even the British Empire, on which the sun was said never to set, fell into terminal decline as its constituent nations achieved independence. Other nations were soon to fill the void but this time principally motivated by ideological expansion. The first and most significant of these was caused by the overthrow of the Russian Tsar and the subsequent formation of the powerful Soviet Union (USSR), built largely on the philosophy of Karl Marx. Thus from 1917, European countries were exposed to the threat of Communism, which in only two decades would escalate to threaten world peace; a threat, possibly more perceived than actual, that would continue to dominate the foreign policies of European countries and the United States of America for over seventy years.

The trauma of World War I demoralised the majority of Europe's political classes. A more optimistic minority believed the future lay in a united Europe freed from the traditional nationalistic aggression. Hence, in 1923, the Austrian Count Coudenhove-Kalergi founded the Pan-European Movement. Three years later, he managed to bring together diverse political figures for the First Pan-European Congress, held in Vienna. In 1929, Aristide Briand, French Prime Minister, addressed the Assembly of the League of Nations at which he presented the idea of a federation of European nations based on solidarity and on the pursuit of economic prosperity and political and social co-operation. The stated goal of the proposed federation was the unity of a Christian Europe, free of "nihilism, atheism and immoral consumerism". Thus, Kalergi's concept of a European union was the first step in creating a political bulwark against Communist expansion. The Union was banned, in 1933, by the Nazi hierarchy who had their own visions of European unity[5]. The Union was resurrected after the war. Following the death of Count Kalergi, in 1973, Archduke Otto von Habsburg, ardent supporter of European unity, became International Honorary President until 2004. It may be significant to recall that the Holy Roman Empire, a monarchy that extended over most of central Europe, was ruled by the Habsburg dynasty, from 1452, for nearly 500 years.

This apparently benign attempt at European unity was followed by a very much more sinister one, the ambitions of Adolph Hitler and the National Socialist Party. Ostensibly to reunite the German-speaking people, Hitler embarked on the invasion and annexation of several neighbouring countries, followed by a rapid expansion into the majority of other European countries. Hitler's campaign was given support by Italy's fascist dictator, Mussolini, who despite a background as a Socialist declared himself to be an ardent defender against Communism. Spain, although remaining neutral throughout the war, also embraced fascism. Following a coup in 1936, followed by three years of bitter fighting, the Spanish government fell to General Franco who imposed a fascist dictatorship that lasted until his death in 1975. Spain's neutrality proved to be extremely useful to both the Allies and the Nazis during and after the war.

The rise of such militant fascist power was viewed with alarm by many of Europe's political leaders. But when Germany's Non-Aggression Pact with the Soviet Union collapsed, others regarded the Nazi regime as a convenient defence against Communism, the worst of the two evils. Communism was considered an unacceptable political philosophy by the West, since it rejected the concept of the 'free market', and by the Judeo-Christian Churches for whom there was no place in this state-controlled society. So it is less of a surprise to discover the level of support given to the Nazi war machine by Allied banks and commercial enterprises; the rationale being that a ferocious battle between Hitler and Stalin would weaken them both to the point that either would be easy prey to Allied forces. This was not to be and for forty years this clash of ideologies between the Soviet Union and America cast a dark shadow over Europe and threatened, at times, to lead to a third world war.

But prior to 1939, there were those who looked in admiration at Hitler's 'economic miracle' and the renewed pride of the German people; just as Hitler admired the achievements of the British Empire. We must not forget the close family ties of the British Royal Family and some of the aristocracy to Germany. Furthermore, Germany's domestic programme of building a modern infrastructure and a military machine required vast funding and resources, and since to coin a phrase 'business is business', there were great opportunities for European and American banks and corporations. Operating indirectly and covertly, often through subsidiaries, their involvement was unseen and it was not until well after the war that the extent of this exploitation of market opportunities became public knowledge. But this is not a new business phenomenon; financial and commercial interests have backed both sides of a conflict throughout history.

This fear of Communist expansion into Europe provided justification for various clandestine activities of Western Intelligence agencies, which, perhaps naively, opened the door to unethical behaviour, political opportunism, and even criminal activity. We have seen how the Allies, with the co-operation of the Catholic Church set up the Ratlines by which thousands of Nazis, some wanted for war crimes, escaped prosecution and justice. A great many of these Nazis were considered to have specialist knowledge in Intelligence, science and technology, business administration and banking, and other spheres useful to other nations; some just bought their way to freedom using plundered Nazi gold. Consequently, the Allies were to gain extensive Intelligence of the Soviet Union, providing the United States with the science to build a nuclear bomb and launch a space programme, and South American dictators the wealth and expertise to maintain their police states.

Closer to home, the Communist fear gave rise to the strategy known as Stay-Behind operations commonly called Gladio. Principally comprised of secret arms caches and specially trained urban guerrilla forces (into which were recruited crack former SS soldiers), established throughout Europe under the overall control of NATO, Gladio's anti-Communist invasion objective was to give way to a more domestic political agenda. Denied for over thirty years, official recognition of Gladio operations has finally been given by most European governments. What they do not admit to, however, is the subversive role played by Gladio in influencing the choice of domestic governments. A prime example of this was P2 in Italy, which, as we saw, was to have major repercussions in the political and financial worlds.

The exploitation of the secretive neo-Masonic lodge P2 with its mainly right-wing membership is only one example of the strategy of infiltrating secret societies for political and even criminal purposes. The fundamental structure and philosophy of secret and occult groups creates a vulnerability to such infiltration and exploitation. With a leadership to whom are accorded grandiose titles such as Grand Master, Imperator, or Grand Prior, and a closely ordered hierarchy that demands obedience and deference from ordinary members, these groups are perfect vehicles for those seeking power and influence. Hiding behind diversionary cloaks of chivalry, spiritual enlightenment, charitable works, and other avowedly noble aims, some unscrupulous members within these societies are able to engage in activities as unpalatable as paedophilia, fraud, the pursuit of extreme right-wing agendas, racism, and subversion. That is not to say that most secret societies or their members are engaged in anything less than honourable activities, only to point out how vulnerable they are to such abuses.

There have been secretive societies set up deliberately to serve a hidden agenda, especially in the field of occult politics. Although their presence is known, great efforts are taken to protect the true nature of their aims. It is in this category that we find the Pinay Circle. In 1969, Antoine Pinay, a French cabinet minister and later Prime Minister, Jean Violet, a Parisian Lawyer, and Archduke Otto von Habsburg, a key figure in international right-wing para-politics, combined to form the Pinay Circle, also known as the Cercle Violet. The leadership of the Circle was heavily involved with two other right-wing movements, the Pan European Union and the Centre Européen de Documentation Internationale (CEDI), founded in 1949 by Archduke Otto and Alfredo Sanchez Bella, one of Franco's ministers, said to have been head of Spanish secret service operations in Europe and, like his brother, a leading member of Opus Dei. Jean Violet's prominent role in this political milieu adds weight to the claim that he had been a member of the Deloncle-Abellio CSAR (examined in chapters 14 and 16), and was yet another ardent supporter of Opus Dei.

It was not long before the Pinay Circle was at the heart of a network of movements and representatives of Western governments, with an Atlanticist (supporters of close political ties to the United States) and right-wing agenda. As secretive, and perhaps sinister, as the Bilderberger Group, the Pinay Circle became a right-wing organisation of serving and retired Intelligence officers, military officers, and politicians that, amongst other aims, has conspired to affect changes in government. There is ample documented evidence to suggest that the group was behind the attempted destabilisation in Britain of Harold Wilson, Jeremy Thorpe, and Edward Heath; and later engineered the election of Margaret Thatcher, a devotee of free market economics and a close ally of US president, Ronald Reagan.

At the time of the Socialist François Mitterrand's first unsuccessful bid for power, in 1974, the head of the French secret service was Pinay member, Alexandre de Maranches. It appears more than mere coincidence that when Mitterrand finally became elected in 1981, Maranches resigned immediately. Politicians of other countries are thought to have experienced similar fates, but there is no available evidence to confirm them. The proven examples do, however, clearly demonstrate an abuse of power by hidden power, and are an affront to the democratic process.

So far, our focus has been limited to the conflict between the forces of Communism represented by the old Soviet Union and the Capitalist, Democratic Free Market of the United States of America. But recent world events have revealed another power that for nearly 150 years has remained largely unknown in the nebulous and shadowy world of occult politics. First coined by Saint-Yves d'Alveidre in the late 1800s, the proponents of Synarchy, and its modern variants, have become a new, but less tangible, enemy to the United States and its allies.

We saw how, during World War II, Synarchist groups, such as X-Crise and the Uriage schools, emerged in and around the Vichy government; although of different names and methods, they shared the same political philosophy. The end of the war didn't bring an end to their aspirations, and as we have seen in the case of ex-Nazis, Synarchists have continued to pursue their own agendas, but in the modern environment of occult politics and covert finance. Furthermore, the recent advances in information technology have allowed previously disconnected groups to network, bringing together surprisingly diverse cultural traditions that share the Synarchist philosophy. So the battle today is now between three ideological and political powers, a new style Russian federation that is rebuilding itself from the ashes of the Soviet Union, the free market Democracy championed by the United States, and a Synarchist fusion of a European New Right, traditional Islamic and Eastern cultures, and those opposed to an unregulated free market and progressive liberalism, considered to be the cause of social disintegration.

As is so often the case in the political world, interpretation and perception have a greater impact than the facts. Frequently the sound-bite that makes the headlines is a distortion of the actual message. This can be a tactic, commonly referred to as 'spin', deliberately employed by politicians; on the other hand, it can be the failure of one culture to 'read' the message accurately. The current political stance of the United States Republican government and its allies can be summed up by a quote from the Project for the New American Century[6].

The Project for the New American Century is a non-profit educational organisation dedicated to a few fundamental propositions: that American leadership is good both for America and for the world; and that such leadership requires military strength, diplomatic energy and commitment to moral principle. This is interpreted by the Russian philosopher, Alexander Dugin[7], in the following terms. He understands, in his words, that the dominant US political philosophy rests on four essential principles:

1. Economical: the ideology of the New World Order presupposes a complete and mandatory establishment of the liberal capitalist market system all over the planet, with no regard to cultural and ethnic regions. All socio-economic systems carrying elements of "socialism," "social or national justice," and "social protection" must be completely destroyed and turned into societies of "absolutely free market." All past flirtations of mondialism with "socialist" models are coming to a complete halt, and market liberalism is becoming the single economic dominant on the planet, ruled by the World Government.

2. Geopolitical: the ideology of the New World Order gives unconditional preference to countries comprising geographical and historical West in contrast to countries of the East. Even in the case of a relatively Western location of one country or another, it will always be favoured in comparison with its neighbour to the east. The previously implemented scheme of geopolitical alliance of the West with the East against the Centre (for example, capitalist West, together with communist Russia against national-socialist Germany) is no longer in use by contemporary mondialism. Geopolitical priority of Western orientation is becoming absolute.

3. Ethnic: the ideology of the New World Order insists on utmost racial, national, ethnic, and cultural intermixing of peoples, giving preference to the cosmopolitism of large cities. National and mini-national movements, used earlier by the mondialists in their fight against "greater nationalism" of the imperial type, will be decisively suppressed, as there will be no place left for them in this Order. On all levels, national politics of the World Government will be oriented towards intermixing, cosmopolitism, melting pot, and so forth.

4. Religious: the ideology of the New World Order is preparing the coming into the world of a certain mystical figure, the appearance of which is supposed to sharply change the religious-ideological scene on the planet. Ideologists of mondialism are themselves convinced that what is meant by this is the coming into the world of Moshiah, the Messiah who will unveil laws of a new religion to humanity and will perform many miracles. The era of pragmatic use of atheist, rationalist, and materialist doctrines by mondialists is over. Now, they are proclaiming the coming of an epoch of "new religiosity."

Whether this interpretation is fully or partially correct, is unfortunately less significant than the truth since it is believed to be true, not just by a Russian political philosopher and activist, but by a network of occult political groups and individuals opposed to unfettered Capitalism, or seeking a past golden age.

In contrast to the American stance, the Synarchist position is best summed up again in the words of Alexander Dugin. The ideology radically opposed to mondialism can also be described on four levels:

1. Economical: priority of social justice, social protection, and "communal," national factor in the system of production and distribution.

2. Geopolitical: a clear orientation towards the East and solidarity with the easternmost geopolitical sectors in considering territorial conflicts, and so forth.

3. Ethnic: allegiance to national, ethnic, and racial traditions and traits of peoples and states, with a special preference for "greater nationalism" of the imperial type in contrast to mini-nationalisms with separatist tendencies.

4. Religious: devotion to original and traditional religious forms – most importantly, Orthodox Christianity and Islam, which clearly identify "new religiosity," New World Order, and Moshiah with the most sinister player in the eschatological drama, the Antichrist (Dadjal in Arabic).

It is immediately obvious that a clash of these competing ideologies could not have been avoided since they are diametrically opposed with little if any common ground; where the West is largely practical and progressive, the Synarchist is idealistic and traditional. The current conflicts with factions of the Islamic world can be explained to a large extent by their entrenched ideological differences.

But what of the Communist threat? Since the fall of the Berlin Wall in 1989, the Communist threat for Europe and the wider world has been significantly reduced. The most populated country on Earth, the Communist, Peoples Republic of China, does not appear to have expansionist ambitions; indeed, in recent years it has shown a willingness to engage in world trade and modern diplomacy. A new Russia is emerging out of the ruins of the old Soviet Union, one that despite embracing elements of Democracy and free market economics, is actually dedicated to rebuilding its power base and to becoming again a major force in world politics[8]. In the *Daily Telegraph*, 2 December 2000, an article entitled 'Will the Russian Bear Roar Again', outlines Russian political ambitions. These ambitions include a Europe–Asian axis between Russia, India and China. Furthermore, President Putin has pursued overtures with North Korea, Libya and Iraq. A paper by Putin entitled 'Russia always felt itself as an Eurasian country', describes in greater detail the steps that will be taken to consolidate Russia's economic and political growth. The key theme is that of Russia's role in creating a new Euro-Asian power block, following the geopolitical theory proposed by Alexander Dugin.

The Eurasianist Party was founded by Dugin in 2002, and is said to receive financial support from the office of President Putin. Borrowing from the ideology of a movement created by the Russian émigrés in 1920, Eurasianists believed that Russia's civilization owed more to Asia than Europe. We can see from Dugin's writings (translated from the original Russian), that he favours a new Russian Empire in which the constituent nations co-operate at various levels without sacrificing any of their cultural independence. In addition he states that 'The new Eurasian empire will be constructed on the fundamental principle of the common enemy: the rejection of Atlanticism, strategic control of the USA, and the refusal to allow liberal values to dominate us. This common civilisational impulse will be the basis of a political and strategic union.'

It is thus not surprising to find that the philosophy behind Eurasianism is warmly embraced by Synarchists who share many of the fundamental principles. But what of the mystery of Rennes-le-Château and the Priory of Sion? We have travelled a long way from the dusty village nestled in the foothills of the Pyrenees to the arena of international politics; and from the somewhat anachronistic Priory of Sion to the modern world of global power blocks.

Despite the wonderfully inventive account of their history, the founding of the Priory of Sion only dates from about 1956, when for the first time their statutes were deposited with the authorities near Geneva, in accordance with French Law. Its principal architects, Pierre Plantard, Philippe de Chérisey, Gérard de Sède, and Louis Vazart, are now dead. Of the remaining known Priory members, Gino Sandri is still active, and their initial promoter to national and world fame, Jean-Luc Chaumeil, has assumed the role of critic and debunker; inevitably their accounts differ. So we will probably never know the absolute truth of the nature and motives of this enigmatic organisation into which so much time, energy, and thought, has been expended with apparently little reward. Without doubt, the Priory was involved at some level in the world of occult politics. Our only recourse has been to examine their own publications, looking for signs and symbols, and to place them in the context of the prevailing political climate.

From his writings in the wartime journal, *Vaincre*, we can see that Plantard had an interest in, and knowledge of, prominent occult groups and the embryonic New Age movement that sought to embrace the mystical and idealistic Age of Aquarius. To this was fused a belief in the politics of Marshal Pétain and the Vichy government for the salvation of France, in which he desired to play a key role as Pierre de France. Thus, the Priory of Sion emerged from the shadow of Vichy politics, at a time when French nerves were still raw from the collaborationist activities of many of its citizens, and when the Russian Bear cast a long shadow over Europe. Having witnessed, within thirty years, two of the bloodiest conflicts in world history on their own soil, and been occupied by a brutal foreign power, it is understandable why many French citizens were disenchanted with their former leadership and administration. President de Gaulle offered himself as the new saviour of France, more in the role of the Grand Monarch than a political appointment; François Mitterrand was to do the same, both realising that portrayal of a sense of destiny and tradition is key to the French psyche.

A sense of national pride and destiny, and the legacy of centuries of glorious, though at times turbulent, history have profoundly shaped French culture. A key element is the tendency towards the esoteric and the liberal use of symbolism, exemplified in French literature. It is for this reason that so many esoteric and occult societies were either born or at least flourished in France; and the sphere of occult politics is as accepted and widespread as the orthodox. This is in marked contrast to Britain and the other Anglo-Saxon nations. Without appreciating this fundamental difference in psychology and culture, we will never understand the nature of the Priory of Sion and similar organisations.

How influential the Priory was, or still is, will probably never be known unless new unpublished documents are discovered. But occult societies form a network, and the influences are subtle, so it is possible that ideas generated within the Priory have permeated into other groups and from there to wider political levels, and vice-versa. An illustration in *Vaincre* reveals an aspiration towards a United States of the West, 1937 to 1946, from Brittany to Bavaria. A knight, riding along a road towards the rising sun in which can be seen the symbol of the Age of Aquarius, holds a flag with the Cross of the South surrounded by seven stars. Published in 1942, this reveals Plantard's support for the concept of a united Europe, with a Franco-German axis, even during a time of great conflict. The same hope was at the heart of the Pan European movement and the dreams of Jean Monnet, father of the European Union, both of which believed in a strong Franco-German axis. Was this not the same motive for Mitterrand's covert financing of Helmut Kohl's German Christian Democrat Party? There have been continuous allegations that the European Union, despite its outwardly democratic structure, is heavily influenced, and even controlled, by covert groups with little regard for democracy.

But what are we to make of the alleged links between the Priory and the mystery of Rennes-le-Château? Despite the unsubstantiated claim that the Abbé Saunière was visited, in 1891, by members of the Priory of Sion who informed him of the presence of a secret treasure buried somewhere within his parish, any genuine link between the Priory and Rennes-le-Château has yet to be confirmed. A nine page booklet entitled, *Un trésor mérovingien à Rennes-le-Château*, by Antoine l'Ermite (patently a Priory pseudonym), reportedly published in 1961, is in fact a direct copy of an extract from a chapter of Robert Charroux's *Trésors du Monde*, published in 1962. To add to their mythology, Plantard declared, at a meeting in 1979 with the authors of *the Holy Blood and the Holy Grail*, that the Priory of Sion did hold the lost treasure of the Temple of Jerusalem. He further stated that it would be 'returned to Israel when the time is right'. Plantard insisted, however, that the real treasure was not material but a spiritual secret, the revelation of which could facilitate a dramatic social change.

Since these declarations, taken at face value, are obviously untrue, either they are the delusional ramblings of an eccentric or they need to be interpreted on a different level. This investigation would tend to favour the latter. Certainly, Plantard was convinced of the existence of the treasure. His purchase of land, in which it is thought to be buried, is confirmation. It is probable that the Priory references to the treasure were a recruitment tactic, aimed at those who may have information or the means to help search for it. Perhaps more significantly, the Priory's mythology contains a multitude of signs and symbols, frequently employed by occult groups, which convey hidden, possibly subliminal, messages. Messages designed to attract individuals with an interest in occult politics, most specifically to promote the right-wing orientated Synarchist model.

Conflict and turmoil continue in the realm of international politics with the so-called War on Terror, the desire to secure energy sources, the stark clash of cultures, the insatiable needs of the free market, and the quest for a better world. In all of this, the conventional military powers are being joined by new forces influenced by occult philosophies and empowered by ideas. Ideas, born and nurtured in cyberspace, are networked throughout the world via the internet. Due to this powerful technological tool, global politics will never be the same again. Only one thing is certain, no-one can accurately arrange or predict the future: but if we could, what future would we choose?

Sitting on the ramparts of Saunière's folly in the shadow of the emblematic Tour Magdala, it is hard to believe that this tumbledown village, and its history, has become the focus for one of the world's greatest treasures, and the symbol of a powerful manifestation of occult politics. But politics are about perception – and, as we have seen, sometimes deception. Whether a veritable treasure of Solomon does rest under or near this small hill-top village is of lesser importance than the belief that it does; in the symbol-filled world of occult politics, with its Masters of Deception, truth and reality are of secondary importance. In fact, there is little place for the truth in their seductive fantasies, carefully constructed to obscure the pursuit of their ambitions, the drive for real geopolitical influence, and the ultimate victory of their ideology. In the conspiratorial world of occult politics, Fiction is often more important – and revealing – than Truth.

~

Notes

Chapter 1

1. The account of 2 Chronicles, ch 9 mentions the presence of the most incredible treasures of gold, silver and precious gems, much of which was supposed to be a gift of the Queen of Sheba. However, most of this was to disappear in the sackings of Jerusalem by the Egyptian pharaoh Shishak in about 930 BC and later, in 586 BC, by the Babylonian king, Nebuchadnezzar. 2 Chronicles, ch 36 also reports that at that time all the city's residents were taken into captivity in Babylon. Great emphasis is placed on the fate of the treasure, and in verse 18 it is recounted that, "all the vessels of the house of God, great and small, and the treasures of the house of the Lord, and the treasures of the king, and of his princes ; all these he brought to Babylon". Before leaving the city, the Babylonians broke down its walls, and set fire to the Temple and the all the royal palaces.

   'Three score and ten' years later however, the Jews were to return to Jerusalem. In Ezra, chapters 1, 2 and 3, it is reported that under the direction of Cyrus, King of Persia, not only was the Temple reconstructed, but also an enormous quantity of treasure was returned to its precincts.

   The most important source of information about the Roman campaign comes from the writings of Josephus, a former Jewish commander who had been arrested in Galilee in 67 AD. A shrewd and persuasive man, he managed to gain the confidence of the Emperor Vespasian and even became a military adviser to the Roman commanders given the task of overseeing the destruction of Jerusalem. Taken to Rome after the fall of Masada, he spent his days compiling detailed histories of the times. In his Jewish Wars against the Romans, Josephus confirms the pillaging of the Temple treasure: 'Among the great quantity of spoils, the most remarkable being those that had been taken from the Temple of Jerusalem, the Table of Gold that weighed several talents and the golden Chandelier made with such skill to make it worthy of the use to which it was destined'.

2. Confirmation of the existence of a huge treasure, deposited in and around Jerusalem, was found in 1952 during the excavations of an important religious settlement by the Dead Sea. In a cave at Qumran, researchers discovered a scroll of rolled copper upon which had been engraved an inventory of the nature and locations of this treasure. The exact sites were not easily identifiable to modern researchers, but a considered estimate of the actual quantity of treasure revealed some sixty-five tons of silver and twenty-six of gold. These were secreted within and around the precincts of the Temple, just prior to the Roman invasion.

3. *The principal focus of the Roman attack was the magnificent temple that dominated Jerusalem from its position straddling the hill of Mount Moriya, to the south of which is Mount Sion. The Temple of Jerusalem was less of a military target than a symbolic one: it represented the heart of the Jewish nation itself. The building under siege had been erected on the command of King Herod, who had reigned over Judaea immediately before the birth of Jesus. But it had been constructed on the foundations of a much older temple, which in turn is alleged to have replaced the legendary Temple of Solomon, built to house the Ark of the Covenant.*

   Around 35 BC, dissatisfied with the existing temple, Herod, on his accession, decided to build a more splendid replacement intended to rival Solomon's Temple of legend. Though little now remains, the dimensions of Herod's Temple are impressive; the temple buildings were built on a platform approximately 470m long and 300m wide, about nine and a half times the area of St. Peter's Basilica in Rome. But Herod's Temple no longer housed, in its Holy of Holies, the Ark of the Covenant, that most symbolic of all the ancient Jewish artifacts. This disappeared from all accounts sometime between 750 BC and 650 BC. The power of the symbolism of the ancient Temple is still in evidence today, as thousands of orthodox Jews pray in front of the Wailing Wall, its oldest surviving part.

4. *Evidence that the Visigoths had possession of an immense treasure is borne out not only by the Guarrazar artefacts (a magnificent collection of jewelled crowns and crosses, known as the Treasure of Guarrazar, on display in Madrid's National Archaeological Museum), but from commentators and historians including Procopius, El Macin, Fredegaire, and the Englishman, Gibbon. That this included the spoils of Rome is confirmed by their references made to the Missorium, a magnificent jewel-encrusted golden plate weighing about 100 pounds, and also to the Emerald Table with its gold stands and pearl inlay.*

5. *The Franks then turned their attention to the Visigothic fortress of Carcassonne. According to the Greek historian, Procope of Caesarea, in his De Bello Gothico, the Franks too were fully aware of the treasure, which they also believed to have come from the ancient Temple of Jerusalem. While at this point physical documentary record of the fate of the treasure becomes obscured, the prevailing legend supported by the historian Firmin Jaffus and the archaeologist Cros-Mayrevieille, affirms that the treasure was now removed from Carcassonne.*

6. *Among the region's extensive cave networks, two in particular are worthy of mention. Right in the heart of the Hautes-Corbières is to be found the tiny village of Auriac, a name that recalls its association with ancient goldmines (the French for gold being 'or') as does the hamlet, L'Auradieu, and the little stream the Aurio. Close to the village is another steam, the Rec de L'Érmita, which emerges from a cave network around which are ancient*

mines, one of which is called L'Hérmita, possibly derived from L'Ermite, the Hermit. The church at Rennes-le-Château, renovated in the late 19ᵗʰ century, is decorated with many symbols that refer to both caves and hermits. Just south of Rennes-le-Château is the Grotte du Carla.

Like many of the other cave networks, both of these have proved difficult, dangerous or even impossible to explore fully from their known access points. It may well be that some of these caves are more safely accessible from other ways yet to be popularly discovered. Interestingly, the words *carla* and *aven* (cave) appear in a message decoded from a cryptogram found at Rennes-le-Château after the death of its priest in 1917. It is a curious message containing direct references to the Hautpoul family, the Visigoths, the Templars, treasure, and a dead king.

7. According to the chronicle *Vita Arbogasti* Dagobert did have a son called Sigisbert but he died a little before his father in 678. Another source claims Sigisbert died shortly after his father. It appears, therefore, that official history states that he died between the 678 and 680. Nothing more is known of this young prince for certain, thus providing the opportunity to create an alternative and persuasive history.

8. The Knight's Stone, generally considered to be of the Carolingian era, is currently on display in the museum at Rennes-le-Château. It is badly eroded from weathering, having been placed in the church garden in front of 'un croix de mission' by Saunière in 1905. Its present condition has prevented an accurate interpretation of the original relief.

9. There is some evidence to suggest that the Merovingians were of Semitic origin. Linguists have studied the mutation, Levi – Clovis – Louis. The name Mérovee-Levis can be shown to have given rise to Levis-Mirepoix. There is also the story of Frederick the Great, who when showing the Duc de Levis Mirepoix a canvas representing the Virgin Mary, said, 'Ah Levi, my dear friend. I won't tell you anything about your grandmother that you don't know already.'

Chapter 2

1. The suggestion (in the Gnostic Gospels) that Jesus and Mary Magdalene were married and had children has given rise to the secret 'Bloodline' theory initially expounded in the *Holy Bood and the Holy Grail* by Baigent, Leigh & Lincoln. This theory, with some variations, has been the subject of many publications, documentaries and films, and is regarded by many authors and researchers as lying at the heart of the Saunière/Rennes-le-Château mystery. However, to date there is no substantial evidence to confirm this theory.

Chapter 3

1. *Castrum de Blanchefort* can only refer to the so-called Château de Blanchefort situated on a rocky outcrop at the entrance to the valley of Rennes-les-Bains. The name 'Blanchefort', in English, means 'White Fort', which must derive from the chalky terrain. Opposite Blanchefort is Cardou, a kaolin hill.

2. The history of the village has been exhaustively researched by local historian, George Kiess, founder of a well respected Templar research association, CERT. Georges was born and still lives at Fa, a tiny village close to Campagne-sur-Aude.

3. Other military-religious Orders were also active in Jerusalem. For instance the Order of Lazarus cared for lepers; the Order of St. John ran hospitals, and are still active today; and within fifty years, the German orientated Teutonic Knights were established. All the Orders espoused a call to duty as defenders of Christianity, but it is the Knights Templar who have entered the realms of fact and fiction as the archetypical noble warriors. Dressed in full armour with a long white mantle on which was emblazoned a blood red cross, mounted on armoured war-horses and carrying their black and white chequered battle standard, the Beausant, these Knights must have created an awesome sight to both their allies and adversaries.

4. See appendix A – Palestine Exploration Fund, Freemasonry & British Israelites.

5. The magnificent 12th century castle, of the kings of Majorca, stands in the heart of Collioure, a coastal town in the heart of Roussillon, about 20km from the Templar Commandery, Mas Deu. A few kilometres further along the coast towards the Spanish border is the town of Banyuls. An important Templar port, their extensive wine cellars still survive.

6. There is an alternative theory concerning the disappearance of both the Templar fleet and their treasure. It is claimed that the Templar fleet sailed from La Rochelle, on the west coast of France, with the Order's wealth to either Scotland or America depending on which version one reads. This, and other Templar legends, appears to have arisen from spurious archives that surfaced in the 19th century Templar revival. No authentic evidence exists to support any of these theories. Since the Templar fleet has never been discovered, the most logical reconstruction is that the convoy never reached the shore – suggesting that if it was carring anything, it disappeared en route.

Chapter 4

1. The Cathars are known to have accepted the possibility that Jesus was married to Mary Magdalene. They were Dualists who believed Jesus had two independent natures, a spiritual Christ and a physical Jesus. It was consistent with this theology that Jesus would succumb to normal earthly behaviour. Cathar documents show a belief that Jesus had married Mary Magdalene, and that the body of Jesus had not ascended into heaven.

2. Due to their linguistic similarity, Arques is a name that has been associated with the Ark of the Covenant. Despite a complete lack of evidence, some clandestine groups today believe that it was indeed the Ark that the Templars had found during their excavations under the temple of Jerusalem; and that it may well have found its last resting place in this region.

3. An alternative theory of the source of Pavillon's wealth is comprehensively explored by Franck Daffos in his book Rennes-le-Château, Le Secret Dérobé. In essence, he maintains that the legend of the shepherd Jean (or Ignace Paris), discussed in chapter five, is true. The shepherd revealed his discovery of a cache of gold coins in an underground chamber to his local lord, Baron Blaise Hautpoul. For reasons of expediency, the Baron decided to share the fruits of this discovery with his bishop, Nicolas Pavillon. Daffos develops a sophisticated and well-researched theory tracing the secret of the treasure from its discovery in 1645 to the period of the Abbé Saunière. Despite some remarkably detailed information, there are nevertheless too many unsubstantiated and speculative links to make the theory entirely credible.

Chapter 5

1. Jean-Pierre Deloux and Jacques Brétigny were present at a meeting in mid-April 1982 between the authors of the Holy Bood and the Holy Grail and, Pierre Plantard, and other members of the Priory of Sion. They co-wrote the book, Rennes-le-Château: capitale secrète de l'histoire de France, published in 1982, that presents a collection of previously unpublished material on the history of the village and its priests.

2. see Chapter 4, note 3.

3. In 1886, Saunière presented a magnificent antique chalice to his friend the Abbé Grassaud, priest of Amélie-les-Bains

4. Gérard de Sède wrote L'Or de Rennes (1967), the first book dedicated entirely to the secret history of Rennes-le-Château. He wrote a number of books on this and other related

themes. The strange life of the Abbé Saunière was first publicised in a series of three articles that appeared, in January 1956, in the newspaper La Dépêche du Midi.

5. *In 1865, Maurice Leblanc was baptised in the diocese of Rouen. The archbishop, Mgr de Bonnechose, and his personal assistant, the abbé Felix-Arsene Billard, were in attendance. Mgr de Bonnechose had been Bishop of Carcassonne and, in 1881, appointed Billard to that post. Billard was to appoint Bérenger Saunière as priest of Rennes-le-Château in 1885. Throughout Leblanc's stories there are remarkable similarities and references to the mysterious history of Rennes-le-Château, especially in his choice of names. It is hard not to conclude that Leblanc had somehow received inside knowledge, possibly through these priests. By a further coincidence, Leblanc's sister, Georgette, was a close friend of the great opera singer, Emma Calvé.*

6. *The original of this Act was in the possession of Roger-René Dagobert.*

7. *The Hautpoul-Blanchefort family occupied the castle adjacent to the church at Rennes-le-Château. Marie de Negrè, who married François d'Hautpoul, was the last of the line of this ancient family that plays such an important role in this mystery. Her enigmatic tombstone will be seen to be a key factor.*

8. *In 1745 the Lodge of the King's Chamber was constituted, made up mainly of officers of His Majesty's staff and even the King's Chaplain. One army officer, Luc-Simeon Dagobert, and his two brothers, themselves officers too, founded the Lodge of the Three Brothers at the court of Versailles, into which the royal Duc d'Orleans, cousin of Louis XVI, was also initiated. Posted to the Royal Italian garrison at Perpignan, Captain Dagobert was initiated into the Scottish Primitive Rite branch of Masonry by his uncle Hector, Governor of the Fort at Salses, between Narbonne and Perpignan. He also initiated the Vicomte de Chefdebien, who came from an ancient minor aristocratic family, formerly of Brittany, with medieval connections to the Lords of Rennes in the Corbières, but which was now established at Narbonne.* ·

9. *According to available sources, the first French lodge was founded in 1725 by Charles Radclyffe (Earl of Derwentwater), Patrick O'Heguerty, and Sir James Hector Maclean, in Paris. Sir James Hector Maclean, head of the Clan Mclean, was an ardent Jacobite, as was the Radclyffe family and the lodge's first Grand Master the Duke of Wharton. It has been suggested with some authority that this lodge was part of an extensive Jacobite network that would facilitate communication between Jacobite supporters in Scotland, England and France. Following the Battle of the Boyne, in 1690, James II had been forced to find refuge in France. He was granted the use of the castle at St. Germain-en-Laye, outside Paris, by the French king.*

10. Known as the Larmenius Charter, this document, largely regarded as a fake, lists a succession of Grand Masters and Regents of the Order from 1314 until 1705 and then to the election of Fabré-Palaprat himself. This is only one of several spurious versions of the alleged continuation of the Knights Templar.

Chapter 6

1. In a detailed examination of the interior of Saunière's church, architect Paul Saussez shows the possible entrance and dimensions of a crypt. His findings and three-dimensional computer images can be viewed at www.renneslechateau.com/francais/saussez1.htm This is the most comprehensive investigation and report on the changes to the church made as a result of Saunière's renovation.

2. Since access was through a door disguised as a wooden panel, it would appear that the room was intended to be secret. From the outside, however, the additional room is very obvious as it has been formed by the construction of an external, curved wall linking the side of the sacristy to the church wall. There is even a small circular window in the wall. Since there was no attempt to conceal the room from the outside, perhaps only its purpose was intended to be secret. One theory is that the room concealed an entrance down to the crypt, but this has never been publicly explored. It is nevertheless interesting that the secret room has a sand soil floor – allowing for easy digging.

3. So where did the parchments that appear in de Sède's book come from? De Sède claims that they were not ancient. M. Debant, Director of the Department of Archives of the Aude, agreed, adding that they had been compiled merely to transmit a secret message by someone with a knowledge of ancient languages. It is suggested that this may have been one of Saunière's predecessors, the Abbé Bigou.

Philippe de Chérisey, a member of a secret society, claimed to have concocted two parchments in which he encoded two messages. He stated that the texts were composed from existing Gospel texts taken from the Dictionary of Archaeology and Christian Liturgy published in 1903. It has been discovered, however, that the texts were taken from the Codex Bezae, first published in 1895.

This discovery tends to dismiss de Chérisey's claim and also the alternative suggestion that the parchments were composed by the Abbé Bigou in 1781. It does raise the possibility that, if genuine, they were composed by Saunière himself, and those illustrated by de Sède were copies of originals. The complexity of the code used to hide the message in the longer parchment has also fuelled the debate, as has the nature of the message itself. Despite claims and counter-claims, no definitive conclusion has yet been achieved.

4. *The mock gothic tower, the Tour Magdala, was built to house Saunière's library. After his death all the contents disappeared. Fortunately, notebooks, account books, receipts, bills, and letters, have been discovered in the Departmental Archives of Carcassonne.*

Within this pile of papers is a hand-written list, apparently in Saunière's writing, of 377 book titles, some with information of the publisher, date of acquisition, and cost. Several of the titles are worthy of particular attention and demonstrate the nature of his reading material. Saunière was apparently aware of many of the aspects that have contributed over the last fifty years to the mystery of Rennes-le-Château. The following are a small selection: La Légende d'or; Ce qu'étaient les Albigeois; La Vérité sur le pape Clément V; Le Procès des Templiers; Le pape Jean XXII; Le sac de Rome, par l'abbé Augustin Devoille; Le Trésor du souterrain, par l'abbé Jean Grange. Examination of the titles revealed here shows that Saunière was widely read on a diversity of subjects. Interestingly, there is a novel concerning the search for an underground treasure. It appears to contain many of the same features found in the current stories of Saunière's alleged treasure find. It can also be seen that Saunière was disposed to Royalist propaganda. He also had works of classical adventure such as those of Walter Scott.

The small fraction of his library revealed here is proof that Saunière had an intellectual interest in religious, historic, scientific and esoteric subjects. The nature of the existing bookshelves seems to indicate that his library was far more extensive than this list suggests.

Chapter 7

1. *Despite the prevailing 19th century belief to the contrary, the original Rosicrucian Brotherhood of the 17th century was never a formal society. According to the late Dame Frances Yates, the term Rosicrucian referred to a specific philosophical vision shared by many intellectuals and free-thinkers. The name was taken from their mythical founder Christian Rosenkreutz. For a full account see The Rosicrucian Enlightenment by Frances A Yates, 1972.*

2. *See Appendix B – Cult of the Sacred Heart; Confrèrie du Sacré Coeur de Rennes-le-Château.*

3. *No independent evidence exists to confirm Saunière's trip to Paris, but the choice of Abbé Hoffet as the object of the visit is a remarkable coincidence. Hoffet, at the time of the alleged visit, was only a novice priest; however, he did become an expert in occult and secret societies. We will see how he reappears as a significant character in the unfolding of the mystery. See also note 6, and Chapter 8, note 3.*

4. A document survives that shows that Emma Calvé was involved in the Paris occult circles. The document is a Diploma of Honour offered to Papus on 11 November 1892, in Paris, by the principal members of his esoteric study group. Emma Calve's signature is accompanied by S.I. (Superieur Inconnu), the Martinist third degree. Papus was head of Martinism at that time. For more details see Appendix C. The document may be viewed on www. rennes-le-chateau.com on the 'characters' page.

5. Sensational details of the Abbé Saunière's mysterious world first appeared in a series of three newspaper articles in La Depêche du Midi, January 1956. The L'Or de Rennes by Gérard de Sède, published in 1967, was the first book to reveal much greater detail of the secret history of Rennes-le-Château and the unusual activities of Bérenger Saunière. The source of this information is said to come from the archives of a secret society called the Priory of Sion.

6. The League of Antiquarian Booksellers does indeed exist. Baigent, Leigh and Lincoln published the result of their investigations in The Messianic Legacy (1986), (p. 317), although they established that the League was based at 39, Great Russell Street, London, opposite the British Museum. In 1956, the address was occupied by a bookseller, Henry Steven, Son & Stiles, and did still serve as the headquarters of the League, details of this 'parchment' episode, however, were impossible to confirm. It has been suggested that some unknown individuals, connected to SOE or wartime Intelligence services, used the name of the League as a cover to hide their illegal activities. These activities included the removal of precious documents and possibly treasure from France.

7. The basic aim of Synarchy is a world controlled by one institute/government based on spiritual and social principles, in contrast to Anarchy and Free-Market Capitalism. In Synarchy, the social entity is led by an Authority that controls Religion, Military, and Education.
The foundation of the philosophy consists of three elements:
1. EDUCATION 2. LAW 3. ECONOMY
The Authority belongs to 'the Wise', according to this philosophy.
Culture, Art, and Science belongs to the fundamental element "Education".
Court, Police, the Army and Foreign Affairs belong to the element "Law".
Unions, the Government, and the working class belong to the third element "Economy".
The highest ambition of the philosophy of Synarchy was a classless society. Furthermore, in a Synarchic society the responsibility of the politicians, who deal with day-to-day issues, would be in the hands of the "Wise", the "specialists".

Synarchy would play a major role in the philosophical view on society of almost all of the mystics of the first half of the 20th century. The view on society of the Martinist-Order *was centred on the philosophy of Synarchy. There was even a Synarchic-Martinist Order founded in 1921 by Victor Blanchard, the Ordre Martiniste et Synarchique, which still exists today in Great Britain and Canada (the French branch merged in 1960 with the Ordre Martiniste de Paris of Philippe Encausse, son of Papus). The O M & S today looks upon Synarchy as a heritage from the past; it is not implemented any longer in its teachings.*

Papus, Philippe Nizier, Victor Blanchard, Emille Dantinne and many others in the esoteric community were all followers of the Synarchic Movement. Rudolf Steiner used Synarchy as a major influence when he developed his own ideas for his own movement, the "ANTRO-POSOFISCHE GESELLSCHAFT", out of which came the philosophy that is known today as Anthroposophy.

The Synarchic Movement was also represented among the nobility at the court of the Russian Tsar, where Martinism was introduced by Papus at the end of the 19th century. As we will see in a later chapter, the Synarchic Movement was persecuted during World War II by the Nazi's, and many members were either killed (the Martinist Grand Master, Constant Chevillon was executed) or imprisoned in a concentration-camp. After the Second World War the Synarchic Movement fell into decline but still remains in political ideology and theory.

Synarchy was developed from the ideas of Saint-Yves d'Alveydre (1842-1909). He was a follower of the school of Jean-Philipe Dutoit-Membrini (a.k.a. Keleph-ben-Natha, 1721-1793) and Fabre d'Olivet (1762-1825). Saint-Yves d' Alveydre, together with contemparies like Eliphas Levi, Maitre Philippe (Philippe Nizier), and Fabre d'Olivet, belonged to the most influental spiritual teachers of France in the 19th century. Gérard Encausse (Papus) saw Saint-Yves d'Alveydre as his intellectual teacher (Maitre Phillipe was Papus' spiritual teacher). Saint-Yves may be considered a 19th century profound thinker, philosopher and mystic. He corresponded with all the well-known occultists of his time. In 1885 he was visited by a group of Eastern initiates, one of them named Prince Hardjij Scharipf. Their mission was to inform Saint-Yves on Agartha, a spiritual and political organisation. Their visit led to his final publication, entitled Mission de L'Inde en Europe, mission de L'Europe en Asie. La question des Mahatmas et sa solution. This book was dedicated to: "Au souverain Pontife qui porte la tiare aux sept couronnes au Brahatmah actuel de l'antique Paradésa du Cycle de l'Agneau et du Bélier". The book would never be published, because Saint-Yves changed his mind (he considered the actual content of the work too precious to share it with a profane society) and tore it up. One copy survived, and was published in a limited edition in 1909.

As mentioned, Saint-Yves d'Alveydre developed during his lifetime the principle of Synarchy that would influence the political view of many of the leading occultists of the first half

of the 20th century, especially in continental Europe. For instance, the FUDOSI implemented the philosophy of Synarchy into its basic philosophy.

Alexandre Saint-Yves d'Alveydre died in Versailles on Februari 5, 1909 and was buried at
the graveyard of Notre-Dame. Saint-Yves' ideas for the concept of Synarchy were probably
inspired by earlier works, such as Tomasso Campanella's Civitas Solis (City of the Sun),
which was published in 1623. Writings like Civitas Solis were based upon an Utopian
worldview (other writings in this genre: Thomas Moore's Utopia, 1516; Johann Valentin
Andreae's Christianopolis, 1619; Francis Bacon's Nova Atlantis, 1627.

8. The Spear of Destiny was considered a powerful talisman by the Habsburgs. In their turn,
the Nazis were committed to finding sacred artefacts, such as the Spear of Destiny and the
Ark of the Covenant. They believed these held esoteric power. In the search for such artefacts, they were known to have undertaken widespread investigations and excavations.
These activities will be explored in a later chapter.

Chapter 8

1. See Appendix C – Martinism.

2. See Appendix D – Investigation of Saunière's wealth.

3. See Appendix E – Hièron du Val d'Or – Hoffet – Paul Le Cour.

4. Outwardly, the Polaires appeared as a harmless, if slightly eccentric, esoteric group in
pursuit of spiritual aims. But yet again, in this strange world of occult politics, we find
unexpected connections. Victor Blanchard was President of the Polaire Brotherhood
from 1933. A year later he was also elected Grand master of the Ordre Martiniste et
Synarchique, thus clearly demonstrating a connection between these two influential occult
groups. Furthermore, we will see in chapter 10 how, in contrast to their avowed spiritual
aims, a Synarchic political plan evolved from the beliefs of these two organisations.

5. RA Gilbert – see Chapter 3, note 2.

Chapter 9

1. Parsival is based on the medieval writings of Wolfram von Escenbach, who himself claims
to have based it on the poetry of a Provençal troubadour, Kyot (or Guyot). The troubadours, who travelled from court to court as entertainers, were the principal purveyors

of ideas from place to place; their gentle ways and sense of humour gave them free and unimpaired access and rights of passage. Within the story, there is some artistic disagreement as to the location of the Grail castle (Montsalvat, in Parsival). Von Eschenbach and Kyot placed it in Toledo, whilst Wagner favoured the Pyrenees. Not surprisingly, Rahn followed Wagner's lead, and formed the view that the Grail castle was in fact the isolated château perched on the top of the mountain of Montségur. The identification of Montségur as the Grail castle had first appeared in Le Secret des Troubadours by Josephin Péladan, published in 1906; Otto Rahn would have been familiar with this. It therefore also seemed logical to him that the Cathar treasure and the Holy Grail, whatever they might have been, would have been hidden in the nearby caves at Sabarthez in the Ariège valley, which had long associations with the Cathars.

Furthermore, Rahn considered that the characters appearing in Parsival were modelled on the actual medieval personalities who had been prominent in the region. For example, he believed Parsival was le Vicomte de Carcassonne Trencavel; Repanse de Schoye was Esclamonde de Foix; and the hermit Trevrizent, Parsival's uncle, was the Cathar Bishop Guilhabert de Castres. This coincided with a widespread belief amongst the Languedocian nobility that they were indeed of Germanic blood, on account of their descent from the Visigoths. As we have seen, among these noble families are those whose ancestors had inherited the secret of the ancient treasure.

2. For a extensive investigation into the life of Otto Rahn and an alternative explanation of his 'death', see Otto Rahn: the real Indiana Jones by Nigel Graddon, 2008.

3. The French Milice was a paramilitary unit created by the Vichy government, on 30 January 1943, ostensibly to combat terrorism which they equated with the Resistance. They collaborated with the work of the German Gestapo. An anti-Republican, anti-Communist, Fascist organisation, the Milice will be seen to play a key role in the immediate post-war occult politics.

4. Buechner does not cite his sources for this report and so it must be treated with caution. However, he has a distinguished record as a soldier and medical professional and so his ᵃwritings cannot be simply dismissed. Colonel Howard A Buechner was born in 1919, in New Orleans, Louisiana. He was formerly a Professor of Medicine and an internationally acknowledged expert on tuberculosis and other diseases of the lungs. During WWII, he was a medical officer with the 3rd Battalion, 157th Regiment, 45th Infantry Division. This unit liberated Dachau Concentration Camp. Dr Buechner was the first medical officer to enter the camp. Amongst his many decorations are the Army Commendation Medal, and the War Cross and Distinguished Service Cross of Louisiana. He is the author of a medical textbook, approximately 200 scientific articles, and a number of non-medical works.

He also teamed up with Kapitan Wilhelm Bernhart, a man claiming to be a German Naval officer during World War II, and wrote two books about Hitler's involvement with the Holy Lance, Adolf Hitler and the Holy Lance and Hitler's Ashes, Seeds of a New Reich.

5. Skorzeny's audacious activities continued after the war. He surrendered to the Americans, underwent a brief trial for war crimes at which he was acquitted, but remained in Allied hands until July 1948. Apparently with inside help, he escaped. In 1950, he settled in Madrid, with a friendly welcome from Franco. From here he was to run a network of ex-Nazis who were working in finance and industry. In 1952 he made the largest post-war deal between Spain and West Gemany. Through the intermediary of his father-in-law, Hjalmar Schacht, he arranged for the delivery of five million dollars' worth of railway stock and machine tools. Living the life of a lord, Skorzeny would hold court at one of Madrid's best restaurants, run by a former favourite of Goring. It was here that most of Franco's inner circle would take lunch. It is said that he went on to run a multi-million dollar empire of hundreds of companies throughout the world run or infiltrated by ex-Nazis. He was also on very friendly terms with the President Peron of Argentina. The Research and Analysis branch of OSS reported in March 1945, "The Nazi regime in Germany has developed well-arranged plans for the perpetuation of Nazi doctrines after the war. Some of these plans have already been put into operation and others are ready to be launched on a widespread scale immediately upon termination of hostilities in Europe". A more detailed account of these activities can be found in, The Bormann Brotherhood by William Stevenson.

6. Although he was never found, it is claimed that Bormann did escape to South America, as did many high ranking Nazi officers. He had sent about two tons of gold coins to Argentina by submarine, where on arrival they were placed under the protection of Eva Peron. For more information, see Martin Bormann and the Fourth Reich, by Ladislas Farago, 1974.

Chapter 10

1. Saunière's heart attack, or stroke, occurred on 17 January 1917. This date appears to have some symbolic importance as it is frequently found throughout this story. Some of the dates can be verified but many are unconfirmed and could have been deliberately chosen as a symbol. Almost all Priory publications and correspondence carry this unique date. The exact reason for the choice of this date still remains a mystery.

2. The Lateran Treaty of 1929 was a master stroke of political expediency by Mussolini, ensuring the support of the Catholic Church. It agreed that the Pope should have complete control over an independent Vatican state; that Catholicism would be the official state religion and the teaching of religious instruction would be compulsory in all schools. But

in return the Catholic Church agreed to recognise the Italian government of Mussolini.

3. *The name Bayard appears in several different contexts in publications relating to the Rennes-le-Château mystery. The castle chosen by the Uriage group was named after the 15th century knight, Pierre Terrail, Lord of Bayard, otherwise known as The Chevalier Bayard. The subject of numerous literary works and paintings, Bayard is the quintessential knight, equivalent to the British King Arthur.*

4. *In an attempt to undermine his early political activity, Plantard has been associated, in a derogatory sense, with the Scouting movement. The Catholic scout movement, however, was considered to play an important role in the education of young people and received the Vatican's blessing. Scoutisme, by Jacques Sevin (3rd edition published in 1934), reveals that a principal aim of this movement was to create dedicated and chivalrous Catholic citizens. Scouts were encouraged in their campfire discussion to learn about Merovingian history and the concept of knighthood, of which the knight Bayard was considered the ideal. It is possibly unnecessary to point out that the Catholic scout philosophy was echoed in that of the Ecoles Nationales d'Uriage, and in the articles of Vaincre. The possible connection between Plantard and the Scout movement, though unconfirmed, cannot be readily dismissed.*

5. *In July 1941, Joseph Darnand established the right-wing military group, Service d'Ordre Legionnaire. The organisation supported Henri-Philippe Pétain and the Vichy government and offered its help to round up Jews, and to fight against the French Resistance. Eighteen months later, the Service d'Ordre Legionnaire was transformed into the Milice, the secret police in Vichy. Darnand was given the Waffen SS rank of Sturmbannfuehrer and took a personal oath of loyalty to Adolf Hitler. Darnand expanded the Milice and by 1944 it had over 35,000 members. Essentially French, the organisation played an important role in investigating the French Resistance. Like the Gestapo, the Miliciens were willing to use torture to gain information. They swore an oath to Pétain that included, 'I swear to fight against democracy, against Gaullist insurrection, and against Jewish leprosy.' Many of the Milice were practising Catholics and considered themselves, 'Soldiers of Christ'.*

6. *Interestingly, De Gaulle and Segonzac had been classmates at a Catholic school in the rue de Vaugirard in Paris, where De Gaulle's father was Préfet des Études. The students at the school came mainly from strict, traditional-minded, provincial nobility whose fortunes at that time were more modest. As expected from this background, the young De Gaulle was a monarchist and became a supporter of Action Française led by Charles Maurras, who wished to see a return to a hereditary monarchy and the imposition of a more authoritarian regime.*

7. Papus died in 1916, and the Martinist Order was soon to become divided. Papus was succeeded by Charles Detre, better known as Teder, who was assisted by Victor Blanchard, Deputy Grand Master. Teder was a keen Freemason of the Memphis-Misraim Rites, and under his Grandmastership the Order began to acquire a Masonic outlook. Teder died in 1918, leaving Blanchard as Grand Master designate. Because of the Masonic tendencies of which he disapproved, he declined the Grandmastership and Jean Bricaud was duly appointed to office. Bricaud altered the Constitutions of the Order and decided to admit, as Martinists, only Masons of the Third Degree (Master Mason) of any Rite. The headquarters of the Order were transferred to Lyon.

Some Martinists did not accept these changes and those who did not approve of Bricaud's directions carried on with the work in the spirit of the original constitution, acting as "Free Initiators." They remained independent for a time, but eventually Victor Blanchard, Deputy Grand Master under Teder, decided to gather all those Martinists who adhered to the original Constitution into a new organisation that would not impose the Masonic prerequisite for membership. He became the Grand Master of this branch of the Martinist Order, which in 1934, was renamed Ordre Martiniste et Synarchique to distinguish it from the Masonic Ordre Martiniste whose headquarters were in Lyon. During the war, the Ordre Martiniste was headed by Chevillion who had succeeded Bricaud in 1934. Chevillon was assassinated in 1944.

Chapter 11

1. De Gaulle had actually studied under a Great War hero and famed military strategist Pétain, at the military school of Saint-Cyr, and was known to have had some admiration for the old soldier, which was reciprocated. De Gaulle even ghost-wrote books on military strategy for Pétain.

2. The turmoil of war provided opportunities for unsavoury pursuits, ranging from involvement in the black market (illegal trading in rationed goods), the settling of old scores, downright criminal activity, and the pursuit of political power. After the war, many of these activities were publicly exposed, especially those of collaboration and profiteering, creating great difficulty to the cause of French unity. A prime example was the allegation by Henri Frenay that one of General de Gaulle's leading supporters, Jean Moulin, had been secretly working for the Communists. In response, Moulin's former secretary, Daniel Cordier, attributed a manifesto to Frenay that showed him to have been a Pétainist, anti-Semitic, a collaborator and supporter of Vichy's National Revolution.

3. Nicolas Bonnal's work explores Mitterrand's penchant for symbolism, particularly il-

lustrated in his thoughts on architecture, a prime example of which can be found in the construction of the Louvre pyramid. It appears that Mitterrand was guided by a strong spiritual sense of mission to restore France to its former greatness. This sense of mission was to transcend his politics so that this Socialist politician would appear to act in ways more expected from a conservative traditionalist.

4. His services to Vichy were obviously of some note, as he was decorated with the Françisque Gallique, a medal awarded by Pétain as a mark of personal favour for contributions to him and to his country. To avoid embarrassment, Mitterrand was later deliberately vague about this award.

5. The following extract is taken from an essay published by the research group CESNUR, founded by Dr. Massimo Introvigne:
"In 1937, Plantard dropped out of high school and established, with some of his friends, the Union Française (French Union), a youth group inspired by the ideas of Eugene Deloncle. The seventeen-year old Plantard also started to show a penchant for mysticism and symbols. He regarded as significant that his group had been founded in 1937, because 1937 (1937 is also the date found in the Vaincre illustration representing the ideal of a chivalric United States of the West) contains the same numbers of 1793, the year in which the French anti-Monarchist persecution period known as the Terror started during the Revolution. The founding of the French Union was, thus, a way of mystically "reversing" the effects of the French Revolution through numerology.
Plantard was a reasonably effective student leader. Thanks to the support of his vicar, a priest called François Ducaud-Bourget (1897-1984), who many years later became well-known as an associate of the splinter Catholic arch-conservative movement of Bishop Marcel Lefebvre (1905-1991), Plantard managed to became the parish leader for the Catholic youth group, Groupement Catholique de la Jeunesse. In 1939, he led 75 students of this group on a camping vacation at Plestin-les-Grèves (Côtes du Nord, Brittany). According to police reports, some of them were eventually recruited into his French Union. He also addressed a conference of young people organised by the Catholic youth group, on 20 June 1939, at the Villiers Hall."

6. Plantard actually made his living by working as a paid sexton in the Catholic Church of Saint-Louis d'Antin, in Paris. His mother, a concierge by trade, and with whom he lived, moved from one building to another, and in the second building Plantard met new friends, including two well-known radio actors, Jacques Thereau and Suzanne Libre, as well as Jules-Joseph-Alfred Tillier (1896-1980), a respected employee of the Compagnie des Forges et Acières de la Marine d'Homécourt and a friend of Paul Le Cour (1861-1954). Although Le Cour was a quite heterodox esoteric Christian, and one anticipating several ideas later associated with the New Age movement, he was also a participant in

the Masses organized by Father Ducaud-Bourget in the church where Plantard worked, for a circle of right-wing intellectuals, including philosopher Louis Le Fur (1870-1943) and Orientalist Count Maurice de Moncharville (1860-1943). Whether Le Fur, Moncharville, and Le Cour actually contributed to Vaincre or whether Plantard adopted their names for his own articles is unknown. However, given that the sentiments expressed in the articles are largely representative of their ideas, and that it is known that Plantard did receive contributions from Robert Amadou (then only a young man of seventeen years but who was to become a distinguished esotericist), it is possibly that they were genuine. Louis Le Fur, a right-wing pan-Europeanist, was one of the influences on the Kreisau Circle and Robert Schuman. Also mentioned in Vaincre is Jean Mermoz, a famous aviator, and member of right-wing organisation "Croix de Feu" (Cross of Fire). He disappeared in 1936, in an aeroplane intriguingly called "Croix du Sud" (Cross of the South).

7. *The first mention of Georges Monti is in the Vaincre articles. Despite his alleged connections with Péladan's Rose-Croix circle, there is no reference to him in any of the related publications. A biography of Monti was later published by Gérard de Sède, who claimed to have obtained this information from the Abbé Hoffet's archives. The authenticity of these archives has not been possible to verify.*

8. *By what may be only a coincidence, the Martinist Grand Council of 1889 included Georges Montières. It is possible that the character Monti was deliberately created to draw attention to Georges Montières. Certainly, a strong Martinist thread binds all the diverse aspects of this investigation. Furthermore, Georges Montières, in 1931, was Grand Master of AMORC (Ancient & Mystical Order of the Rose Croix).*

9. *The Kreisau Circle was largely formed from members of established Prussian aristocratic families, many of whom had had distinguished military or political careers. Helmut von Moltke, whilst studying Law at the Inner Temple in London, had established contact with important members of the British Establishment; even before the outbreak of the war, he had expected support for opposition to Hitler. In June 1942, he wrote to an English friend indicating his utter despair for Germany under Nazi domination and the bloodshed to come.*

10. *Not only does this symbol connect Plantard's ideas with that of the Hièron du Val d'Or, but we know that Plantard was acquainted with Paul Le Cour who had founded the Order of the Divine Paraclete that had effectively replaced the Hièron. See appendix E for details.*

Chapter 12

1. *Le Grand Monarch, also known as the 'Roi Perdu' (Lost King), or Rex Mundi (King of the World), is a symbolic leader that will unite his people in peace and prosperity (as seen in the stories of the British King Arthur). The prophecies of Nostradamus refer to such a king who will appear at a time when France is threatened by great danger. Historically, the Grand Monarch is expected to be of either the Merovingian line, the first kings of France, or from the Carolingian line in the model of Charlemagne. In addition to his temporal power this unique king will also fulfil the function of priest, thus bringing together earthly and spiritual power. Interpretation and exploitation of this powerful, idealistic, archetype ranges from extreme esoteric belief, held by those commonly referred to as New Age, to a more practical political level.*

2. *Nostra magazine publishes articles on esoteric, unexplained, and supernatural themes. Many of these include well-known subjects such as UFOs, reincarnation, and parapsychology.*

3. *During his research for the Holy Blood and the Holy Grail, Michael Baigent obtained, from Pierre Plantard, a photograph of the receipt for Saunière's coffin. The original receipt is in the possession of the Corbu/Captier family. This would suggest that Plantard met, or was in touch with, Noël Corbu in order to obtain the photograph.*

4. *Plantard bought three tracts of land in 1967, and a further five in 1972.*

5. *Pierre Plantard and Anne Lea Hisler were married in 1951 and allegedly divorced in 1956. However, it is known that they were still in close contact in 1960 and 1963. Her articles reveal significant and controversial information about her husband.*

6. *The unusual choice of 'Way' as a pseudonym has not previously been explained. Its true significance may become apparent by the following discovery. In mid-1948, a Soviet funded international youth movement held a conference. The result was the creation of the World Assembly of Youth (WAY) with HQ in Paris. It was soon taken over by career-minded potential politicians who, mindful of the power of youth politics, steered it away from its communist roots. In the 1950s and 60s, the national committee remained in the hands of the Right. Money came from the Foundation for Youth and Student Affairs – a CIA front organisation. In 1952, the International Youth Campaign formed a political wing called the European Youth Campaign that led a propaganda campaign for a united Europe amongst the youth. It was most active in the mid 1950s. In view of Plantard's known activities with youth groups in the 1940s, the 'Way' pseudonym may well indicated continued involvement with youth politics.*

7. *Despite presenting itself as a publication of the 'Federation of French Forces', CIRCUIT was actually a publication of the Priory of Sion. Its managing-director was Pierre Plantard, at that time secretary-general of the Priory. In the second edition of CIRCUIT (August 1959), Adrien Sevrette wrote an article concerning problems faced by governments, and called for new political methods and new men (political leaders), since in his opinion the current 'politics are dead', especially the economic situation. In issue 4, there is a comprehensive plan for government reform, ranging from the reorganisation of the administrative regions, to import taxes, work and production, health, and education. These are not idle reflections but a genuine analysis of the political situation in France at the time and a manifesto for change. Thus we can see that, in parallel with his esoteric and occult interests, Plantard had a very strong and clearly defined political philosophy revealed first in Vaincre, 1942, and later in CIRCUIT, 1959. Whatever the truth of the allegations, the publications of Plantard and the Priory are liberally interspersed throughout with political statements, symbols and references. There is no doubt that there was a powerful political motive, albeit idealistic and fanciful, behind the promotion of the mythology of the Priory of Sion.*

8. *Le Cour saw in the Age of Aquarius a Second Advent of Jesus, albeit perhaps Christianity without its original Jewish roots. But, perhaps unwittingly, he reveals a contradiction in this view. There is a difference between the first and second editions of his book, Ere du Verseau (Age of Aquarius), which in fact gave rise to a charge of anti-Semitism. The first edition contains a chapter in which Le Cour writes, "One of the great events of the Age of Aquarius must be logically the reconciliation of the Jews and the Christians". And that a 'Temple of Solomon' would be restored. This chapter is removed from the second edition. However, it must be born in mind that the second edition was published in the early 1940s when France was under Nazi occupation.*

Chapter 13

1. *The list of Grand Masters of the Priory of Sion is identical to the list of alleged 'Imperators' of the neo-Rosicrucian Order, AMORC, which circulated in France around this time. This is less surprising since Plantard, Paul Le Cour, Camille Savoire (said to be doctor to Georges Monti), were studying the monographs of AMORC, having made contact with Jeanne Guesdon, a leading member of the French branch. Plantard never became a member of AMORC, but he did become a friend of a later AMORC head, Raymond Bernard. (Source: CESNUR)*

2. *This account cannot be accurate since the pillar, which supported the old altar in which the 'parchments' are alleged to have been found, is not hollow. There is a small recess in*

which a holy relic could have been placed, according to Church custom. In his *Mythologie du Trésor de Rennes*, René Descadeillas confirms that Elie Bot did witness the discovery of some documents during the dismantling of the altar but claimed that they were almost illegible. Thus it is probable that the hollow pillar story of the find, and the nature of the documents, are a later embellishment.

3. As we saw in chapter 6, a crypt is known to exist from entries in the Old Parish Register of 1694. The register details a number of people interred in the crypt, referred to as the 'Tomb of the Lords', between 1694 and 1726. Surprisingly, the deaths of two Bishops of Alet are also recorded in the Register, which implies that they had a special connection to the village.

4. By yet another coincidence, the Juniorate at which Emile Hoffet undertook his religious training was situated next to the Basilica of Sion, reconstructed in 1741, on the hill Sion-Vaudémont. It is the history, traditions and events of this site that form the basis for *La Colline Inspirée* by Maurice Barrès, first published in 1913. The popular paperback was published in 1961.

5. Viscount Leathers, Major Hugh Murchison Clowes and Captain Roland Stansmore Nutting, are all genuine people of some note. They all had business interests with connections to the City of London, especially in the fields of insurance and shipping. During World War II, each of them had experience and information of value to SOE and British Intelligence. Other names mentioned in Priory documents include Lord Selborne, Sir Thomas Frazer, Sir Alexander Aikman, Sir John Montague Brocklebank, and Lord Blackford. The researches of Baigent, Leigh & Lincoln published in *The Messianic Legacy* reveal interesting connections between some of these names and SOE. The nature of Intelligence is secrecy, thus making detailed research very difficult. If this story is entirely fabricated, why and how did the Priory of Sion choose these people, who did have a genuine (indirect) connection to covert wartime activities in France?

6. Philippe de Chérisey, in an interview with Jean-Luc Chaumeil, emphasised that the documents found by Saunière and deposited in a London bank since 1956, were three genealogies and not the two infamous coded parchments that he claims to have fabricated. However, he claims to have based the false parchments on an ancient work of Dom Cabrol found in the Bibliothèque Nationale. This conflicts with recent findings that the small parchment was in fact based on the Codex Bezae.

1. *The young François Mitterrand was an activist in Croix-de-feu's youth movement, crying 'France aux Francais' (France for the French), the catchphrase of Edouard Drumont and his followers. On 2 February 1935, Mitterrand demonstrated against the 'envahissement des meteques' – the invasion of foreigners, in this case foreign medical students. Launched in 1928, Croix-de-feu was an extreme paramilitary nationalist organisation, headed from 1931 by Colonel François de la Roque. While Action Française worked closely with the Front National, la Roque did not permit Croix-de-feu to join it. Croix-de-feu had now become the largest and most important opponent of the republic, eyed jealously by Taittinger and Maurras. See Bad Faith: A Forgotten History of Family & Fatherland, pp. 104, 116/7.*

2. *François Durand de Grossouvre, son of an aristocratic banker, was born at Vienne in 1918. He studied under the Jesuits before training as a doctor. At the outbreak of World War II he initially joined a Moroccan regiment as an auxiliary doctor. In 1943, Grossouvre married Claudette Berger of the wealthy Berger Sugar family and was appointed PDG of Sucres Berger. There are conflicting versions of his later war record. He maintained that he was a skier in the Vercors, in 1944, with the Maquis, FFI de Chartreuse. It is here that he met Captain Bousquet, also known as 'Chambert', who created one of the first networks of the ORA, the Resistance army. We must recall that it was in this region that the Ecoles Nationales d'Uriage were operating.*

   Other sources maintain, however, that he was an Action Française supporter and a member of Darlan's Service de l'Ordre Legionaire (SOL). Joseph Darlan was a member of the Cagoule and created the secret society, Compagnons du Glaive (Companions of the Sword), in Nice. Grossouvre claimed that he had joined SOL, from 1943, but only as an infiltrator on behalf of the Resistance. In 1952, he entered SDECE (French Intelligence) but left in 1961 only to rejoin in 1965. He used the pseudonym 'Canjean'. The SDECE archives disappeared in 1966 so it is not known for how long his affiliation continued. SDECE, founded in 1946, is considered to have had a chequered history, with many allegations of corruption, including drug dealing, until its re-organisation in 1982. Under the code name of 'Leduc', he became chief of the French 'stay-behind' network Arc-en-ciel, established by NATO and part of Operation Gladio. More detail on the career of Grossouvre can be found in Guerres Secrètes à l'Élysée by Capitaine Paul Barril, 1996.

3. *The following is a digest taken from the International Herald Tribune article, 1 February 2002, reporting on the on-going ELF Investigation:*
   "This African-based system of money-laundering was created in the 1950s by President Charles de Gaulle and his key adviser, the late Jacques Foccart, according to French scholars. Mr. Foccart saw these networks as a way of using oil wealth, via Elf, from newly

independent colonies in West Africa. The system of split commissions afforded a way of maintaining French influence and later subsidizing Gaullist political activities."

The chief heir to the Foccart system, according to French analysts, was a Corsican, Charles Pasqua, 74, a right-wing Gaullist who served twice as interior minister. He has been caught up directly in the Elf case by evidence that he used Elf corporate jets or charter flights on more than 70 occasions, allegedly taking trips for private or political purposes, including some during his 1992 campaign against the Maastricht treaty on European monetary union. The free travel was said to have been arranged by a sometime Elf adviser named André Guelfi, 82, a free-wheeling tycoon known in Paris as "Dede-la-Sardine" because he made his first fortune with an Africa-based fishing fleet. Guelfi has extensive international business connections, thanks largely to contacts he made as a key promoter and intermediary for the International Olympic Committee. André Guelfi was a close friend of former Spanish ambassador to Moscow, and IOC president, Juan Antonio Samaranch, graduate of Opus Dei's prestigious business administration school, IESE, in Barcelona. It is claimed that by implementing the business practices that he learned at IESE, Samaranch turned the Olympic movement into a formidable money-making machine. Interestingly, Charles Pasqua would become personally involved in the drama of the suicides of the Order of the Solar Temple. Before the apparent suicide, the victims sent their passports to Pasqua, then Interior Minister, claiming they held him responsible for their deaths. Later testimony claimed that one of the two policemen known to have "suicided" the members, before committing suicide himself, had been driven to Paris, for meetings with Pasqua, or some of his aides.

Chapter 15

1. *According to further research, Major Otto Dickmann was actually Major Adolph Diekmann. The error arose through inaccurate reporting.*

2. *Mackness refers to this bank as Banque Léman. A Jewish bank founded by Chaim Mankowitz (another pseudonym) and part of the Harton Léman holding company that specialised in dealing in gold and precious metals. Mackness mentions that the PA to Mankowitz was the son of the chairman of one of Geneva's most exclusive banks where many right-wing ex-politicians (former collaborators) were said to have accounts.*

3. *According to Mackness, Raoul was born Raphael Denovicz, in 1923, in Leipzig. His Jewish parents owned a successful jewellery business. With the rise in anti-Semitism in Germany, the family changed its name and was forced to move first to Alsace and then again Agen, near Toulouse. Mackness does not reveal Raoul's actual name. In 1940, Raoul's father sent him to a college in Pau, where he met his future wife Janine. Through Janine's contacts, in*

1941, Raoul drifted into minor Resistance activities in the Pyrenees.

4. *The occupation of the Vichy zone by the Germans, in 1943, motivated more intense Resistance activity. Raoul underwent further training in the course of which he was taken to Castelnau sous l'Avignon, where he spent time with the deputy mayor, M. Gaston, a retired Belgian mining engineer. Gaston was in fact English SOE agent George Starr, code-named 'Hilaire', who ran 'Wheelwright', the largest Resistance network in France. The area covered by 'Wheelwright' included Montauban where the Panzer tank division, Das Reich, was stationed. So it was Hilaire's men who were keeping a close eye on the division's activities and carrying out acts of sabotage whenever possible.*

5. *Pierre Bergé was the lover of Yves Saint Laurent, whose cosmetics business, YSL, he had helped to finance. In 1987, he launched the magazine, Globe, which supported the candidature of François Mitterrand. He took part in all Mitterrand's campaign meetings, and later became the president of the Bureau de l'Association des amis de l'institut François Mitterrand.*

6. *The forest of Troncais is one of the most beautiful and extensive (10,000 hectares) oak woods in Europe. It is situated in the north of the Allier department, located in the geographical centre of France. The forest is about 100km north-west of Vichy at the edge of the unoccupied 'free' zone.*

7. *The Cressac family moved to Château de Lussac in 1913. Bernard's father was Emile de Cressac de la Bachelerie. The family originated from Périgord but split into two branches in the 12th century, 1) Périgord – Bourdelle, and 2) Quercy – Luzech (Lussac). In 1876 the Vicomte de Cressac was head of the Royalists of the Vienne and were supporters of the Comte de Chambord (Source: Notice sur le Château de Lussac, by Bertrand de Cressac).*

8. *Founded by Heinrich Himmler and colleagues in July 1935, the Ahnenerbe was a Nazi government study group that presented itself as a 'study society of Intellectual Ancient History'. With over fifty different departments, the Ahnenerbe concentrated on archaeology, interpretation of ancient writing, anthropology (especially the search for racial purity), collection of sacred artefacts, and the creation of a new German culture.*

9. *This information was given to Roger-René Dagobert by the proprietors of the Château de la Borderie who had acquired it, in 1985, after the death of Bertrand Cressac in the previous year.*

Chapter 16

1. *The biographical details of Jean-Pierre François have been drawn mainly from two sources, Vol d'Identitié, by Jean-Pierre François, Éditions Albin Michel SA, Paris, 2000, and L'Ami Banquier, by Bernard Violet, Éditions Albin Michel SA, Paris, 1998.*

2. *In a dispatch dated 7 January, 1942, U.S. Ambassador Anthony J. Drexel Biddle revealed to President Roosevelt the magnitude of the Synarchist financial control of the Vichy government that had been working with Germany.*

   Prior to the founding of the Banque Worms in the 1920s, the Worms group was primarily involved in industry, especially shipping. The shipping company of Hippolyte Worms handled much of the oil shipments for the Anglo-Dutch conglomerate, Royal Dutch Shell. The Paris branch of the Lazard banking interests helped establish the Banque Worms on behalf of the French Synarchist industrialist Hippolyte Worms. Thus was created a very tightly knit network of Synarchists, ultimately reporting to this Anglo-Dutch financial oligarchy, but working through both the Lazard bank and Banque Worms. French intelligence documents from the 1930s identified Hippolyte Worms as one of the original twelve members of the secret Synarchist Movement of Empire, a group at the heart of the Nazi collaboration.

   By 1948, all of the leading Synarchists had been freed from jail in France, and the entire network was in the process of being reconstructed under a renovated Anglo-American ownership. The Banque Worms began hiring back a number of people who had been among the most visible pro-Nazis inside the Vichy government. Georges Albertini, who had been a top official of the Labour Ministry under Vichy, was released from jail after four years of hard labour and immediately hired by Banque Worms. Albertini oversaw a funding mechanism that was set up so that Banque Worms, in France after the war, became one of the major sources of funding for Synarchists under the cover of the 'Congress for Cultural Freedom'. Furthermore, he set up an Institute for Historical Studies, a major Banque Worms-funded Congress for Cultural Freedom propaganda outlet, producing anti-Communist tracts, to exaggerate the Communist threat, in the period of Truman and the emergence of the Cold War, after Roosevelt's death.

3. *Information on the Matesa affair is taken from Their Kingdom Come: inside the secret world of Opus Dei, by Robert Hutchinson, Doubleday, 1997; Chapter 12.*

4. *According to: The Occult, Chambers Compact Reference, 1991. Georges Soulès – Raymond Abellio, (1907-1986), developed a syncretic philosophy that involved a synthesis of the Cabbala, the phenomenology of Husserl, the thinking of Guénon and an early form of*

242

structuralism. His thinking ran along parallel lines which he often confused – the meta-physical and the political. He believed that the West should reverse its apparent decline. His outlook was typical of an extreme right-wing form of esoterism which sought to 'renew the tradition of the West', replacing Liberty, Equality, Fraternity with Prayer, War, Work. Abellio desired a society founded on an absolute hierarchy; the principle found at the heart of Synarchy.

5. Gérard and Sophie de Sède, L'Occultisme dans la Politique, 1994.

6. In spring 1951, Abellio decided to return to France, but due to the death of JPF's wife he delayed his decision for some months. He is said to have been helped by General Pierre de Bénouville and the lawyer Jean-Baptiste Biaggi. In February 1952, Abellio was called to a military tribunal in Paris. With help from JPF and the General, he was cleared of collaboration. It was said that he provided precious inside information on the MSR to the General and Jean de Castellane who had both belonged to the 'camelots du roi', activists of the right-wing Action Française, but claimed not to approve of the activities of Déat's RNP and the Cagoule.

   Abellio and his friends effectively rewrote their wartime afiliations, denying Collaboration and substituting Resistance activities. Eugene Schueller, owner of L'Oréal, Monsavon and Valentine, was also called to account but managed to escape justice.

7. See: Entretiens avec Abellio, by Marie-Thérèse de Brosses, Jean Mabire, 1967.

8. Antoine Pinay was a member of Pétain's Vichy government, but at the end of World War II, he helped General de Gaulle to power. He was Prime Minister of France in 1952, and has been rumoured to have been an Opus Dei supernumerary. Jean Violet is reported to have been a member of Deloncle's CSAR. For more details on the Pinay Circle, its most prominent members, and its effect on European politics, see the articles by David Teacher and Scott Van Wynesburghe, Lobster magazine, No. 18, 1989. Also David Guyatt, Circle of Power, 1999.

Chapter 17

1. According to the title page of Les Descendants mérovingians et l'enigme du Razès, by Madeleine Blancassal, the work as published by the Grande Loge Alpina. In another publication, also believed to originate from the Priory of Sion, a key figure in the text, Leo Schidlof, is alleged to been a dignitary of the Grande Loge Alpina. The Priory of Sion leadership evidently wished to connect their organisation with the Grande Loge Alpina, the premier Masonic Lodge in Switzerland. See also Chapter 13.

2. *The Ordre Renovée Temple was founded by Raymond Bernard, in 1970. From an interview with Bernard we learn that membership of the ORT was reserved for AMORC members only. Bernard was world leader, Imperator, of AMORC, the Rosicrucian society that had interested Pierre Plantard and Paul Le Cour. Plantard became a friend of Bernard and would most likely have known of his activities.*

3. *Several reports on the tragic events of the Order of the Solar Temple have been compiled by CESNUR (Centre for Studies of New Religions). In their papers, the role of Princess Grace is rejected, as are some of the other more sensational allegations regarding the fate of Solar Temple members. Indeed, although there is no independent evidence that Princess Grace attended meetings of the Order of the Solar Temple, her involvement in the Sovereign Order of the Solar Temple is well-attested. A key figure in these reports is Jean-François Mayer, a Swiss cult information expert, who played a major role in the investigation into the mass deaths. Mayer is a friend of CESNUR founder, Dr. Massimo Introvigne, and has associated himself with CESNUR reports on other cults. Several websites, investigating CESNUR, make a range of allegations against it, including links to extreme Catholic and right-wing organisations and individuals.*

4. *In Le Trésor des Templiers by Jean-Luc Chaumeil, 1984, Plantard's associate in the Priory of Sion, Philippe de Chérisey, claimed that the Château Valcros, situated in the Vallée de Croix, Verdon Gorges, was intimately connected to the history of Rennes-le-Château. It appears that he believed that the site of the ancient town of Rhedae could be found in the Vallée de Croix.*

5. *In 1963, Alfred Weysen founded the Nouvelle Observence Templière, in Nice.*

6. *Extensive research on FUDOSI, by Milko Bogaard, can be found on the website: www. hermetics.org/fudosi.html.*

7. *There are several websites dedicated to revealing the membership and history of the Groupe de Thebes. One must treat such information with caution since some website hosts have agendas, lack objectivity, and deal more or less favourably with the subject.*

8. *Giulio Evola (1898 – 1974) was an Italian traditionalist. He anticipated the 'New Right' philosophy in his views. A follower of René Guenon, he influenced Italian Fascism and became interested in eastern Tantrism which led to an interest and belief in sexual magic, on which he wrote a number of books. In 1943, he fled the collapsed and discredited Italian regime to Nazi Germany where he worked with the Ahnenerbe on research on Freemasonry. He has become an inspiration for many extreme right-wing groups today.*

Chapter 18

1. *Roberto Calvi, born in Milan, 13 April 1920, was an Italian banker dubbed by the press as "God's Banker", due to his close association with the Vatican. Calvi was the chairman of Banco Ambrosiano, which collapsed, causing one of modern Italy's biggest political scandals. His bizarre death in London, in June 1982, has been the source of enduring speculation. His death, initially declared a suicide, was finally ruled as murder after two coroner's inquests and an independent investigation. In June 2007, five people were acquitted of his murder after a trial in Rome.*

2. *Giulio Andreotti (born 14 January 1919, in Rome) is an Italian politician with a prolific but tainted career. He served seven periods as Prime Minister of Italy. He was also appointed Foreign Minister between 1983 and 1989. Andreotti has sat in Parliament without interruption since 1946, when he was elected to the Constituent Assembly. He was almost continuously re-elected to the Chamber of Deputies, until President Francesco Cossiga appointed him Senator for life in 1991. During his early political life, he was closely connected to the Christian Democratic leader Alcide De Gasperi and served as a Deputy Minister in Italy's Post War governments. He was the last Christian Democratic prime minister of Italy, serving from 1989 to 1992. His last term of office was marred by the revelation of the corruption that ultimately destroyed the party. On October 24, 1990, he acknowledged, before the Chamber of Deputies, the existence of Gladio, a NATO secret anti-communist structure. In April 1993, he was investigated for having mafia relations. The following year, the party of which he was a predominant figure, vanished from the political sphere.*

3. *Licio Gelli, born 1919, is a multi-facetted political activist and intermediary. To understand his career, one must understand the complex post-war years of Europe. The biggest threat to Europe in pre-war times was Communism – it was the great fear of Communism that gave birth to the Fascists and the Nazis. Though both sides were dreaded, the Fascists represented right-wing government, while the Communists represent left-wing government. It was the right-wing that the United States and the Catholic Church desired over Communism – because Communism would destroy the capitalistic system. This is why the CIA and the Vatican initiated Operation Paperclip, the recruitment of top Nazis. The Nazis had massive amounts of Soviet intelligence, had infiltrated Communist partisans, and this could not be allowed to fall into the hands of the Soviet Union.*

Gelli worked both sides. He helped to found the Red Brigade, spied on Communist partisans and worked for the Nazis at the same time. He helped establish the Ratlines, which assisted the flight of high ranking Nazi officials from Europe to South America, with passports supplied by the Vatican and with the full acknowledgment and blessing of the United States intelligence community. While on one hand, the US participated in the war crime tribunals of key Nazi officials and maintained an alliance with the Communist Soviet Union, secretly, the US was preparing for the cold war and needed the help of Nazis in the eventual struggle the US would have with the Soviet Union. Gelli's agreement with US intelligence to spy on the Communists after the war was instrumental in saving his life.

The Vatican provided support to Nazis and Fascists because the Communists were the real threat to the Church's survival. The Italian Communists would have taxed the Church's vast holdings and the Church has had a dismal experience with Communist governments throughout the world – where religious freedom was severely restricted. Gelli had close connections with the Vatican from the days of the Ratlines and also worked for American Intelligence. He formed the P2 Masonic Lodge, which did not follow the direction of any Grand Lodge. Supplied with a sum of $10 million a month by the CIA, its membership was a Who's Who in the Intelligence, Military and Italian community. So extensive was Gelli's influence, that he was even a guest of honour at the 1981 inauguration of President Ronald Reagan.

When required, Gelli used blackmail in order to recruit prominent members to his P2 lodge; its membership was estimated at 2400 members, including 300 of the most powerful men in the Western World.. He was a close friend of Pope Paul VI, Juan Peron of Argentina, Libyan Dictator Muammar el-Qaddafi, and many high officials in the Italian and American governments. He is also reported to have had some financial dealings with the George Bush snr. for his presidential campaign.

Gelli and his P2 lodge had staggering connections to banking, intelligence and diplomatic passports. The CIA poured hundreds of millions of dollars into Italy in the form of secret subsidies for political parties, labour unions and communications businesses. At the same time the Agency continued its relationship with far-right and violent elements as a back-up, should a coup be needed to oust a possible Communist government. This covert financing was exposed by the Prime Minister of Italy in a speech to Parliament, at which he stated that more than 600 people in Italy still remain on the payroll of the CIA.

Operation Paperclip was terminated in 1957, when West Germany protested to the United States that this project had effectively stripped the country of "scientific skills." Paperclip may have ended in 1957, but by then numerous Nazis had been employed, through the agency of Licio Gelli, as CIA agents, engaging in clandestine work with the likes of George Bush, the CIA, Henry Kissenger. (Edited extract from: www.proutnewsnetwork.org)

4. Elected to the Papacy on the 26 August 1978, at the age of 65, Albino Luciani died in bed thirty-three days later on 28 September. Officially diagnosed as a heart attack, no autopsy

was performed and the body was embalmed within twelve hours of death, eliminating any possible investigation for poison. The only medication that Luciani had been taking was Effortil, a liquid medicine that he had been taking for some years to counteract low blood pressure, and a course of adrenalin-stimulating injections. Suspicion still surround his sudden death not least because he had passed a full medical examination in Venice just prior to his attendence at the Conclave.

5. *Prominent Knights of Malta include John McCone, CIA Director; William J Casey, President Reagan's Director of the CIA; Alexander Haig and Vernon Walters, members of Reagan's inner circle; William Wilson, US ambassador to the Vatican; Alexandre de Maranches, French Intelligence chief; Umberto Ortolani; and a great many more involved in the worlds of Intelligence and Diplomacy. Former Nazi, General Reinhard Gehlen, Head of the West German secret service, was awarded the Knights' highest honour, the Grand Cross of Merit.*

6. *For additional information on Gladio: Gladio: the secret US war to subvert Italian Democracy, Arthur E Rowse; Gladio article from Searchlight, January 1991; Operation Gladio, David Guyatt, 1997.*

Chapter 19

1. *Hitler and the Nazi party were influenced by the Thule Society. Taking their name from a mythical island that once existed in the north Atlantic, Thulists believed they had inherited occult wisdom from Atlantis and of the Northern Mystery Tradition. Much of their teachings were based on The Secret Doctrine by Madame Blavatsky, founder of the Theosophical Society. Her belief in 'root races' provided the impetus for the Nazi political theory of Aryan racial superiority. Blavatsky's work has provided a foundation for many occult societies since the late 1800s. As a model for the SS, the Teutonic Knights were considered the ultimate example warriors in the defence of Aryan supremacy. See The Occult Conspiracy by Michael Howard, 1989, for more details.*

2. *An extensive investigation into Black Gold has been carried out by David Guyatt, a former international banker based in the City of London.*

3. *See – www.bloodlinethemovie.com*

4. *In the mid 16th century, a French physician and astrologer, Michel de Nostredame, more popularly known as Nostradamus, made a series of cryptic predictions concerning the fate of Europe. His Quatrains (four-line, rhymed verses) have been endlessly interpreted,*

resulting in many different conclusions concerning the details.

It is perhaps less surprising that in his predictions he placed France at the centre of European events. He was born in 1503, in Provence, and though Roman Catholic, he was of Jewish descent. Given a basic classical education by his grandfathers, he was sent to Avignon and thence to the University of Montpellier to study medicine. After graduation, he exercised his medical knowledge in dealing with an outbreak of plague in Montpellier and Narbonne. Continuing his studies, he earned a reputation for absorbing knowledge in many different disciplines, including astrology; as a result of which he compiled his prodigious divinations. However, living in a France held in the grip of the Inquisition, he was forced to encode his writings and prophesies in order to avoid any charges of heresy.

Being an educated man, of traditional Jewish heritage despite his Catholic up-bringing, and with his roots firmly embedded in this ancient region, it is hardly possible that Nostradamus could have travelled throughout the region without becoming aware of its great legends. Legends that must have included the secret of the lost treasure of the Temple of Jerusalem. In fact, there is a persistent local assertion that he stayed at the house of a relative in the village of Alet-les-Bains; a village intimately connected with the history of the Corbières, the village of Rennes-le-Château, and the lost treasure. There are at least ten verses that deal specifically with gold, of which Century VIII, verses 28, 29 and 30 refer to gold and treasure from antiquity that one day, would be discovered in this region.

Though the prophecies, and especially the numerous interpretations, should only be accepted with some caution, they are legitimate writings within the context of 16th century France. Furthermore, Nostradamus specifically identifies certain cities such as Avignon, Barcelona, Narbonne, Carcassonne, Toulouse, Lyon and Perpignan. These were cities that were not only renowned centres of learning in his time, but that have also played such a crucial role in the occult history of France.

Whatever the truth of the source or explanation of his prophecies, they have continued to play a sigificant role in the occult world, at times exploited as justification by those with less than benign intentions.

5. *For an extensive investigation into the Nazi visions of political and economic European unity, see The Tainted Source, by John Laughland, 1997, chapter 2. In his erudite examination of the roots of the present European Union, Laughland exposes the influences of Fascist, Nazi and Eurasian philosophies. Furthermore, he suggests that students from the Uriage school, during the Vichy period, have obtained positions of political power from which they have been able to influence policies adopted by the EU.*
6. *Among supporters of the PNAC philosophy can be found Michael Ledeen. Born on 1*

August 1941, Ledeen is a resident scholar at the American Enterprise Institute and a contributing editor to National Review. He was a founding member of the Jewish Institute for National Security Affairs and he served on the JINSA Board of Advisors. He holds a Ph.D. in History and Philosophy and is a former employee of the Pentagon, the State Department and the National Security Council. His ideas are believed to have influenced the thinking and foreign policies of the Bush administration since the Twin Towers tragedy. He has attracted some criticism for his apparent approval of some aspects of Italian fascism. He is certainly an admirer of Machiavelli, who he considers to be a great political thinker.

In his latest book, The War Against the Terror Masters, Michael Ledeen wrote: 'Creative destruction is our middle name, both within our own society and abroad. We tear down the old order every day, from business to science, literature, art, architecture, and cinema to politics and the law. Our enemies have always hated this whirlwind of energy and creativity, which menaces their traditions (whatever they may be) and shames them for their inability to keep pace. Seeing America undo traditional societies, they fear us, for they do not wish to be undone. They cannot feel secure so long as we are there, for our very existence – our existence, not our politics – threatens their legitimacy. They must attack us in order to survive, just as we must destroy them to advance our historic mission.'

But Michael Ledeen's contact with right wing politics has a long and surprising history. In 1984, Ledeen was found in Rome in the company of Italian Military Intelligence chief, General Giuseppe Santovito and Francesco Pazienza, a consultant to Roberto Calvi. An associate of Pazienza, Frederico Federici had known Ledeen since 1968. They had discussed Federici's plan for the publication of a book of Licio Gelli's memoires. Pazienza and Ledeen were to handle diplomatic relations between the administration of Ronald Reagan and the Italian government. According to the sworn testimony of Federico Umberto D'Amato, Pazienza had mediated in secret talks between the Vatican and the Palestine Liberation Organisation, and knew Marcinkus and Ledeen well.

7. *Born on 7 January 1962, Alexander Dugin is a Russian political activist of the Russian school of geopolitics commonly known as Eurasianism. He appears to be an advocate for National Bolshevism and is known for his anti-Semitism and Russian nationalism. His father, a former high-ranking officer in Soviet Military Intelligence, helped him get a job in KGB archives. It was here he discovered topics that really interested him: Eurasianism, world religions, and mysticism.*

8. *Perhaps more significantly, in mid-August 2007, Putin ordered Russian bombers to resume daily patrols, as a clear statement of Russian military and economic resurgence.*

Appendix A:

Palestine Exploration Fund, Freemasonry & British Israelites

In 1864, Lt Charles Wilson (later to become Major General Sir Charles Wilson, Royal Engineers) was sent to Jerusalem to undertake the city's first detailed survey. But perhaps more significantly, between 1867 and 1870, excavations of the Temple Mount were initiated by Sir Charles Warren, at that time a lieutenant and a member of the Palestine Exploration Fund (PEF), founded in 1865. The PEF and subsequent excavations were funded by the prominent bankers, Rothschild, United Grand Lodge, and other establishment figures including Church of England archbishops, members of the aristocracy, and political leaders, many of whom were members of the PEF. Lieutenants Warren and Wilson published the results of their archaeological activities in 1871 in *The Recovery of Jerusalem*. Warren eventually became president of the PEF.

He was also a high-ranking Freemason, a co-founder and first Grand Master, in 1884, of the Masonic research lodge, Quatuor Coronati. At that time, Quartuor Coronati supported the following aims: the founding of a new State of Israel initially under the British; the reclamation of the Temple Mount; and the rebuilding of the Temple of Jerusalem. Many of its members belonged to the PEF.

There are numerous allegations connecting this episode of excavation in Jerusalem and the role of prominent Freemasons today. It is very difficult to establish the genuine facts partly through lack of documented evidence and partly due to denials from those involved. There are certain facts and events, however, which do suggest that not all the allegations are completely untrue. The higher degrees of Masonry themselves do reveal a mindset that is not at variance with many of these claims.

Today, it is claimed that the agenda of an inner core of Masonry associated with Quartuor Coronati, the Canonbury Research Centre, *Cornerstone Masonic* magazine, and British Israelites appear to include:

- the rebuilding of the Temple of Jerusalem and the symbolic recreation of the Temple cult;
- the restoration of the "Jewish" treasure, ie the Ark of the Covenant, Menorah and other precious artefacts;
- the promotion of a universal religion based on the Jewish mystical Cabbala; the one God concept of Ahkenaton but re-invented as the "Great Architect"; the ethical framework of Masonry.

These claims are dismissed by the official publicity department of United Grand Lodge.

Sir Charles Warren was appointed Chief Commissioner of Police from 1886-1888, the period of the infamous Jack the Ripper murders. The case, which some allege involved Jewish/Masonic rituals, has attracted accusations of a cover-up by Sir Charles to protect the Brotherhood. As an aside, the infamous Satanist, Aleister Crowley, one-time member of the Hermetic Order of the Golden Dawn, was alleged to have known the identity of Jack the Ripper.

The Golden Dawn was founded in 1887 by McGregor Mathers, a Jacobite and British Israelite. The Jacobites believed that the Scottish and Irish nobility were descended from the High Kings of Tara, who themselves were descended from Biblical or Egyptian characters. The Golden Dawn was involved in Cabbalistic magic. Today, the acknowledged world authority on the Golden Dawn and Jewish Cabbala is Robert A Gilbert. He is also said to be interested in the British Israelites. Gilbert was introduced into the research lodge Ars Quartor Coronati by his close friend Spencer Douglas David Compton, 7th Marquess of Northampton, currently the second most senior Mason in United Grand Lodge. Gilbert is the librarian of the former Golden Dawn library, now the library of the Societas Rosicrucina in Anglia (Soc Ros) housed in Stansfield Hall, Hampstead. The Societas Rosicrucina was founded by members of the Golden Dawn but became absorbed into Masonry later on. In 1890, Dr. Wynn Westcott, a member, and Magus, of the

Societas Rosicrucina, became Master of Quartuor Coronati.

In 1995, Professor Guiliano di Bernado (former Head of Italian Grand Orient Freemasonry), established the Jerusalem Lodge in a location adjacent to the Temple Mount. It is said that Lord Northampton was a co-founder of the lodge and is a supporter of British Israelitism. He has also expressed an interest in the Golden Dawn and Jewish Cabbala, which he believes holds some ancient secrets truths relating to individual and social enlightenment. He further believes that old British Jewish families have preserved the Cabbalistic tradition and is the founder of the Canonbury Masonic Research Centre that meets at the Canonbury Tower, which he owns. The centre promotes Masonic and Cabbalistic studies and at a lecture in summer 2001 the lecture hall was decorated with signs depicting the twelve tribes of Israel – typical of the Royal Arch degree. The Royal Arch theme is the finding of ancient scrolls and/or the Ark of the Covenant in a vault beneath the Temple Mount.

British Israelites generally believe that:
- the British are descended from the ten 'lost' tribes of northern Israel;
- the British royal family is of Davidic/Solomonic descent. There is a connection to the legend surrounding the Stone of Destiny and the ancestry of the Jacobites;
- the State of Israel is a prophesied destiny.
They are Protestant but anti-Catholic, believing that the Catholic Church has corrupted Christianity. They believe in the Kazar connection and in the Sephardic descent from Judah. They make a distinction between Israel, representing the other tribes, and Jews, which come from Judah. These beliefs have existed for centuries, though the first formal society to promote these views was the Anglo-Saxon Assoc. founded in 1879.

The British Israelite World Federation (BFWF) had its original headquarters at Bove Town, Glastonbury; the Somerset town to which they believed Jesus had visited. William Blake and Swedenborg had contacts with Dr. Stukely who promoted the British Israelite association with Druids (as did Blake). Blake's works deal with the theme of Messianic Government, Swedenborg's dream of biblical prophecy.

The British Empire was considered by the British Israelites as a fulfilment of the promises given to Abraham by God. Some leading members of the British Establishment were British Israelites. British Israelites believed that sections of the British nobility, aristocracy and others were directly descended from the dispersed northern tribes of Israel As a result they maintained that British had a more legitimate right to occupy/govern the Holy Land than either the Jews or Palestinians.

For Christians the Temple Mount represents a holy site. For the 'religious', it is a symbol of their faith. Certain extreme sections of secular Jews are unconcerned with the religious dimension of the site but use it as a justification of their political aim – total control of Jerusalem and Israel. The modern State of Israel provides a focus for the unity of worldwide Jewry, and for both Christians and Jews is seen as the last frontier or foothold in the Middle East at the heart of Islam.

According to writer/researcher Barry Chamish, some modern Knight Templar Orders, including the NATO Templars and the Automonous Order headed by Simon Lefebvre, wish to put all Jerusalem's holy sites under international (NATO) control – a move strongly opposed by Orthodox Jews, Zionists and Palestinian Arabs. Though partly to protect the site from Islamic development, international control of Jerusalem would be a step towards the fulfilment of the new "Masonic" religion subtly promoted by the Canonbury Centre. Historically, the Templars were by definition anti-Islamic, a trend that predominates today. The Temple Mount, site of the legendary Temple of Solomon, is a physical symbol and a focus for the new "Masonic" religion. Universal Judaism/Jewish Mysticism is open to all people, but the original Biblical Jews are considered to be the people chosen by God to hold the keys. Freemasonry is considered as a parallel or extension of Jewish Mysticism, hence the use of the same symbols.

But we have a footnote to this extraordinary network of people involved with the themes of biblical prophecy, restoration of the Jerusalem temple, and establishment of a universal religion. Robert A Gilbert was co-author with Walter Birks of the *Treasure of Montségur* (1987), the book that explored the Grail quest of Otto Rahn in the very area considered to be the last resting place of the lost treasure of the Temple of Jerusalem.

The Cult of the Sacred Heart and the Mystery of Rennes-le-Château

Abbé Bérenger Saunière arrived as priest of Rennes-le-Château in 1885. From July 1886 onwards, he started to renovate his church; and from 1900 commenced the creation of a private domain near the castle that was formerly the home of the aristocratic de Voisin, Hautpoul and de Fleury families.

Symbols of the Cult of the Sacred Heart are prominently displayed throughout Saunière's constructions at Rennes-le-Château:

- a statue of Jesus in the Sacred Heart pose can be seen on the front of the Villa Bethania;
- a bas relief on interior west wall of church;
- the "In hoc signes vinces" inscriptions – on the church porch, and on the Devil's statue ensemble;
- inscriptions around the Calvary Cross plinth;
- the fleur de Lys on the Villa's gable ends are monarchist symbols.
- a stained-glass window above front door of Villa depicts the conventional motif of the Sacred Heart (This is one of a pair of windows that also depicts the Immaculate Heart of Mary. Both these symbols can be fond on the Mirculous Medal struck to commemorate the apparitions of the Rue de Bac, Paris, in 1830)

There is a record, in the diocesan archives, that Saunière purchased a statue of the Sacred Heart for his private oratory in the Villa Bethania.

It was after Saunière's return in July 1886 from his temporary post as tutor at the Petit Seminaire de Narbonne that he expressed his interest in the Sacred Heart. According to local archives the motto of the Cercle Catholique de Narbonne was 'In hoc signes vinces', which suggested a link to the Sacred Heart movement.

This display of devotion to the Sacred Heart, taken together with other activities, will be seen to be a clear sign of Saunière's support for the restoration of the Monarchy. This was an absolute-style Monarchy supported by a specific traditionalist faction of the Catholic Church. Furthermore, we will see how and why the Cult of the Sacred Heart and its ramifications, have been woven into the mythology created by the mysterious Priory of Sion.

Devotion to the Sacred Heart has been a key aspect of the Roman Catholic Church for many centuries. Specific devotion arose in the fervent atmosphere of Benedictine and Cistercian monasteries. Medieval and Renaissance Christian mystics (including St. Bernard) had meditated upon the symbol of the Sacred Heart as an expression of Christ's human and divine love – although initially this was combined with devotion to the Sacred Heart of Mary. For believers in esoteric Christianity, the Sacred Heart was identified with the Sun, thus associating Sacred Heart Devotion with far more ancient religious traditions than that of the Christian era.

However it was brought into sharper focus following the Visions of Sister Magaret-Mary Alecoque (1647-1690) at Paray Le Monial in 1673. As early as the 10th century, a Benedictine monastery had been established at Paray. The main part of its church was constructed in the 12th century and is considered a valuable example of Cluniac architecture, since its model at Cluny has virtually disappeared. The Benedictine Order was founded at Cluny in 910. Despite this heritage, Paray-le-Monial came to prominence primarily because of the series of visions experienced by Saint Margaret-Mary Alacoque. Her spiritual director, Claude de la Colombiere (1641-1682), Superior of a Jesuit house at Paray, encouraged her and, from 1875, interpreted and publicised her visions.

On 26 December, 1673, she claimed that Christ revealed the mystery of His heart to her for the first time saying: "My heart is so full of love for men... that the flames of its ardent love can no longer be contained, but must be poured out through you". Other apparitions followed in 1674. Then in June 1675, Jesus, revealing His heart, said "Behold this heart which has so loved men...", and asked that a feast be instituted in honour of His heart. But more importantly, other visions contained specific references to Christ as King, clearly intended to associate Jesus with Monarchy.

Margaret-Mary died on 17 October, 1690, but she was not canonized until 1920. In 1765, Rome authorised the institution of the feast of the Sacred Heart of Jesus in France; this was extended in 1856 by Pope Pius IX to the Universal Church. In 1899, Pope Leo XIII consecrated "all Mankind" to the Sacred Heart – underlining the exalted status in which Sacred Heart devotion is held. Later in 1925, the Church introduced the feast of Christ the King.

Thus we can see how devotion to the Sacred Heart became clearly identified with Monarchism, especially amongst Royalist Catholics. Following the French Revolution, the image of the Sacred Heart became a key symbol for them. As such, devotion to the Sacred Heart became as much a political statement as a spiritual one. In 1870, Rohault de Fleury led a movement to revive the tradition of the prophetic visions of Paray-le-Monial almost a century earlier. But was his true motivation, political, spiritual or esoteric? Interestingly, he was of the same family that had acquired through marriage the former Hautpoul/Blanchefort lands at Rennes-le-Château and Rennes-les-Bains.

In 1871, the Royalist dominated National Assembly voted to offer reparation for the sins that had led to France suffering its heavy defeat in the Franco-Prussian War (especially the capture of Paris and the murder of the Archbishop). Their political aim was a restoration of the Christian Bourbons, enlisting Christ's help by dedicating themselves and the French nation to His Sacred Heart at the symbolic town of Paray-le-Monial. Furthermore, it was proposed to construct a huge church dedicated to the Sacred Heart on the hill of Montmartre in Paris – Le Sacre Coeur de Montmartre.

The architecture of the Sacre Coeur is of some interest: of the 78 entries in the competition for its design, the one chosen was by the architect named Abadie. He was already well known for his restoration of the Saint-Front Cathedral in Périgueux. The plans for the new basilica called for an edifice of Romano-Byzantine style, evident today with its great onion-shaped domes – very different from La Notre Dame and France's other great medieval Cathedrals. Although the first stone of the Sacre Coeur was laid in 1875, only the foundation had been completed when Abadie died in 1884. Completed in 1914, it was not consecrated until 1919 when the First World War had ended. The final cost was forty million francs. Although originally the fund raising was by public subscription, in 1873 the National Assembly declared its construction to be a state undertaking. However, the largest single contributor (500,000 Frs) was the Comte de Chambord, thus clearly associating himself with the Sacred Heart movement and promoting himself as the saviour of France.

Henri, Duc de Bordeaux and Comte de Chambord, was the only Legitimist Bourbon claimant to the throne of France, the last of the senior branch descended from Louis XIII. Chambord had enjoyed close support from the Hautpoul family: Félines d'Hautpoul had been a tutor to the young Comte and the Marquis Armand d'Hautpoul was a close and trusted supporter who in 1843 accompanied Chambord on several foreign visits. Despite being offered the crown three times, lastly in 1873, he declined; refusing to reign under the shadow of the Tricolour – the Republican flag. He left France for self-imposed exile in Austria until his death. Many of his Legitimist supporters could not believe that he had thrown away the opportunity to take the throne on just such a point of principle. Was there perhaps another reason?

Chambord died in 1883 leaving no direct heir. In 1886, Saunière noted in his diary that Chambord's widow, the Archduchess Maria-Thérèse of the Habsburg dynasty, had donated 3000 Frs to the restoration of his church. It is reasonable to conclude that at least initially Saunière had been a loyal supporter of the Chambord claim.

There was however an alternative Bourbon claimant to throne of France, Karl Wilhelm Naundorff. In 1833, Naundorff came forward to claim the title of Louis XVII, son of the Bourbon king, Louis XVI. It had been generally accepted that in 1795, the young Louis XVII had been murdered in prison at the age of 10. According to the historian Philippe Boiry, Naundorff appeared in Germany with no birth certificate and no known parents. He was, however, the most plausible of all the characters (at least 100) that claimed to be Louis XVII because he was apparently recognised by the Dauphin's nurse and the Minister of Justice under King Louis XVI. The Dauphin's sister was told of his strong resemblance to the family. However, she refused to see him because at the time she was a strong supporter of her uncle, King Louis XVIII. Her refusal to see Naundorff combined with the story of his rescue from prison in 1795 evidently gave credence to his claim. (A claim considered by most modern historians to be false – recent DNA evidence casts further doubt – but at the time the Naundorff claim attracted widespread support.) In 1845, Karl Wilhem died; his eldest son, Charles Louis, would continue his father's mission.

The Naundorff claim received support from a series of apparent visions that occurred in 1846, at the village of La Salette near Grenoble. The Virgin Mary was assumed to have appeared to two young shepherd children, Melanie Calvat (15) and Maximin Giraud (11). The vision was later proved in court to be a hoax perpetrated by a former nun and Royalist, Constance de la Merlière. Nevertheless, the RCC continued to exploit the potential of La Salette as a sacred site for pilgrimage. The "visions" were later carefully publicised specifically to give support to the restoration of the French monarchy and to encourage greater devotion to the Catholic Church. Furthermore, an underlying political message, the restoration of the Roi Perdu – Lost King – was identified with the Naundorff cause. This powerful Royalist archetype, Le Roi Perdu, also known as the Grand Monarch, had been referred to in many of the famous prophecies including those of St. Malachy and Nostradamus. In these prophecies, both King and Pope are accepted as having divine authority.

The Virgin Mary allegedly told Melanie that "Rome (Vatican) would lose faith and become the seat of the anti-Christ". This was partly a subtle attack against the trend of modernisation in the Roman Catholic Church.

In 1865, the Comte de Chambord met with Maximin, who died in 1875; it is alleged that Maximin told him that he would not be king. It is further claimed that Chambord then gave his endorsement to the Naundorff claim. Does this offer a better, although contoversial, explanation for Chambord's reluctance to take the throne?

An answer may lie in a key figure of the time – Philibert de Bruillard, Bishop of Grenoble, 1846-1852. In his earlier days, Bruillard had been a confidant of Louis XVI and Marie Antoinette; and would have known the young Dauphin. Following their execution, he went into hiding and continued to work with an underground network of aristocrats for the Restoration of an "Ancien Regime" style Monarchy. Much later, using his position as Bishop of Grenoble, he was able to manipulate the publication of the visions of La Salette. Evidently convinced of Naundorff's claim, Bruillard actively promoted La Sallette in support of his cause. In fact, the present Naundorff descendent – Charles Eduoard Bourbon – claims to possess a letter from Melanie Calvat that shows her support for Charles Naundorff.

After the death of Chambord (1883), some Royalist support switched to the Orleanist claimant, whilst other more militant groups followed Charles Loius Naundorff. He immediately launched a more public campaign culminating in a speech made at Paray-le-Monial in 1884. Here he presented himself as a traditional monarch and a traditional Catholic. He gave staunch allegiance to the devotion of the Sacred Heart and adopted the motto "In hoc Signes Vinces" (featured on his flag along with the symbol of the Sacred Heart – embroidered by the Sisters of Paray-le-Monial), the very words displayed by Saunière in his church at Rennes-le-Château.

Appendix C:
Saunière and the World of Martinism

One vigorously debated aspect of the Rennes-le-Château mystery is the possibility of Saunière's involvement with the world of Occult societies. It is now known that in 1900, Saunière attended at least three meetings of a Martinist lodge in Lyon. Pages of the Lodge minute book reveal his presence as an honourable guest.

To be invited to a lodge meeting as an honourable guest, Saunière must have been a member of a Martinist lodge elsewhere. Though this might be surprising, we know that at this time most Martinists were clerics; but what attracted them to Martinism and how could they reconcile occult activity with their faith? To attempt to answer these questions, it is necessary to start by looking at the nature of Martinism and those involved with it.

Although not known by this name until much later, Martinism developed out of the Masonic-affiliated Order of the Elus Cohen founded by Martinez de Pasqually around 1750. In 1768, Louis Claude de Saint Martin, known as the Unknown Philosopher, became his secretary and eventually took over the Order after Pasqually's death. At this time there was no centralised administration but a number of independent lodges practising his system.

Pasqually's book *Traite de la Réintegration* explains his belief in the theory of Reintegration. The central belief of this doctrine was that Man can return to the divine state that he was assumed to have possessed before the 'Fall'; that is, he can become closer to God. The system of ritual designed to achieve Reintegration employed a specific style of magic called 'theurgy'. Theurgy was the merging of the personal Will with God's Will and was called in authentic Martinism the Inner Way or the Way of the Heart. It was believed that the creative power of Man was a gift from God, the ultimate Creator; and that Man can acquire the ability to will something to happen or to manifest. But as a Theurgist, the initiate would invoke

God's Will to bring about a manifestation or happening. Thus Man becomes an agent of God's Will.

Saint-Martin rejected some of Pasqually's magical rites, which employed the intercession of spirit beings, as being medieval, and substituted a more Christ- and God-centred Theurgy that he called "Magism of God". The ultimate aim, as stated by Saint-Martin, was to "restore order, peace and life in the world". He further claimed that it was the duty of the individual to work for Reintegration: a reaffirmation of Pasqually's teaching if not his methods.

There was a Gnostic dimension summed up by the belief that Man's wisdom (Sophia) blossoms when the individual recovers his 'sensitivity', that is his spirituality, which is normally submerged in his inner darkness. Thus with the progress towards Reintegration came increased spiritual knowledge: a greater understanding of Man's divinity and God's purpose.

Saint-Martin died in 1803; there were a number of attempts to reform and although many other Rose-Croix and esoteric orders were formed at this time, it wasn't until about 1890 that Martinism itself underwent a major revival in the form of the new Ordre Martiniste. The Grand Council based in Paris included such notable occultists as, Papus (Gérard Encausse), Stanislas de Guaita, Sedir, Maurice Barrès, Georges Montieres and Josephin Péladan.

Appointed Grand Master, Papus began to unite the various Martinist lodges creating a more structured movement. As a young man, Encausse spent a great deal of time at the Bibliothèque Nationale studying the Cabbala, the Tarot, the sciences of magic and alchemy, and the writings of Eliphas Lévi. Papus also studied material that came from Charles Nodier, writer, occultist and chief librarian of the famous Arsenal Library in 1824. Papus became aquainted with a circle of Gnostics, Rosicrucians, and 'older' Martinists, all students of the late Eliphas Levi.

His meeting with Philippe de Lyon in ca. 1886 upsets his vision of the world. From this time on Papus became the propagator of Christian Mysticism and the Way of the Heart, which Saint-Martin called the Inner Way. The core of this philosophy, as described by Papus, is published in his *The Cardiac or Mystic Path*. Papus deals in this publication with the importance of simplicity and the purification of body, soul and mind in one's spiritual quest.

On the purpose and aim of the Martinist Order, Papus wrote: "the Order, as a whole, is especially a school of moral knighthood, endeavouring to develop the spirituality of its members by the study of the invisible world and its laws, by the exercise of devotion and the intellectual assistance and by the creation in each spirit of an all the more solid faith as it is based on observation and science." Papus actively sought an alliance between the clergy and occultists to restore the forces of tradition against the trend of modernisation that he considered was responsible for a loss of social order.

So far we have not encountered anything that could be considered contradictory to the Faith of a traditionalist priest. And certainly the socio-political message would have been equally acceptable to the Catholic Church. But could there have been another aspect that may have attracted Saunière and other priests to Martinism?

Spiritualism, popular in America, had taken hold in Europe in the second half of the 19th century and had become a key feature of Martinist ritual. We know that Papus himself held seances for contacting spirits. One can easily see how attractive such activity would have been to a questioning priest. Despite being outlawed by Rome, direct contact with the dead would have held a fascination to those whose lives were dedicated to preparation for the afterlife.

Papus and his involvement in esoteric movements became widely known amongst those with an interest in occultism. In 1905, Papus was summoned to the court of Tsar Nicolas II to hold a Spiritual Séance at which the spirit of his son Alexander III was raised. The Russian Court had been witness to many seances arising from the interest of Tsar Alexander II and his wife in occultism. In fact, as early as 1861, the Scottish medium DD Home, accompanied by the French writer Alexander Dumas, held seances at the Winter Palace in St Petersburg for the Tsar, his courtiers and other Russian aristocrats.

It is during this episode that the notorious Protocols of the Elders of Zion were first circulated. Allegedly the minutes of the World Zionist meeting that took place at Basle in 1897, they caused quite a stir at the Russian Court where they were used to cast a slur on certain political factions. Contrary to popular belief, they are not a forgery, or a fiction; but neither are they of Zionist origin. In fact they formed the basis of a Martinist plan for Synarchic government. Papus himself wrote of such a plan as a necessary counter to what he saw as creeping Anarchy. Aware of their political potential, they were used by a faction of dissident Russian exiles to discredit Russian noblemen involved in Freemasonry who were believed to be involved in a conspiracy to influence the Tsar. This Martinist document was then seen by Sergei Nilus, who confused the Martinist symbol – a six-pointed star – with the Zionist Star of David. He immediately interpreted the document as being a Zionist plan and part of a Zionist conspiracy. The Martinists were duly attacked as belonging to this illusory Judeo-Masonic plot. Anti-Semitic tendencies of the time greatly helped to fuel this confusion and added to its propaganda value that continues even until today.

But the indefatigable Papus had other interests and beliefs. In 1896, he published the *Tarot of the Bohemians*. A look at the preface to the book reveals some of his other occult beliefs: "The Tarot pack of cards, transmitted by the Gypsies from generation to generation, is a primitive book of ancient initiation. […] The uninitiated reader will find in it the explanation of the lofty philosophy and science of ancient Egypt." Papus further states that the wisdom of the Caballa, the Freemasons and the ancient Egyptians had been kept alive by the Tarot of these nomadic gypsies. Very influenced by Freemasonry, Papus evidently believed in the transmission of sacred wisdom and occult science, which had been handed down, as he saw it, through the gypsies, Rosicrucians, Templars, Christ, the Old Testament, and ancient Egypt, from the Garden of Eden and the Fall of Man. His quest was to discover and reveal the Synthesis that in his words "condenses in a few simple laws the whole of acquired knowledge."

This essentially defines the element of Gnosis found at the heart of Martinism. We can now more easily understand the role of Cathar enthusiast Jules Doinel in this esoteric world and its connections to Saunière.

In 1888, while working as archivist for the library of Orleans in France, Jules Doinel discovered an original charter dated 1022, which had been written by Canon Stephan of Orleans, a schoolmaster and forerunner of the Cathars who taught Gnostic doctrines (He was burned for heresy that same year). Doinel had a vision in which the "Aeon Jesus" appeared, who charged him with the work of establishing a new church. Doinel was a "Grand Orient Freemason" and a practising Spiritualist. "In May of 1890, Jules Doinel attended a séance in the oratorie of the 'Duchess of Pomar (The Countess of Caithness). [...] It is said that the disembodied spirits of ancient Albigensians, joined by a heavenly voice, laid spiritual hands on Doinel, creating him 'Valentinus II, Bishop of the Holy Assembly of the Paraclete (Holy Ghost) and of the Gnostic Church.'"

Thus the Eglise Gnostique was founded by Jules Doinel in 1890. In 1892, Doinel consecrated Papus as Tau Vincent, Bishop of Toulouse; he also consecrated other Martinists, such as Paul Sedir and Lucien Chamuel. These three men formed the 'nucleus' of the newly built Gnostic Universal Church. Jules Doinel, Patriarch of the Gnostic Church entered into Papus' Martinist lodge in 1891. As we saw, he made Papus Gnostic Bishop of Toulouse and in 1893, he founded the Ordre Gnostique de la Colombe du Paraclète. In 1896, he was appointed Archivist/Librarian at Carcassonne and two years later became Secretary to the Society for Arts and Sciences in Carcassonne: at which time he is thought to have visited Rennes-le-Château. This becomes an even more credible possibility since Saunière's colleague, Henru Boudet, Curé of Rennes-les-Bains, was also an erudite member of the Society. But most interestingly in 1900, the year when Saunière attended Martinist meetings in Lyon, Doinel became Gnostic Bishop of Mirepoix – which include Montségur, and of Alet-les-Bains – which included Rennes-le-Château.

It is not known how long Saunière was a Martinist. However, the inextricable link between the Gnostic Church and Martinism offers some interesting possibilities. "In 1908 a schism occurred within the Gnostic Church: the branch at Lyon under JEan Bricaud took another name; 'Église Gnostique Catholique' (EGC); later changing again to the 'Eglise Gnostique Universelle' (EGU). The EGU would later change its name once more to 'Eglise Gnostique Apostolique' (EGA). In 1911, the EGA headed (since 1908) by Jean Bricaud, Patriarch of the Gnostic Church, became the official church of Papus' 'Ordre Martiniste'. Furthermore, Jean Bricaud himself was later to become head of this Marintist Order.

But were Martinist's beliefs, or those of the Gnostic Church, in conflict with the doctrine of the Roman Catholic Church? Jules Doinel, the founder of the first Gnostic Church had dreamed of a Church that would give back to Christianity its gnostic dimension. But gnosis needs to be defined so as not to confuse the very holy gnosis that, as Clement of Alexandria said, does not oppose faith but perfects it, with the "gnosis whose name is a lie" denounced by Saint Irenaeus in his treatise against heresies in the 2nd century. Thus, many of the Gnostic Churches can be considered heretical, but significantly, those that have remained true to Doinel's tradition are not.

Appendix D:
Saunière's Wealth

The source of Saunière's wealth has been a subject of continuous debate especially as he clouded his activities in secrecy. The more sceptical researchers have advanced the theory that Saunière indulged in the trafficking of masses. That is, the saying of an excessive number of masses for money. The following facts, however, cast doubt on the credibility of this explanation.

From René Descadellias: *Mythology of Treasure of Rennes-le-Château:*
- The accusation against Saunière for trafficking in masses was not upheld by the Vatican. (p. 40)
- Bishop de Beauséjour lifted the sentence on Saunière, imposed in December 1911, but did not publicise it as he didn't want Saunière to resume his position as priest of Rennes-le-Château. (p. 40) See below*
- Saunière was a good and charitable man, much liked by his villagers. (p. 42)

Descadeillas offers a reason for his trouble with the bishop: that the traffic in masses alone had not brought in sufficient sums for Saunière to have created his domain and to have lived as he did. There had to be another source of his income. (p. 42) Saunière himself wrote that he had received donations from people who wished to remain anonymous. He could not therefore reveal the complete source of his income. (p. 42/43) It is known that his brother, a Jesuit priest, solicited donations for him – he had connections with the aristocracy.

Saunière did write directly to religious communities throughout France and Europe requesting funds to rebuild his ancient church and to build a retirement home for priests, but many of his subsequent receipts were given as donations. The Vatican response would tend to support the probability that his receipt for the saying of masses was not beyond permissible limits (Saunière does confirm that he gave some of these requests to his neighbouring colleagues) and that the remaining receipts were genuine donations for works that Saunière could account for.

From Dominique Dubois: *Rennes-le-Château, L'Occultisme et Les Societes Secretes:*

* Bishop de Beauséjour having failed to secure a judgement against Saunière for "trafficking in masses", exhorted one of his colleagues to find something with which to condemn Saunière (p. 91). (This would appear to have been motivated by Saunière's attitude and apparent disobedience to his Bishop.)

A note written by Saunière in his private memoires claims that the specific accusation of trafficking in masses in such quantities was unsustainable as the details mentioned would have been impossible. He would have to have received requests for about 150,000 masses. The existing lists shown by the sceptics and allegedly proving this wholesale traffic, are in fact lists of all his correspondence, sent and received, containing references to "Demands for Masses", "the Sending of Masses", and general letters. They are far from conclusive.

One must ask the following questions:

1. How could he have persuaded so many people from all over Europe to send him money to say masses? Why did they not use a local priest or one that they knew personally? What did Saunière write, in his advertisements, that was so effective and persuasive? It is said that some of these advertisements survive, but I have not been able to find any.
2. If Saunière was indulging in activities contrary to Cannon Law, why did he keep such meticulous notes that could incriminate him? Either he would have found a coded way of maintaining records or he would have destroyed them as soon after their usefulness as possible. The only conclusion can be that Saunière did not consider these records to be incriminating.
3. Why did a colleague of his write a letter, in 1910, supporting his actions and absolving him of any immorality or illegality regarding the sources of his income. Furthermore, he endorses Saunière's decision not to reveal the sources. It is not

clear from this letter whether the source was through donations or a treasure find, but it cannot have been trafficking in masses.

4. If he was guilty, why did he not admit to this earlier on and suffer the probably more lenient consequences rather that suffer the emotional ravages of a prolonged battle with the Bishop that resulted in his poor health? Saunière himself comments on the toll that this dispute had on him.

One can only conclude that he may well have taken full advantage of the rules governing the saying of masses – even passing on the excess to his colleagues. This may have not been in the true spirit of the rules, but was not illegal. Bishop de Beauséjour was leading a personal campaign against Saunière. Saunière was aware that whatever he did, he would never satisfy the demands of de Beauséjour.

Appendix E:

The Hiéron du Val d'Or and Esoteric Christianity

Concurrent with the conventional religious devotion to the Sacred Heart is an alternative political and esoteric interpretation. But are there any signs that Saunière had such political and esoteric interests?

Occult and esoteric societies tended to be orientated towards the Right. Many were monarchists with a romantic vision of the 'Ancien Regime' which represented tradition and social order. They were therefore anti-Republican and looked forward to the restoration of a traditional Catholic monarchy as a better system for realising their ideological ambitions. They tended to operate in secrecy.

We must now enter the world of Esoteric Christianity, the adherents of which held the belief that the Catholic Church was in fact a repository for wisdom and traditions from antiquity. And that more could be learned from its symbols and rituals than its dogma. Amongst those symbols was the Sacred Heart.

Central to this alternative interpretation of the Sacred Heart is an institution, with its own esoteric and political agenda, located at the very core of devotion to the Sacred Heart. The Hiéron du Val d'Or was founded at Paray-le-Monial in 1873; the very year that Chambord refused the throne and offered his support to Naundorff. Paray-le-Monial, we must recall, was the site of the Sacred Heart apparitions and thus the centre for devotion to the cult of the Sacred Heart. The Jesuit Victor Drevon (1820-1880), together with the baron Alexis de Sarachaga (1840-1918), established a research centre called Hiéron du Val d'Or at Paray-le-Monial. Sarachaga was a Spanish nobleman linked to the Russian Imperial Court on his mother's side and related to Saint Theresa of Avila on his father's side. He was interested in aspects of Esoteric Christianity, as well as in the political/social ideas of Christ in the role of the ultimate divine monarch. As already mentioned, the Grand Monarch concept of an earthly ruler with Divine Right, was a common feature of esoteric belief.

Perhaps unsurprisingly, Sarachaga was also a Naundorffist. By 1877, the Hiéron was a group of extreme devotees of the Sacred Heart and of the doctrine of the "social reign" of Christ the King – an aristocratic paternalistic socialism. Outwardly, the Hiéron was a museum dedicated to art and artefacts connected to the Eucharist. But the movement had a separate agenda.

The Hiéron's aims and philosophy can be ascertained from the writings of two contributors to its in-house magazines Regnabit and Rayonnement Intellectual. They are the renowned esoteric writers, Louis Charbonneau-Lassay and René Guenon, who was not only a Martinist but, as we have seen, became a bishop in Doinel's Gnostic Church.

According to them, the Hiéron's stated aims were:

1. to investigate the antiquity of Christianity which was considered to have originated in Atlantis and continued through the ancient Egyptian religion, Celticism and Druidism. The teachings of Jesus were considered to be an affirmation of the ancient tradition. According to devotees, the shrine of Paray-le-Monial was considered sacred due to a belief that, fifty years after Noah's flood, a great fire swept across Celtic Gaul from the Pyrenees and only stopped when it reached Paray. Celtic Gaul was thus considered to enjoy a special relationship with the Sacred Heart of Jesus; vestiges of its proto-cult are believed to be preserved in many pre-Christian pagan sites. For this reason the Hiéron sought out Celtic religious sites, where they thought they could see prefigured the cult of the Sacred Heart. Were Rennes-le-Château and Rennes-les–Bains considered as possible sites?

We must recall that Saunière's close colleague Boudet, priest of Rennes-les-Bains and author of the enigmatic Le Vrai Langue Celtique, was very much concerned with the apparent Celtic history of the region and the existence of an ancient sacred Celtic temple in his parish.

2. to create a synthesis of Christianity with Eastern philosophy and Western occultism. This included working towards a reconciliation of the Roman Catholic
and Orthodox Church – later confirmed by the visions at Fatima (1917) that
"The Sacred Heart will triumph". Russia is to be encouraged to return to the
Church. Russia was considered to be the third Rome after Constantinople, the
second, an important inheritor of the Byzantine tradition. According to some
writers, the Byzantine design for the Sacre Coeur Basilica was deliberately chosen as a symbol of this reconciliation.

3. the creation of New Holy Roman Empire – with a French temporal and spiritual
head in the manner of the Grand Monarch – an association of European nations bound by a common law and dedicated to advancing the mission of Christ
the King. According to Jean-Luc Chaumeil, the Hiéron's agenda was 'the creation of a new Habsburg and Catholic Holy Roman Empire'. This may explain the
visits between 1888 and 1890 of the Archduke Johan Salvator von Habsburg to
Saunière; and the later visit and interest in Rennes-le-Château by the Archduke
Rudolph in 1975.

The aim of creating a renewed Holy Roman Empire receives unexpected support
from an allegation found in the researches of Jean Robin, author of *Rennes-le-
Château: La Colline Envoutée,* and *Operation Orth,* and other writers including
Charbonneau-Lassay. They claim the existence of a secret parallel Catholic tradition called L'Eglise d'Avignon. In this Avignon tradition, the medieval Papacy,
installed at Avignon from 1309 to 1378, had continued in secret with a Pope who
represents the esoteric aspects of the Catholic Church. L'Eglise d'Avignon is said
to act as an intermediary between the Roman Church and the Orthodox Christian
(Byzantine) traditions. For a full account, see the book *Montmartre* by Phillipe
Julien. Unsurprisingly, amongst supporters/believers of the Avignon tradition are
found Gallicans, Péladan's societies and many other individuals and groups involved in the esoteric world of the Sacred Heart and Naundorffism.

But returning to the world of the Hiéron du Val d'Or, we are now introduced to another very influential figure, Paul Le Cour, who will be seen to play a role in the later development of the mystery. When Baron Sarachaga died, the Hiéron was re-organised by Georges and Marthe de Noaillat, who mainly fought for the institution of the Feast of Christ the King; that they finally obtained in 1925, from Pope Pius XI (the encyclical Quas Primas). For a long time, Noaillat's colleague, Jeanne Lépine, had been in correspondence with Paul Le Cour (1861-1954), who, in 1927, founded the association and magazine *Atlantis,* in which he tried to pick up some of the topics which had interested Sarachaga. From Jeanne Lépine, Le Cour was to inherit Sarachaga's gold signet ring; his followers considered this act as a sort of succession.

After the death of the Noaillats and then Jeanne Lépine on 5 February 1926, the reality of the Hiéron du Val d'Or came to an end, but still remained an inspiration for further activities. Le Cour went on to found the Order of the Divine Paraclete which effectively replaced the Hiéron.

Among those who had regularly attended the research centre at Paray-le-Monial, there was Father Félix Anizan, Oblate of the Virgin Mary, who since 1909 had dedicated his spiritual mission to the devotion and the doctrine of the Sacred Heart. And it was he who had decided to found a scientific review that would deal with this subject from dogmatic, moral, ascetic, mystic, liturgical, artistic and historical points of view. The first issue of *Regnabit,* the Revue Universelle du Sacré-Coeur ("Universal Review of the Sacred Heart") appeared on June 1921. It was supported by a committee whose chairman was the cardinal Louis-Ernest Dubois (1865-1929), Archbishop of Paris, and by fifteen other prelates from all continents, and on 10 March 1924, obtained a special apostolic benediction sent from the Pope by the State Secretary Cardinal Pietro Gasparri (1852-1934). It is interesting to note that the Hiéron with its declared esoteric political agenda received such heavyweight support from the Catholic hierarchy. Whatever the individual agenda of Hiéron devotees, it was obviously of advantage to the whole Roman Catholic Church to support them. In fact unification of the Roman and Orthodox

Churches would certainly have increased Catholic political and spiritual power.

We have seen that René Guenon and Louis Charbonneau-Lassay were among the first contributors to *Regnabit,* but possibly even more interesting is the Oblate of the Virgin Mary, Emile Hoffet (1873-1946). We must recall that in 1891, Emile Hoffet was a novitiate whose uncle was Director of the Seminary of St Sulpice and it was he to whom Saunière allegedly confided the famous "parchments" for translation and interpretation. Gérard de Sède claimed to have acquired a significant portion of the Abbé's extensive archives that included a prolific research on esoteric and secret societies. Can it be mere coincidence that Hoffet is written into the Saunière mystery through the dubious parchment episode? Or is there a more specific reason?

~

Bibliography

- Discoveries from the Time of Jesus: Alan Millard, 1990, Lion Publishing, Great Britain
- Penguin Atlas of Medieval history: Colin McEvedy, 1961, Penguin Books, London
- Encyclopedia Brittanica: The Bible – Masonic Edition: W.M.Collins Sons and Co. Ltd., 1947, The Masonic History Company, Chicago, Illinois
- The Sign and the Seal: Graham Hancock, 1992, William Heinemann Ltd., London
- The Holy Blood and the Holy Grail: Michael Baigent, Richard Leigh, Henry Lincoln, 1982, Jonathan Cape Ltd., London
- The Messianic Legacy: Michael Baigent, Richard Leigh, Henry Lincoln, 1986, Jonathan Cape Ltd., London
- The Hiram Key: Christopher Knight, Robert Lomas, 1996, Century, London
- The Dead Sea Scrolls Deception: Michael Baigent, Richard Leigh, 1991, Jonathan Cape Ltd., London
- L'Héritage de l'Abbé Saunière: Claire Corbu & Antoine Captier, 1995, Belisane, 11570 Cazilhac, France
- L'Or de Rennes: Gérard de Sède, 1967, Julliard-Tallandier, Paris
- Rennes-le-Château - Le Dossier, Les Impostures, Les Phantasmes, Les Hypothéses:
- Gérard de Sède, 1988, Éditions Robert Laffont, Paris
- The Woman with the Alabaster Jar: Margaret Starbird, 1993, Bear & Company, Sante Fe, New Mexico
- Dictionary of British Kings and Queens: Brockhampton Reference, 1995, Brockhampton Press, London
- Jesus: The Evidence Ian Wilson, 1984, Weidenfeld & Nicolson, London
- A Jewish Princedom in Feudal France: Prof. Arthur Zuckerman, 1972, Columbia University Press, New York
- The Templars, Knights of God: Edward Burman, 1986, Crucible, London
- The Monks of War: Desmond Seward, 1974, Eyre Methuen, London
- Le Comté de Razès: (Reprint from 1880 original edition), Louis Fedié, 1979, Lajoux frères, Carcassonne
- Les Templiers du Bézu: Abbé M.R.Mazières, 1957-59, Philippe Schrauben, Rennes-le-Château
- Histoire Générale de Languedoc (Tome 3): Benedictine Monks of St. Maur, France, 1742
- The Knight and Chivalry: Richard Barber, 1974, Revised ed. 1995, Boydell & Brewer, New York
- The Knight in History: Frances Gies, 1987, Reprint ed. Harper-Collins, London
- The Hiram Key: C.Knight, R.Lomas, 1996, Century, London
- Alet-les-Bains – Les Portes du Temps: Franck Marie, 1984, Alet les-Bains, France
- The Elixir and the Stone: M.Baigent, R.Leigh, 1997, Viking, London
- Parzival: Wolfram von Eschenbach, edited by André Lefevre, 1991, Continuum, New York
- Moorish Spain: Richard Fletcher, 1992, Weidenfeld & Nicolson, London
- The Assassins: Prof. Bernard Lewis, 1987, Oxford University Press
- Massacre at Montségur: Zoe Oldenburg, 1997, Weidenfeld & Nicolson, London
- Languedoc and Roussillon: Andrew Sanger, 1989, Christopher Helm, London
- The Land of the Cathars: Georges Serrus, 1990, Éditions Loubatières, 31120 Portet-sur-Garonne
- The Encyclopedia of Heresies and Heretics: Leonard George, 1995, Robson Books, London
- Visitors Guide to Rennes-le-Château: Tania Kletzky-Pradere, 1983, 11500 Quillan, France
- The Treasure of Montségur: W.Birks & R.Gilbert, 1987, Crucible, London
- Vicars of Christ: Peter de Rosa, 1988, Bantam Press, London
- Rennes-le-Château: L. and P. Fanthorpe, 1991, Bellevue Books, Ashford, Middx
- The Occult: Chambers Compact Reference, 1991, W&R Chambers Ltd, Edinburgh
- Barricades and Borders, Europe 1800-1914: Robert Gildea, 1987, Short Oxford History

- The Mythologies of Secret Societies: J.M.Roberts, 1972, Secker & Warburg, London
- Jules Verne – Initié et Initiateur: Michel Lamy, 1984, Payot, Paris
- Arsène Lupin – Supérieur Inconnu: Patrick Ferté, 1992, Guy Trédaniel Éditeur, Paris
- Franc-Maconnerie, Templière et Occultiste: R le Forestier, 1970, Éditions du C.N.R.S., Paris
- Le Roi Dagobert: Roger-René Dagobert, 1996, Cercle Général Dagobert, Nantes
- Napoleon – Master of Europe: Alistair Horne, 1979, Weidenfeld & Nicolson, London
- The Court of France, 1789 – 1830: Philip Mansel, 1988, Cambridge University Press
- Mystery of Rennes-le-Château – A Concise Guide: Gay Roberts, 1995, Llanidloes, Wales
- Le Fabuleux Trésor de Rennes-le-Château: Jacques Rivière, 1995, Belisane, 11570 Cazilhac, France
- Refuge of the Apocalypse: Elizabeth van Buren, 1986, Neville Spearman, Suffolk
- Freemasonry – A European Viewpont: Paul Naudon, 1988, EnglishTranslation from French by Joseph Tsang, 1993, Freestone Press, Great Britain
- The Flight from Reason – Sects of the Late 17th Century:, James Webb, 1971
- World History: Geddes & Grosset, 1996, Geddes & Grosset Ltd., New Lanark, Scotland
- Lumières Nouvelles sur Rennes-le-Château (2nd edition): André Douzet, 1995, Éditions Aquarius, Geneva
- A Concise History of France: Roger Price, 1993, Cambridge University Press
- The Prophecy of the Apostles of the Later Times: Jean-Marie Barette, 1998, Editions Magnificat, Quebec
- The Occult Conspiracy: Michael Howard, 1989, Destiny Books, Rochester, Vermont
- Rennes-le-Château: Capitale Secret et L'Histoire de France: J.Deloux and J.Brétigny, 1982, Éditions Atlas, Paris
- Les Dessous d'une Ambition Politique: Matthieu Paoli, 1973, Éditeurs associés, Nyon, France
- The Treasure of Montségur: W.Birks, R.A.Gilbert, 1987, Crucible, London
- Le Mystère Otto Rahn – Du Catharisme au Nazisme: Christian Bernadac, 1978, Editions France-Empire, Paris
- Otto Rahn – Leben unt Werk: Hans Jurgen-Lange, 1997, Arun-Verlag, Engerda
- Otto Rahn – Argonaut or Dupe?: Nigel Graddon, 1998, Penarth, Wales
- The Footprints of Otto Rahn: (article from the Rennes Observer, March 1998), Nigel Graddon, 1998, Penarth, Wales
- Crusade Against the Grail*: Otto Rahn, 1933, French trans. 1974 ed. Stock, Paris
- Lucifer's Court*: Otto Rahn, 1935, French trans. 1994 ed. Pardes, Puiseaux, France
- * note: English translations by Christopher Jones are now available
- In Search of the Holy Grail and the Precious Blood: Ian & Dieke Begg, 1995, Thorson's, London
- Skorzeny's Special Mission – Memoires of the Most Dangerous Man in Europe: Otto Skorzeny, 1997, Greenhill Books, London
- Nazi Gold: Ian Sayer and Douglas Botting, 1984, Granada, London
- Emerald Cup – Ark of Gold: Col. Howard Buechner, 1991, Thunderbird Press, Los Angeles
- The SS – Alibi of a Nation, 1922 – 1945, (1st edition 1956): Gerald Reitlinger, 1981, Arms & Armour Press, London
- The Bormann Brotherhood: William Stevenson, 1973, Arthur Baker Ltd., Great Britain
- A Genius for War – A Life of General George S. Patton: Carlo D'Este, 1995, Harper-Collins, London
- Pétain's Crime: Paul Webster, 1990, Macmillan, London
- Pétain, Hero or Traitor: Herbert L. Lottman, 1985, Viking, London
- A Concise History of France: Roger Price, 1993, Cambridge University Press
- France, Since 1945: Robert Gildea, 1997, Oxford University Press
- Making History – World History from 1914 to the Present Day: Christopher Culpin, 1984, Collins Educational, London
- The Knight-Monks of Vichy France, Uriage 1940-1945 (2nd edition): John Hellman, 1997, Liver-

pool University Press, Liverpool
- The Murdered Magicians – The Templars and their Myths: Peter Partner, 1982, Oxford University Press
- Opération Orth – L'Incroyable Secret de Rennes-le-Château: Jean Robin, 1989, Éditions de la Maisnie, Paris
- Les Archives du Trésor de Rennes-le-Château: Pierre Jarnac, 1987, (2 Vols) Éditions Belisane, Nice
- Rennes-le-Château – La Colline Envoutée: Jean Robin, 1982, Guy Tredaniel, Paris
- The Death of Politics: John Laughland, 1994, Michael Joseph, London
- The Day the War Ended: Martin Gilbert, 1995, Harper-Collins, London
- Hitler's German Enemies: Louis L. Snyder, 1991, Robert Hale, London
- Vaincre Journal (6 issues held in the Bibliotheque Nationale, Paris): published 1942
- Mitterrand – Le Grand Inititié: Nicolas Bonnal, 1996, Claire Vigne Editrice, Clamecy, France
- L'Histoire du Trésor de Rennes-le-Château: Pierre Jarnac, 1985, L'Association pour le développment de la lecture, 66330 Cabestany
- Les Archives de Rennes-le-Château: Pierre Jarnac, 1987, (2 Vols.) Éditions Belisane, Nice
- Table d'Isis: Jean-Luc Chaumeil, 1994, Guy Tredaniel, Editeur, Paris
- Rennes-le-Château et l'Enigme de l'Or: Jean Markale, 1989, Les Editions Pygmalion/Gérard Watelet
- The Templar Revelation: L.Picknett, C.Prince, 1997, Bantam Press, London
- Mythologie du Trésor de Rennes: R.Descadeillas, 1974, Carcassonne
- Researches of C.M.Scargill, BA (Hons) MA
- The Death of Politics – France under Mitterrand: John Laughland, 1994, Michael Joseph, London
- Orador-sur-Glane – Le Drame, Heure par Heure Robert Hébras, 1992, Éditions C.M.D., 49260 Montreuil-Bellay
- Orador: Massacre and Aftermath: Robin Mackness, 1988, Bloomsbury, London
- Les Puissance du Mal: Jean-Edern Hallier, 1996, Editions du Rocher, Monaco
- Guerres Secrètes à l'Elysée: Capitaine Paul Barril, 1996, Editions Albin Michel, S.A., Paris
- Les SS en Limousin, Quercy et Perigord: Georges Beau, 1969, Presses de la Cité, Paris
- Emerald Cup – Ark of Gold: Col. Howard Buechner, 1991, Thunderbird Press, Los Angeles
- Le Monde (18 June 1998)
- Minute (25 September 1996)
- Minute (22 September 1993)
- L'ami banquier Bernard Violet, 1998, Éditions Albin Michel, Paris
- La Mafia des Sectes Bruno Fouchereau, 1996, Édtions Filipacchi, Levallois-Perret
- Vol d'Identitié Jean-Pierre François. 2000, Éditions Albin Michel, Paris
- Their Kingdom Come – Inside the World of Opus Dei: Robert Hutchinson, 1997, Doubleday, London
- In God's Name: David Yallop, 1984, Poetic Products Ltd., London
- The Last Supper: Philip Willan, 2007, Constable & Robinson Ltd., London
- Pourquoi la Resugence de l'Ordre du Temple?: Peronnik, 1975, Editions de la Pensée Solaire, Monte Carlo
- Le Guide des Societes Secretes: Jean-Pierre Bayard, 19, Philippe Lebaud, France
- The Treasure Trove of the Knight's Templar: André Douzet, translated and edited by Filip Coppens, 1997
- Investigation of the origin of the Order of the Solar Temple: Clive Prince, 1997
- C4 Television Documentary 'Secret Lives': broadcast on 29 December 1997, editor Alistair Mitchell
- Operation Gladio: David Guyatt, 1997, re-printed with permission on http://www.copi.com/
- Gladio – The Secret US War to Subvert Italian Democracy: Arthur E. Rowse, 1998, http:// www.worldmedia.com/caq/articles/gladio.html
- Archives of Roger-René Dagobert

- The End of Time – Faith and Fear in the Shadow of the Millenium: Damian Thompson, 1996, Sinclair-Stevenson, London
- Vicars of Christ – The Dark Side of the Papacy: Peter de Rosa, 1988, Bantam Press, London
- The Evening Times (Glasgow, Scotland): 22 July 1996
- Sunday Mail (UK): 18 August 1996
- Wall Street and the Rise of Hitler: Prof. Antony C. Sutton, 1976, Bloomfield Books, Sudbury, Suffolk
- Blood Money: Tom Bower, 1997, Pan, London
- BBC2 TimeWatch Documentary 'Banking with Hitler': editor Laurence Rees, broadcast 1998
- The Hidden Encyclical of Pius XI: Georges Passelecq, Bernard Suchecky, 1997, Harcourt Brace & Co., USA
- The Bormann Brotherhood: William Stevenson, 1973, Arthur Baker Ltd., Great Britain
- La Synarchie – Le Mythe du Complot Permanent: Olivier Dard, 1998
- Librairie Académique Perrin, Paris
- 'Now Nazi gold scandal taints the Vatican': Bruce Johnston, The Sunday Telegraph, 27 July 1997
- The Last Pope: John Hogue, 1998, Element, London
- Nostradamus – The Millenium and Beyond: Peter Lorie, 1994, Bloomsbury, London
- L'Occultisme dans la Politique : Gérard & Sophie de Sède, 1994, Robert Laffont, Paris
- The Tainted Source: John Laughland, Little, Brown & Company, Great Britain, 1997